CW01667263

DRAGON ASSASSIN

VOLUME 3

ARTHUR SLADE

DAVA ENTERPRISES

Cover by Zhivko Zhelev

Map by Garnet Whyte

❀ Created with Vellum

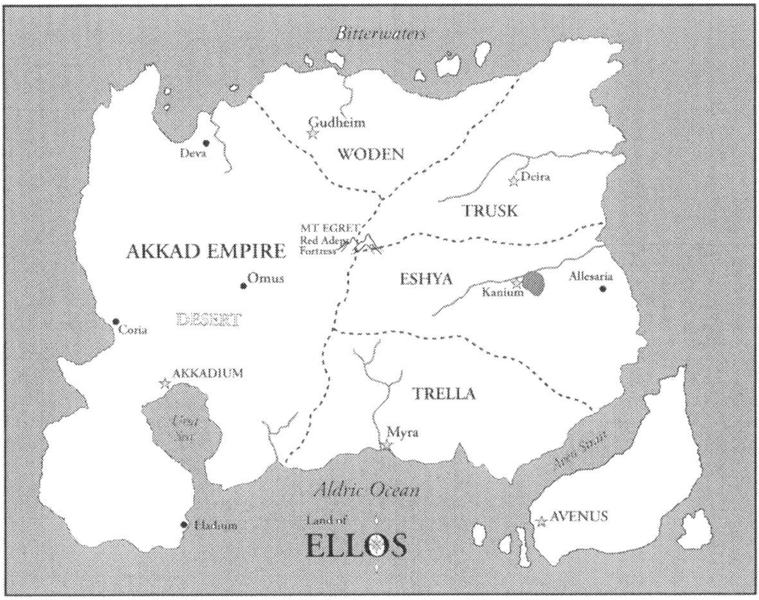
Bitterwaters
Gudheim
WODEN
Deva
Deira
TRUSK
MT EGRET
Red Adept Fortress
AKKAD EMPIRE
ESHYA
Omus
Kanium
Allesaria
DESERT
Coria
AKKADIUM
TRELLA
Myra
Aldric Ocean
AVENUS
Hadum
Land of
ELLOS

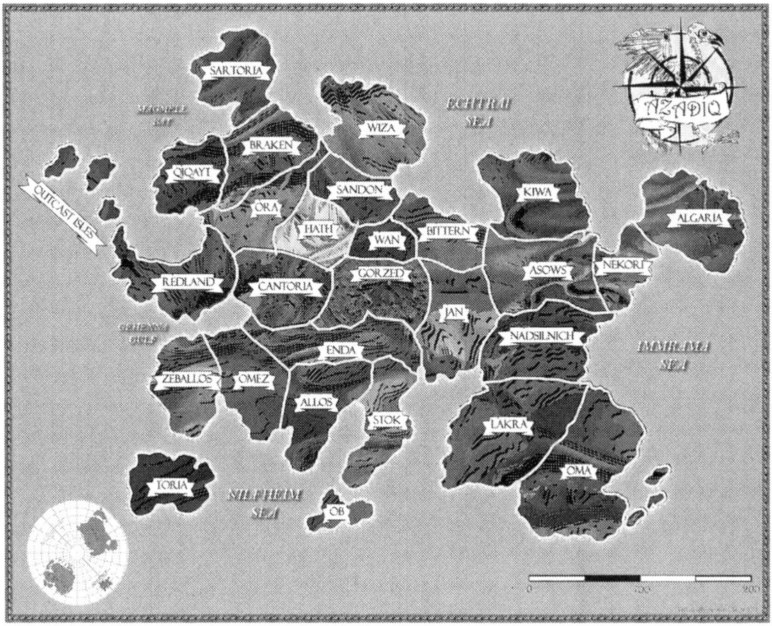
AZADIQ
SARTORIA
WIZA
BRAKEN
QIQAYT
SANDON
ORA
HAITH
WAN
BITTERN
KIWA
ALGARIA
OUTCAST ISLES
REDLAND
CANTORIA
GORZED
ASOWS
NEKORI
JAN
NADSILNICH
IMMRAMA SEA
ENDA
ZEBALLOS
OMEZ
ALLOS
STOK
LAKRA
OMA
TORIA
NILFHEIM SEA
OB

PART 7: HIDDEN POWERS

PROLOGUE

Mysterious Arrival

The giant black swan with the young man tied to her back was dead. She died in flight, her massive heart giving out after many days of traveling westward. She fell through the air like a dark comet. The swan's dull eyes didn't see the mist open below her, nor did she notice that land was nearly within reach. Neither did the young man spot it, for he was unconscious and far from the world. If his eyes had been open, he'd have been staring up at the stars and the half moon.

A gust caught the swan's dead wings and they locked in position so the bird skimmed over the water, waves lapping at its dangling talons. The beast smashed into a beach and the white sand sprayed in an arc from the impact. The swan didn't even let out a final breath.

The waves tried to reach the bird, but failed. Then something stirred in the distance. A shadow along the rocky land overlooking the beach detached itself from the darkness and loped toward the swan and its rider. It padded quietly, licking its lips and sniffing. Another shadow followed and another, and soon there were several shadows moving with sly caution.

The rider groaned and gradually became aware. He'd not had a drink other than rainwater for days, nor had he eaten, and he was wasted and thin. His bonds were loosened by the impact and for the first time in what felt like decades he could move his right arm freely. He touched his face. It was dry and sunburned and caked with blood. And it was real. So much of what he had been experiencing in the last few days felt like he was flying through a dream.

Instead, he touched along his body, finding more rope. *Why am I tied up?* he wondered. The knots were tight, made tighter by the moisture in the air, and they were familiar to him—he had tied similar knots hundreds of times. And he knew, too, that they were nearly impossible to loosen.

The young man had no memory of being bound. His fingers encountered the feathers below him, so he lifted his head enough to see that he was lying on a swan.

A black swan. He was tied to a giant black swan! It also seemed familiar to him, as if he'd known it—or beasts like it—in a past life. But how would he know a giant black swan? He had no memory of this creature before this moment. It took him several seconds to realize it was dead.

He knew, very suddenly, one other thing: he couldn't remember his name. It was such a deeply shocking fact that he drew in a deep breath.

"What is my name?" His words echoed slightly. He sucked in another helping of cool air, but the memory didn't return to him. *What am I, if I can't remember my name? I am nothing. I am no one. I'm lost.* For several sharp seconds he felt on the edge of going completely mad, then he slowly drew in another breath and another, naturally calming himself. His heartbeat thudded to a normal speed. His thoughts were no longer so big and jagged; they were smoother. Easier to handle. It was as if he'd been trained to settle his emotions whenever they grew too wild.

Gather the facts, he told himself. *Then make a plan.*

It was a saying he'd heard a thousand times, though he couldn't remember who had said it to him. So he gathered the facts. He no longer remembered his name or his past. That was a fact. He was tied to a dead swan on a beach in a land that he also didn't know the name of. That, too, was a fact. But his heart was beating and he was alive. That perhaps was the most important fact of all.

So the plan he made was simple. Get off the dead bird.

He grabbed at a knot, trying to find a loose loop, but his fingers were stiff, his muscles sore, and hunger grew in his belly. His throat was parched and that would be the next part of the plan. Get off the bird. Find water. Find food. Find shelter.

He congratulated himself on his plan. A simple plan has the best chance of success, he thought. This was another saying that someone else had taught him, but he couldn't remember who. A simple plan would motivate him and help him to survive. He continued to explore the knots, one by one.

Then came a tiny snapping sound. It originated in the bushes to his left, just beyond where he and the swan had crashed. He lifted his head again and looked in that direction. He noticed that he had to turn quite far before the beach became visible.

Too far, he realized.

And in that moment he knew another fact that nearly

drove him mad. He was blind in his left eye. He'd had to turn too far to look properly at that part of the beach. All the blood and scabs he'd felt on the left side of his face meant his left eye was gone.

He imagined himself flailing, screaming, and tearing at his bonds and very nearly began to do so.

Instead, he remained still. He breathed slowly and deeply. "Gather the facts," he whispered.

He ran his fingers across his left eye and discovered that a deep wound had been gouged along his brow, through his socket and down his cheek. The eye was gone. And there was nothing he could do about that fact now.

He found a small loop in a knot and, after several tugs, it came loose. It didn't change how tightly his left wrist was bound, but it was a start. As he worked, he developed a grudging respect for the knot and the knot tier—it was expertly done, and it would take hours for him to escape. He didn't know if he could go that long without water.

Then he heard a ghost of a sound.

Pat. Pat.

Footsteps. Stealthy and quiet, right next to him. He turned his head very slowly to the right and saw two glowing angry eyes, lips curled back to reveal slaver dripping from sizeable teeth.

A wolf. No—something larger than a wolf had padded around the side of the dead swan and was now growling softly at him.

The knowledge of how to deal with wolves suddenly appeared inside his brain: One should make oneself look big and maintain eye contact. He was certain he'd read that in a book. He also understood that these creatures could see and smell fear. He would show none. There wasn't much he could do about his smell. He hoped the blood was dried enough to conceal his scent.

The eye contact was easy, even if he only had one eye to use. He was surprised to discover he didn't feel the slightest bit of fear looking in the beast's eyes. He had faced down larger creatures. He didn't remember which larger creatures or when, but he had.

As for making himself bigger, well, that was impossible. He was tied to a swan. The wolf was one of the most intelligent animals in the mortal realms, and this brother creature to a wolf would recognize this weakness.

So it was very important to not show fear.

The wolf stared. The young man with no name held his stare. Then after several seconds the wolf backed one step away.

The young man sighed ever so slightly. He had won the contest. He had driven it back with just his eye and his belief in himself. Even without a name, he had won.

Then another *pat pat* came from his opposite side. Wolves traveled in packs. He'd read that, too, and it took all his concentration not to panic. If he broke eye contact the first wolf would be on him in a heartbeat. The other wolf creature was sniffing around his blind side. It would smell the dried blood and that would be disastrous for the young man.

Pat. Pat. Then came a low growl. And another.

There were two wolves on the other side of him. He slowly moved his hand, searching for a blade. He'd had a dagger at one time. He could picture it, but all he discovered was an empty sheath. He was wearing a cloak, and he felt the many pockets, but found nothing inside any of them. His fist was his only obvious weapon.

The growling on his other side was getting louder, and

he knew what that meant. One of those wolves was gathering its courage up for a charge. Challenging him. He only had a moment to respond.

He twisted to see three wolves on his right side. But the moment he broke eye contact with the first wolf, he knew he'd made a mistake.

For that first wolf made no growl.

Instead, there was only a whistling in its nostrils as it launched from the sand and flew through the air.

His body reacted without thought, as if he'd been trained for this very battle. He fought through the stiffness, turning to face that first wolf, reaching out his hand. He shoved it below the teeth and the curled lips and grabbed the scruff of the wolf's neck. It had plenty of scruff and had jumped high enough that by grabbing and twisting he added to its speed, pulling the animal. Its claws scratched his chest as it tried to stop, but with an angry growl it flew over him, striking one of the other wolves and letting out a *yip yip yip* after it hit the ground.

It kept *yipping* and running until it was gone.

The young man smiled. If it was the alpha male, then he had won. The others would not be brave enough to attack.

And it looked like the goddess of luck was smiling on him. For the remaining wolves had raised their hackles but were backing away.

Then a fourth wolf that was larger than the rest strode out of the nearby bush, not bothering with stealth. It passed its companions and they advanced behind the alpha male.

That first wolf creature had just been a desperate skinny scout. This one had eyes that flickered with pride and keen intelligence, and it was a king of beasts.

The young man held its eyes, showing his strength. His bravery. His belief in himself.

But the big wolf continued to advance, its own stare one of absolute confidence.

A light flashed somewhere in the distance behind the young man. A shooting star? It was bright enough to light the wolf's eyes. Perhaps this beast was so powerful it was bringing down the sky one star at a time.

The wolf paused and sniffed the air, and then, without a moment of further hesitation, it attacked.

It was big enough it didn't have to leap. When the young man tried to grab it, the wolf twisted its head, deflecting his arm, and bit hard on his wrist. The youth let out a scream of pain, which only encouraged the other wolves. One grabbed his leg, trying to pull it out of the bonds. The third bit the dead swan.

And all the while, the alpha wolf kept a steady gaze on him as it bit deeper and deeper into his wrist. As if it relished his fear and wanted to soak it in. As if it dared him to continue to fight.

Then its pupils narrowed and its eyes grew bright—everything grew bright. The wolf thing let go of his wrist.

At first the youth didn't know what was happening as the pupils of his enemy grew smaller and smaller and the surrounding land brighter and brighter. Why was it releasing him and trying to flee?

A ball of flame struck the giant wolf creature full in the face and knocked it off the youth. Two smaller flames hit the other wolves. The alpha male shook its head, fur burning. It let out a growl so deep that the beach echoed with it, and then it shook so hard the flames went out. Its face was mostly bare; its skull looked melted. Its eyes held an unfathomable anger.

But it turned away and silently ran along the beach,

smoke trailing from its skin. The others followed it with their tails between their legs.

The young man let out his breath.

"I had a bad sleep," a male voice said as if that explained the sudden appearance of flying fireballs. "It's a good thing I walked on the beach to clear my head or you'd be that dire wolf's midnight lunch."

The young man had not heard the stranger approach, even though he had been trained to hear these things. The youth turned his head.

The speaker was a middle-aged man in simple earth-colored robes. The top of his brown-skinned head was bald, but the sides had two fluffs of white hair. His pudgy face was friendly and he held a tall wooden staff.

"Wh-what—who are you?" the youth asked.

"I am Goran," the man said. "And I am a wizard. But you know that, don't you? Oh, how you know that."

The youth wasn't certain exactly what he meant, but he knew what wizards were. He had seen them before, and he briefly remembered a white tower. A prison for wizards.

"I know you, too," Goran said. "Or at least I know what you are and who rides a bird like this. And I recognize the distinctive cut of your cloak. But what I don't know is your name."

"I-I don't know my name, either," the young man said.

This made the wizard raise an eyebrow. He came closer and the youth lowered his arm, knowing there was nothing he could do if this man wanted to hurt him. The wizard made no motion other than to stare directly into his eye. "You don't, do you? Oh, how odd. The stars have sent me a puzzle and the gods are laughing at us both."

"Do you know who I am?" he asked.

Goran shook his head. "No. But I know what you need:

shelter and kindness. You will come with me and we will tend your wounds and feed you. Come."

He made a subtle gesture with his little finger that the youth almost didn't see. The ropes binding him unknotted themselves, slithered to the ground and disappeared into the bushes.

The wizard offered him a hand and the young man took it and stood on shaky legs.

"Thanks," he said but the wizard didn't reply. Then the youth looked at his mount. She had been a lovely beast: beautiful and powerful. He felt a sudden sadness that she was gone even though he couldn't remember her name. "It's a shame that my swan is dead. Are we just going to leave her body for the wolves?"

"No," the wizard said simply. "She will come with us."

"But she's dead," the youth answered.

"Recently dead. Which makes it easier to convince her to come back to life." He tapped the swan with his staff.

The bird stirred. Her head twitched and she slowly fluttered her wings and rose to her feet. The very sight of that—of a creature that was dead coming back to life—made the young man's guts fill with a liquid fear. It couldn't be real. The swan didn't open its eyes.

"We don't want to look into her eyes, right now," Goran explained. "We'd see the underworld, and that sight causes nightmares and gas. I don't like the gas." His chuckle was friendly and soft. "Can you walk?"

"Yes. I think so," the youth said.

"Then walk with me, my home is nearby." They traveled until they were off the beach and on a path that cut between the rocks. "You know I can't just call you No Name. Or the Swan Boy. Can you think of a name for yourself?"

The youth thought and he thought. "No," he said.

"Then we will call you Nameless," Goran said. "I like it. Mysterious and yet true. Do you accept it?"

The youth nodded.

And so Nameless walked alongside the wizard Goran, away from the ocean. The recently dead swan followed silently.

1

THE SKY

It turns out that riding on a dragon, zipping through the air at top speed and feeling as if you can touch the sun or the stars, gets boring. For three days and three nights, Brax and I had been winging our way east over a roiling, angry ocean. I didn't even know the name of this endless body of water. The dragon-ruled land of Drachia was far behind us, and my homeland of Ellos was even further away.

Thankfully, we weren't alone. Thord and Megan soared along beside us on their giant black swans. They had kept me sane during this endless journey, because talking to a snarky dragon for three days straight would have driven me mad.

"Oh, look, the sun is rising," Brax said. "I wonder if this is the last sunrise we'll ever see. It's so wonderful that I get to spend my final moments with sniveling mortals."

There's an old saying: *Don't let a dragon get your goat.* Some people take it literally, which is wise. Others see it as a warning not to respond to every smart alec sentence to come out of a dragon's mouth. That is even wiser.

So I bit my tongue and didn't answer Brax. Instead, I concentrated on my aches and pains, which were everywhere. My hand was now a claw of tightness, still clinging to the spike on Brax's back. My legs would be forever stuck in a U-shape before the end of this journey.

We were winging this great, dangerous distance because a talking bird had passed on to us the words of a dead mage dragon.

I know that sounds ridiculous. But it was true. To make it even stranger, Vecterix, the aforementioned dead mage dragon, had sent the message with a spellbird before his death and the tiny creature had spoken it to us using the mage's voice: "These mortals and Carmen must fly to the lands in the East that are not on any maps. There is a man there who is gifted at bringing back the dead. I searched the stars for his name, but he does not have one. That man may have the knowledge to bring your sister back."

I wished Vecterix were still alive to give a bit more of a hint about exactly what this man would tell us—if we found him. I'd also ask Vecterix whether we were even going in the right direction. "*Fly to the lands in the East*" were not very exact instructions. One degree north or south and we could miss a whole continent.

But we wanted to go. First, we were hoping to find allies against Emperor Sargon who was marching across Ellos, burning cities and towns every bejeweled step of the way. And second, we intended to bring Brax's sister, Brenna, back from the dead. I had her soulstone on a chain around my neck, hidden under my shirt. She was our silent companion. I absently touched the stone. It was light, but the weight of knowing Brenna was inside that bauble was heavy.

So, we had a lot to do. And all of it hinged on finding these lands in the East.

My tunic was drenched with sweat, and the air grew warmer with each wingbeat. It was entirely possible that there wasn't a land out there with a man who knew how to bring people back from the dead. Vecterix, after all, had been on the edge of madness.

But long before we discovered that island, our winged companions might get so tired that they could no longer fly. The swans, at least, could float, though the last time we stopped to let them rest they took some convincing to take off again and Naga nearly didn't make it into the air. Brax, who could not float, rested his wings as much as possible while making lazy circles in the sky.

I glanced over at Thord and stifled a chuckle. He was asleep—only he could snooze on a flying swan. His mouth was partly open as if he were about to really get into his snoring. Even sleeping, he looked a little rugged and handsome. It would be a perfect pose for a painting if he wasn't drooling. He had been wise enough to tie himself into his saddle.

Thord had been somewhat aloof from me during the trip. It's not like you can have a deep, private conversation while flying with your companions, but I noticed that he looked at me with a bit of reservation, as if he didn't know exactly who I was. That perhaps made sense since I'd spent so much time away from him in the last few weeks and, frankly, I'd changed. I did have a dragon eye. And scales beneath my skin. He'd spent all that time with Megan, deepening their friendship.

I turned toward her. It would be hilarious if she were asleep. She—

"We will die!" Megan said. Near enough and loud enough to make me shudder—she'd quietly drifted above us and was hanging partway down the side of her swan to pull off the surprise. She grinned, showing her teeth and then she sang: "*We will die. We will die. We will die.*" So much time on the back of a swan had driven her mad! She shook her head, making her red hair flow with the blowing wind, then she straightened up and flew slightly ahead so her swan's wings didn't knock me off Brax's back. She had learned, much earlier, to stay out of his back draft.

"Well, let's not be so cheery about our deaths," I said.

"I've had a lot of time to think, lately," she answered.

"You were thinking?" Brax snorted hard enough a flicker of flame came out his nostril. "I thought I smelt something burning."

"You should flap your wings, not your gums," Megan snapped back with an even wider grin.

It was a surprisingly good quip, so I expected Brax to blast her with a quiver-full of insults, but he shrugged—in midair—and said, "Go on, Megan. You obviously have something important to tell us."

Megan spat over her right shoulder. Thankfully it was directed away from me or I might have been smacked with spittle. "I just had to clear my throat," she explained. "Anyway, I realized we're well past the point of no return. If we try to go back to Drachia we'll crash into the ocean and become seafood for a sea monster or a pack of sharks."

"Did you just pop by to cheer us up?" I said.

"I'm one hundred percent against cheeriness." Megan waved a finger as she said this, either emphasizing her point or conducting an invisible orchestra. I worried she might start singing again. Maybe there wasn't enough air up here for her brain. "Anyway, I figured out how to make this trip easier on us all. It is a brilliant idea."

"Oh, a mortal with a brilliant idea," Brax said. "The gods

have paused in the heavens to listen. Amaze us with your brilliance."

"Yes, what is it?" My words sounded snappier than I'd meant them to be. I blamed the muscle spasm that had just jolted up my left leg.

She made a sign with her index and middle finger—a V. She waved it at us for several seconds.

"Is that it?" Brax said. "What in the blazes does that hand signal mean?"

"It means, silly dragon, that we should fly in V formation," Megan said. "Vee. Vee. Vee." Yes, she sang this last part. I grimaced.

"What does the letter V have to do with it?" I shouted loud enough to stop her from singing.

"I just remembered reading about the group missions that assassins would perform—if they were a great distance away, they would travel in a V formation. It cuts down on how much we have to fight against the friction of the air. It's why we see ducks fly like that."

"I'm a dragon, not a duck," Brax snapped. "I don't fly in formation."

"It is a brilliant idea," I said.

"I believe that's the first time you've thought I was brilliant," Megan said. "I'm honored."

"Well, your timing is perfect." I tapped Brax on the back. "My scaly friend is on his last legs...wings, I mean."

"I can fly for months," he growled. "I'll flap circles around these swans. I just need to drop some dead weight off my back."

"This is not a time to dragon up," I said. "We need to conserve our strength since we have no idea how much farther this unknown island is."

"If this magical land with the man who brings people back from the dead even exists," Brax added.

"Vecterix said it exists, so it is there," I said. Even thinking of the dragon mage made my voice catch in my throat. He had been such a kind soul. "We just have to be smart enough to find it."

Brax let out a long sigh and then cleared his throat. "Well, let's try this V formation trick. I'm sure it won't work, but at least you'll shut up about it."

"Then we need to wake up Thord," Megan said.

"Oh, leave that to me." I recognized the gleeful tone in Brax's voice, but before I could react he spat out a ball of flame that arced toward Bolt. The swan, who was flying with eyes half closed, let out a terrified *honk* as the flame burst right in front of him. He performed a sudden dive, shaking Thord awake, who then let out a yell and waved his arms in startled surprise.

"Brax!" I said. "Why did you do that?"

"You said you needed to wake him up," he answered. "I woke him up. Plus, it was hilarious."

"You could have fried him and the swan!" I shouted.

"Oh, you mortals know nothing of flames. That blast was all for show. I barely singed any feathers."

It didn't help my case that Megan was chuckling. "Admit it, Carmen. It was funny."

"Don't encourage him!" I wished I still had a book to smack Brax over the head with. Not that he'd take too kindly to that.

Thord struggled to get himself back in the saddle and then immediately flew up to Brax. "What was that all about?" he said, "Were you trying to kill me?" Bolt squawked after every word, as if adding angry punctuation.

"No, brat," said Brax. "I was not trying to kill you. I just wanted to wake you up. Now get that black beast away from me before I turn it into dinner."

I mouthed *I'm sorry* but Thord still grimaced. He had that look people get when they are sleepy and angry. The best way to calm him down was by telling him our latest plan. It took a bit of explaining, but it worked.

"I'll take the lead," Brax announced.

He pushed forward and the swans found a place where they followed his draft. We discovered that if he went faster, they could too, without having to work much harder. Several hours passed before we switched positions and Brax discovered how much easier it was to fly when one of the swans was cutting through the air first. "I really had a great idea," he said.

"This wasn't your idea, it was Megan's!"

He snorted. "No one will believe a mortal thought of this. Your brains are too tiny! Therefore, it's my idea. I'll call it Brax's Battle Formation. I can't wait to tell the other dragons. Maybe they'll name a mountain range after me."

As the hours passed, hope sprouted a seedling in my heart. Though there was no sign of land or of anything other than water, the traveling was easier and we now had a much better chance of finding our destination. It continued to grow warmer, though that was a bad thing. Our waterskins would soon be empty. All we had to eat was dried fruit and meat provided by the slaves of the dragons, and those stocks were low, too.

The hours continued to tick by, and I couldn't help but notice how small our little winged group was when I looked around at the enormity of the sky and the endless ocean. "How are you doing?" I asked.

"In all honesty," Brax said, "I am fading even with the energy we saved. It is just too far."

"Oh, come on: you flew above the Bitterwaters caked in ice and carrying me on your back."

"That was only for two days. This is much longer. And you've gained some weight since then."

Again, I wished for a book to hit him with. Maybe next time I'd bring a branch.

Naga, Megan's swan, gave out a desultory honk—a warning—and then spiraled down toward the ocean. It was only by kicking and shouting out every swear word under the heavens that Megan got the bird to climb back into the air. Even the gods would blush at her pyrotechnic display of cursing. "I don't know how many times I'll be able to do that," she admitted.

"Let us hope we see land soon," I said. For what must be the thousandth time I wished we could find the same airstreams that the spellbirds used. But that knowledge for this part of the world was lost to us.

My dragon eye spotted a small black thing in the distance. I sat up straight.

"Brax," I said

"I see it."

"But what is it?" I asked.

"It's a bird." Then he drew in a breath. "The first bird we've seen in days."

"If there's a bird there is land," I said.

"Or danger," Brax replied.

"What kind of danger could a bird bring?"

"Close your human eye and focus. Then you'll see what I mean."

I did so, and it took a second for my dragon eye to adjust. But he was right, it wasn't one bird, it was two.

"What is it?" Megan shouted. Both she and Thord were

squinting against the sun, but they would never see as far as Brax and I.

"It's two birds," I said.

"Incorrect." Brax sounded a little haughty. "Keep watching." A moment later another bird appeared, and another and another. In a few wingbeats it became clear that there were thousands of dark, large birds.

Ravens.

But not the message-carrying ravens I'd grown up with in the rookeries of the Red Assassin Fortress. The eyes of these ravens glowed red and many of them looked to have very few feathers. Some were only bones. And yet they stayed aloft.

"Dead ravens," Brax said. "I'm sure this is a really, really terrible omen."

2

A BLACK CLOUD

The smell hit us first.

And with the smell came a bubbling panic—it was a rotten stink of death times a hundred, crawling into my nostrils and deflating my lungs. Each breath became tight in my throat. All the fresh air had vanished from the sky. This reeking cloud was more than just a whiff of decay. It was going right into my body so that my flesh, my nerves, my bones shook and jittered with fear. I wanted to flee.

At the same time Brax, too, shuddered as the vapor hit us. And the two swans gave out simultaneous high-pitched squawks as Thord and Megan uttered wordless shouts of surprise, as if they'd both been punched in the guts.

A stench I could deal with—I'd been trained in the butcher's carcass pits of Ogra, forced by my maestrus to breathe that smell for hours so that the scent of rotting meant nothing. I shouldn't be reacting with such guttural fear. But a rattling sense of horror threatened to gobble up every last sane thought.

Brax shuddered again, and so did I. The birds still hadn't reached us.

Naga and Bolt began flying madly up and down, both Megan and Thord doing their best to control their mounts. But the swans—our highly trained swans—knew death. They recognized that we were flying directly into our own destruction.

My eyes watered and I blinked, keeping one closed, so I looked at the world through my dragon eye. A misty greenish light surrounded us, as if the very smell itself glowed.

Magic! It was magic that forced the stink to make me shudder.

"You see it, too," Brax said. "We are caught in something much worse than an unkindness of ravens. I'm sure whatever comes next will be horrible."

I knew that an unkindness was how people referred to a group of ravens. Today, it was the perfect name. "You always see the bright side of—" I began.

The ravens hit us like a dark cloud of wings and bones and rasping and croaking *caw caw caws*. They came with such speed I thought they'd go right through us, but they turned and spun at the last moment, surrounding us, avoiding Brax's wings. They were a suffocating cloud—the air was choking, not just with the smell but the feathers and falling bones and ashes. The closest ravens had dried eyeballs and bony feet.

"Thord!" I shouted. "Megan! Where are you?"

A muffled yell came from far away.

"What?" I drew in a breath and my throat grew parched so I couldn't even spit out a word, let alone yell.

"C-c-come," the ravens said as one. *"C-c-come."*

We had no choice. They blocked out the ocean and the sky, so that all we saw were their rotting bodies. I couldn't even make eye contact with Brax—the creatures flew that close to me. Only the occasional speck of light shone through.

I don't want to talk aloud, Brax sent the thought to me. *Hold on. I will try to break away.*

I wasn't certain if it was wise, but I hated being trapped in this mass collection of death. I grabbed tight to him with both hands. *Go ahead. I'm ready.*

He twisted his wings, attempting to turn, and we crashed into the birds which broke into dust around us. We cut through the flock, but then other ravens filled in the empty spaces and pressed even closer to us, so that their dry wings tickled my face.

It is no use, he said. *There are hundreds of them below me, just pushing me back into the air. I don't even have to flap my wings, and we keep flying in the direction they want us to go. I do not understand how that works.*

Well, I sent to him, *they haven't killed us yet. So maybe that's a good thing.*

Not dying is always a good thing. Unless they are taking us to a nest for their hatchlings to devour.

What!

Anyway, it's best not to think like that. Fill your tiny mind with sunny thoughts!

That was impossible, mainly because the sun had vanished. The ravens stopped their cawing and all I could hear was their rattling breath and scraping bones and rustling wings. Though I wanted to cough with every inhalation, I gritted my teeth and breathed in slowly. That seemed to help.

Time passed and we continued moving forward, though directions were hard to ascertain. For all I knew, they were keeping us floating in the same place above the water.

Are we even moving? I asked after several minutes. Or hours.

I believe so, Brax said. *But I could be wrong.*

Well, that was a first: Brax admitting that he might be wrong. If only I could take a deep breath and laugh about it, but laughter was not in the cards.

One raven turned so that it glared in my direction. Its dry eyes looked like raisins, but I got a chill when I realized it was looking me up and down. All the other birds faced forward, but this one didn't.

Which made me wonder if someone was looking through those eyes. Someone other than a raven.

The moment I had that thought, the bird turned and pointed its beak in the direction we were travelling. The stink was getting stronger, so strong that it was close to forcing me to jump from Brax's back to escape it.

But would the ravens just lift me up and carry me in their cloud of wings?

Then they let out a horrifying, rumbling *caw* as one and began flapping in all directions away from us. The sun was suddenly bright and very blinding. I covered my eyes with one hand and only after several moments was I able to see.

Brax shook his head, sucking in clean air. Megan and Thord were still on either side of us, both as pale as ivory and coughing like they had the coal dust sickness. Thord gave a shaky wave that I assumed meant he would survive.

He was alive. Thord was alive. And Megan, too. She brushed feathers from her shoulders.

I then noticed the color green.

There was a lush emerald land before us—after so much blue water followed by the darkness of the ravens, this green was shocking to my eyes. The grass was so bright and rich it seemed to glow. And on that grass was a small group of sheep of such a brilliant white they also looked unreal. I blinked several times to be sure it wasn't a dream.

It was while I blinked that I noticed a woman standing next to the sheep. She was in a gray robe and had long gray hair, but her olive face, even from this distance, looked young.

She leaned on a long intricately carved staff, staring at us as if we were curious bugs that had just appeared in the air.

"A witch," Brax and I said at the same time.

3

THE NAME CALLER

The last bit of doubt about her occupation vanished when the cloud of ravens drew up behind her, now silent as moths. They floated there, wings slowly flapping up and down as all their beaks pointed at us. The sheep didn't react to the birds.

She gestured toward a green open spot and we landed in the grass. After so many hours of flying, it felt like Brax would collapse onto the ground, but he soon straightened himself and stretched. I wanted to jump off and just stand, but knew that would be unwise in case we needed to leave quickly. Thord and Megan landed on either side of us, their swans ruffling their wings. I'm sure we looked like a ragged, dangerous crew.

At least I hoped we looked dangerous, despite all the feathers and bone dust decorating us. We'd be in a better bargaining position if we looked mean. The witch showed no sign of being impressed by our appearance, and even the sheep didn't stir or glance our way—they were oblivious to a dragon only yards from where they grazed. A dragon who at this moment was licking his lips.

Don't do that! I sent.

I can't help it. They look so tasty and I'm ever so hungry.

Perhaps the sheep had never seen a dragon and didn't know to fear Brax's mighty gullet.

The witch sniffed in a sneering manner, and the gurgling of snot up her nostrils carried across the distance between us. Maybe she had a cold. She then spat, her spittle landing near our feet. It was an impressive shot. And frightening.

Frightening because the spittle was sizzling and burning through the grass like acid.

"By Belaz," Thord whispered. "That's so incredibly gross. And dangerous."

"I don't think she likes us," Megan added in her own whisper. "I'm pretty sure she hates dragons—she was aiming at Brax."

The spittle continued to sizzle as if it was burning its way to the underworld. The witch looked from one of us to the other and then let a leering smile widen. That grin nearly made my jaw drop open in shock.

She had no teeth! Her mouth looked like a black hole. And then, as my dragon eye focused, I saw that something was glistening there—her teeth were black, large and very sharp. There was a worse fate than being trapped in an unkindness of ravens. It was facing a witch who was unkindness incarnate.

She continued to smirk and then she lifted her staff, slowly, and I braced for some sort of searing spell. I slid one hand down to grab the hilt of my dagger. I could try to throw it before she brought all of heaven down. Or turned us into flowers. Whatever it was that witches did to their victims.

She shook the staff at us, and nothing happened. Then it became clear that she was counting. "Three assassins, two swans and a dragon," she said. Her voice sounded as if she'd spent several lifetimes gargling gravel. "This is an unexpected pleasure."

"What impressive math skills," Brax answered. I was tempted to elbow him and tell him to shut up, but Brax's verbal barbs had caused the witch's smile to widen. The top teeth were particularly sharp. How did this woman not bite off her own tongue?

"Your sense of humor is almost impressive," she said. "If one could call it humor." She spread her arms, displaying long, ragged sleeves that flapped in the slight breeze. "Welcome to Sartoria."

"Is that what this island is called?" I asked, proud that I got a word in before Brax launched another snark attack.

Her chuckle was a low growl. "This is not an island, you stupid tart." Despite my best effort, my hackles raised. I wasn't a tart. I wasn't stupid! "Sartoria is the land from the Bracken River to here. It is *my* land. But this fief—my fief—and all the other fiefs are on a land mass as big as Ellos or Drachia. It is a country. A homeland. A haven. So, I tell you now that you are standing on the fief of Sartoria in the great land of Azadiq." She gave a thunderous sniff as if we were stinking up the surrounding air. "Azadiq means freedom, since I'm certain you don't know the old tongue."

So this was the land where the wizards had fled to after the emperor had tried to kill them all—with the help of my fellow assassins. We'd known that it might exist, but even standing here I found it hard to believe.

"Are there other witches?" Thord asked. "Umm... or wizards?"

"Oh, the brick-brained male speaks!" the witch said. "So you aren't just a pretty face."

"I'm not a pretty face!" Thord snapped. "I mean, I'm more than that. I mean—"

"Oh, winged gods!" Brax hissed. "Please hammer his brain full of wisdom. You're not helping Thord, but your question was a good one. Are there more magical mortals like you, witch?"

She shook her staff at Brax. "I am not going to answer that, Mr. Soft Scales." Brax tensed as if those words had enraged him and, by the shaking of his muscles, they had.

I will fry her! Brax shouted in my head. *FRY HER!*

No! I answered. *Hold your tongue. Hold your fire, too!*

She deserves to be ashes. A pile of smoking ashes!

Just calm down! I wasn't certain if I'd said this out loud, but Brax grew slightly calmer. He didn't stop digging his talons into the earth, though.

The witch turned toward Brax and me and shook her index finger. "You two naughty children are passing notes in class, aren't you?"

"No," I said. "No, we aren't."

"Yes, you are, Miss Nosy." Why was she attacking my nose? There was nothing wrong with it. Well, it wasn't perfect, but—her words were getting right under my skin. Traveling for days without proper food or a rest had left me and my companions vulnerable. And starving. I had to slow this whole conversation down.

"You really like nicknames," I said. "You're good at them." Maestru Alesius had always said that an honest compliment could be the best way to diffuse a bad situation.

The witch continued to point at me. Her fingernails were long and sharp. "Names that nick are my speciality, princess."

Princess! No wonder Emperor Sargon had ordered every wizard and witch to be executed. If they had all been as aggravating as this loudmouth, then thousands of people would have been lining up to swing the beheading axe.

"Speaking of names," Megan said in a calm voice. "May we have yours?"

"No, you brainless clot, you may not," the witch replied. She had moved slightly and the mass of ravens behind her shifted, too, so they were all pointing toward Megan. "If you have studied any of the books in your horrid Red Assassin School, you'll know that wizards and witches protect their names. Our names are the font of our power."

"Then what do we call you?" Megan asked. "Gums?"

I expected each and every one of those ravens to dart forward, going right through Megan and her swan. But the witch let out a great big loud guffaw that echoed around us. "That's a good one! I appreciate your sauciness and in return for your cleverness, I will give you a name that you can use. That name is: Blacktooth."

"But all of your teeth are black," Megan said.

"Yes, but Blackteeth sounds stupid," Blacktooth replied.

"And Blacktooth doesn't?" Brax asked.

"Oh," the witch said. "I see you suckle on your own wounds, baby dragon. That's a bad habit. But I chose Blacktooth as a name because it is easy to remember considering the color of my teeth. And, before you ask, my teeth are not rotting black—they are made of obsidian. My real teeth fell out about hundred years ago. I still miss them." She tapped her teeth and took on a pensive look, as if recalling a wonderful time in her past. "Now, I don't want you to get your feathers or scales ruffled, but I thought I should let you know that I am trying to decide whether or not to kill you all. It is the law."

"Kill us?" I said. "Just because we landed here? What kind of law is that?"

"We have very few laws in Azadiq—we magical types enjoy our freedoms. But one very important law is to kill strangers who land on our shores. We don't want others to know that we and our beautiful land exist."

"Oh," I said. "That doesn't sound fair or kind at all."

"It's neither, but it is logical," she answered. "That said, a witch must make one's own judgments, too. We are individuals. And, because I'm the curious sort, I've magnanimously decided to let you live. Before we go too far down this toothy tale, what are your names?"

"I am Megan," Megan said. "And this is Thord, Carmen and Brax." Naga hissed. "Oh, and Naga below me and Bolt over there." She gestured with a thumb.

"Perhaps I should have started my discussion with the swans," Blacktooth said. "They seem the smartest of the group."

"If they could speak," I said, "they would tell you we have traveled from Drachia, for days and days, and we are hungry and tired and would greatly appreciate food and water."

Blacktooth rubbed her chin. "So it is possible to fly here from Drachia? Interesting. But why would a motley crew travel such a great distance?"

"We will keep our own council concerning that," Brax said.

"Oh, secrets!" She rubbed the top of her staff. "Witches thrive on secrets. It's so much fun to pick at them like scabs. Or rotting scales."

You should have let me fry her, Brax said.

Then we wouldn't know her lovely nickname, I answered. And Brax chuckled.

Blacktooth wagged a finger at us. "Now, now, I told you

not to pass notes. You should speak up if you have something to say. Let us all know what you're thinking."

I shivered. She really could sense when we talked mind to mind. It was such a private communication between Brax and me that I felt slightly vulnerable.

"As I said: we are at the end of our reserves," I continued. "Could we have food?"

"There is plenty here," Brax said, sniffing in the direction of the flock.

"These are prize sheep," Blacktooth said. "Touch one and you'll be boneless in a heartbeat."

I had never heard such a threat delivered to a dragon without the slightest bit of fear. Brax held his tongue and his thoughts.

"That got your attention," she said. "I will give you water, but not food. I'm afraid if I feed you, you will stick around longer than I would prefer. Like stray cats."

"Water will be enough," I said. Brax groaned but said nothing else.

"I am not quite done poking in your business," Blacktooth said. "You came all this way for something. One does not travel vast reaches of ocean without some burning purpose."

"Yes," Thord said before we could have a conversation about what to tell her. "We are looking for a wizard who doesn't have a name."

"None of us have names," she said. "At least not names we share."

"Well then we seek council with your masters," Thord continued. "With your ... your wizard king."

"Kings? Masters? Mistresses of power?" Blacktooth let out a half-mad chuckle. "There are none here. Each of us is his or her own master or mistress. We have left all of our old rulers behind. But you will want to meet with the council, and you're in luck, for they are gathering this evening." She drew a circle in the air with her finger. "I shall announce your presence." A raven broke from the collection of blackbirds and came to her at a blurring speed. It stopped and landed on her outstretched wrist, slowly moving its ragged wings. Blacktooth spoke to it so quietly I couldn't catch a word.

When she was finished the raven flapped a few feet away, burst into flame and arced like a phoenix through the air and was gone.

"So you don't use spellbirds?" I asked.

"No, they're old-fashioned and they're far too insulting," Blacktooth said. "Plus a flaming raven has panache and really gets people's attention. Now. Let me see if I can resurrect some of my hosting skills. I haven't had visitors for years. Not ones who lived, anyway." Though that last sentence made me tremble, she finished with the words I wanted to hear. "Let's get you some fresh water."

4

FALLING HEAVENS

Blacktooth led us down a hill to a pleasant valley where the sun was warm and there was no breeze. My legs were sore and bowed—they felt like they'd stay in this U shape forever. Five days straight of flying had rattled my bones; they cracked and crackled with each step. Both Thord and Megan let out little grunts of pain as they limped along. Thord even paused to rub Megan's shoulder.

I glared for a moment, then looked away. "Want me to rub your shoulder?" Brax whispered, and I shot him a glance I hoped would pierce him like a crossbow bolt.

"Just walk," I said. "Don't talk."

At the edge of a stream sat a wooden home that looked as if it had grown out of the ground. Oak trees had formed straight walls, opening here and there for a window. It was a tall structure with a canopy of green leaves that served as its roof. Many of the ravens settled in the branches above us. The front door was bright red.

"Come, come, my cherished guests," Blacktooth said. It was hard not to stare at her teeth when she spoke. "There is aqua berry juice and water and if you're particularly truthful and polite, I'll let you have mint tea." A kettle was already boiling on a fire near her home—perhaps it constantly bubbled under the direction of a spell. She approached it and filled a cup in the shape of a skull—or a skull in the shape of a cup—with tea. I caught a wonderful scent of mint.

We three mortals sat at a stone table that could have been used for supper or for sacrifices. Brax stood next to me and the swans rested behind us on a patch of green grass, snapping at any large beetles or locusts that they saw.

Blacktooth put her hand up to her mouth and did a fake whisper: "Your dragon is house-trained, isn't it? It won't defecate next to the table, right?"

My eyes widened. Brax slammed his paw into the ground, digging out divots with his talons. "I am not her dragon. And I am not trained like a pet and I don't def—" He stopped and gave a rueful grin. "You are perhaps the greatest mortal I've met with the gift of getting under my skin. And believe me, all mortals are an aggravation."

"I take that as a high compliment," the witch said. "Now, please drink up."

There were three mugs of tea in front of Megan, Thord and me and a bucket in front of Brax and the swans. They had materialized out of the air without a fuss or the slightest flash. "Drink! Drink!" she repeated. "It isn't poisoned. I'm not a lowly assassin. And if I wanted you dead, I wouldn't be so subtle—I'd peel the skin from your flesh and laugh as you scream."

"Well, that makes me thirsty," Megan said. She drank from her cup.

I stared at mine. At least the cup wasn't a skull and the tea did smell divine, and the mint in it might give me some sustenance. I sipped and was surprised by the taste.

"This is wonderful," I said. "The best mint tea I've ever had."

Brax lifted his head from the bucket. "I agree! And I've never had tea in a bucket before. It's both classy and trashy."

"Of course you love the tea." Blacktooth lifted her skull cup in a sort of toast. "I'm known throughout Azadiq for my tea. Well, and my ravens of death and my biting sarcasm and my beauty."

Brax cleared his throat to make a comment on that last declaration, but I kicked him in the leg before he could say anything.

"The cups fill themselves!" Thord had drained his and was now staring down at it. My own cup was also full.

"Of course, simpleton." She didn't say this in a sarcastic manner, which suggested that insults flowed naturally when she spoke. "I wouldn't waste time carrying a pot around. I'm a witch." Blacktooth came over and sat across from me. Her skull cup clinked as she set it on the table. "You have an interesting right eye, child. So... reptilian. What is it that your snake eye sees?"

"The truth," I said, hoping to sound deep and mysterious.

"Well, truth is in the eye of the beholder." She chuckled and then sniffed for about the tenth time since we'd met her. Maybe she had a nasal drip—it was a bad one, judging by the sound of snot gurgling up her nose. "You had mentioned Ellos: what news do you have of the land I once called home?"

"It is in flames," Thord said. "Emperor Sargon has conquered Woden and Trusk, and the other realms will soon bend a knee or fall before his onslaught. Perhaps they have fallen already."

"Emperor Sargon?" Blacktooth pretended to do math in

the air. "I am already two emperors behind. Assuming his older brother was emperor for a heartbeat or two."

"You didn't miss much," Brax said. "A bunch of mortals fighting over a patch of sand, some ugly mountains and sheep."

Blacktooth nodded. "That sums up most of Ellos's history. Now what is the endgame for this baby emperor?"

"To conquer all of Ellos," Megan said. "Sargon won't rest until every last kingdom is under his sandals."

Blacktooth sighed; her breath smelled minty with a hint of decay. "It's the way of emperors—you can't blame him for that. They are raised from babes to grow the girth of their empires. And their bellies, too. Now I—" She stopped and looked to the sky. "It seems the heavens are falling."

All of us looked up.

A black dot was coming down from high in the clear sky, and at such great speed I at first thought someone had fired an arrow from above. The dark blur seemed to be coming straight for me. I lifted my cup to deflect it. Thord put his hand up as a shield. Both useless gestures if this was an arrow.

The blur stopped right above Thord—two wings unfurled and a voice said, "Oh gods! A witch. I thought they were all dead."

A spellbird! It flapped its wings hummingbird quick, keeping its position above the table.

"You *hoped* we were all were dead," Blacktooth said. "You spellbirds are ever so ungrateful for the life your creators gave you."

"Such a life!" The spellbird spat an impressive amount of spittle for such a small creature. "I am so thankful for the endless slavery. It's truly wonderful to spend every waking moment darting back and forth in the heavens, passing inane words from one mortal idiot to the next. If I have to recite any more recipes for pickled herring, I will explode."

Blacktooth made a *tut tut tut*. "Such a travesty! Since you mentioned reciting things, perhaps you have words for one of my guests." Blacktooth gestured toward us.

"That I do." The songbird turned and opened one eye slightly wider, examining us. "Which of you is Thord of the Red Assassins? I have a message from Davin of the Red Assassins." The name wasn't familiar to me. "Would you like me to relay it here or in private?" He glanced back at the witch.

"I'd suggest sharing it with everyone," Blacktooth said. "As payment for the tea. Plus, in all honesty, there isn't a square inch in Sartoria where I can't hear. I have a thousand ears."

"Well, that's a lovely image," Brax said.

Megan patted Thord on the shoulder. They didn't seem to be able to keep their hands off each other. "You might as well let us all hear the message," she said. "It's not like Davin will be giving away any state secrets."

Thord pointed at the spellbird. "Go ahead. Share the message with everyone."

"Here it is." The spellbird cleared his throat. "Make sure you pay attention to the ending. It gets kind of garbled." I'd seen enough of these birds that I thought of them as very tiny actors. He then spoke in a deep male voice. "Thord, this is Davin." I now remembered he was one of the two assassins Thord and Megan had met: Davin and Mai. I'd seen a poster with their faces on it in Akkadium several weeks ago. The poster also had my face. "I assume you are getting this message within a few hours of my sending it. I have bad news. Mai is dead. Immortals, under Scyllia's control, discovered both of us. We fought and escaped, but Mai succumbed to her wounds a few minutes ago. I will have to abandon her body. I do still have her swan." As cold as it sounded, I knew that every swan was an important tactical weapon. "There is something different about Scyllia—they have cast a spell on her. She is stronger and our blades couldn't penetrate her—her flesh. Well, if it is still flesh." The bird took a deep breath. "Sargon's fleet has landed in Myra and they are pushing up through Trella. So that Eshya is caught in his pincers. This also means that Avenus is cut off from supplies. I'm sending this from a hidey hole and hope I can fly across the strait to Avenus." The bird paused and stood still for a second or two, then nearly shouted: "Oh, by Belaz, they have found me! Quick, take this message to Thord of the Red Assassins. Go, bird. Go! Go!" The spellbird sat still for several more moments, and I was just about to say something when it shouted again. "Ugh! You won't take me. I—"

The songbird stopped talking and looked at Thord. "Is there something I can do for you? Do you have a reply?" he said in his normal voice.

"A reply?" Thord asked. "Did Davin survive?"

"Can you mortals survive without your heads?" the spellbird asked.

Thord went pale. "Do you mean what I think you mean?"

"Yes," the songbird said.

"No, we can't," I answered.

"Then your companion did not survive. I did. And I brought his message and now you have heard it. Is there something I can do for you? Do you have a reply?" He coughed again. "And, may I be so bold as to give you a hint? A reply to Davin would be pointless."

Thord was still blinking, staring at the bird. I didn't

know this Davin, but maybe Thord had become friends with him. I patted his hand. It took a moment for his face to regain some color. “No. I don’t have a reply,” he said. “Nor do I have another command.”

“Good, then I am released. Fare thee well and may you forget the summoning spell.” He flapped his wings, about to take off from Thord’s shoulders, when a ball of flame and feathers appeared between him and the witch. But the flame radiated cold instead of heat.

“You… you use a dead burning raven to pass messages!” the spellbird shouted.

“Yes, I do,” the witch said.

“That’s abominable!” the bird shouted.

“They don’t talk back,” Blacktooth said.

The spellbird let out a disgusted grunt, then arrowed straight up into the sky.

Before we could discuss the message we’d just received, Blacktooth spread her arms and said, “Speak, raven. What is the answer?”

“Yes,” the bird growled. The witch gestured and the raven flapped away, though the burning smell clung to the air. Megan coughed.

“And there you have it,” the witch announced. “They have granted you audience to the most powerful circle of witches and wizards in the world. They are—how shall I put it?—excited to meet a group of assassins."

"You got all of that from the bird saying yes?" Brax asked.

"A witch can always read between the lines." She grinned, giving us a flash of those black, sharp teeth. They looked even more grotesque this close up. "You've had your tea. That's all you will get from me. Leave immediately for the Gorzed Circle. You’re the council’s problem now. Begone!”

5

A PLACE OF STONES

Her ravens were our guides.

Thankfully, Blacktooth didn't send the whole flock of ravens. Instead there were seven on one side of us and seven on the other. I had done enough reading at Maestru Beatrix's library to know that seven was a powerful number for magic-using mortals.

"The presence of the ravens will let other wizards and witches know you are under my watch and my protection," she had explained. "You wouldn't want a big ol' bolt of lightning blasting you from the sky. That would be sad and very messy."

Flying with the ravens was almost worse than messy—they still gave off a nauseating stink that sent tendrils of fear scratching at my thoughts. But the dead birds did their job and we flew in a southeast direction over the green lands of Sartoria. As far as I could see Blacktooth's fief was just grass and hills and sheep. No other mortals seemed to live there.

My throat wasn't dry, because I'd drunk more than my fill of tea, but my stomach rumbled with an aching hunger.

Occasionally, even though we were flying with the wind in my ears, I heard Brax's stomach rumble, too.

"She wanted us to be hungry," Brax said. "To be on edge."

"That thought had crossed my mind. Plus, she didn't want any of her sheep to vanish into your gullet."

"There's that, too," he answered. When he spoke the next time, it was loud enough for Thord and Megan to hear. "I just want you all to know that wizards are greedy, power hungry, egotistical and self-centered."

"So you have several things in common with them," Megan said.

"Oh, ha!" Brax replied, but he didn't come up with a clever reply. Instead, he belched with such velocity and power that even Megan crinkled her nose. "I also want you to know that when we arrive at this Gorzed Circle, it is very likely we will be caught in some sticky spell and murdered. I have the most to lose, of course."

"Why is that?" Thord asked.

"Because I have such a lovely hide." He gestured at his scales, which were looking a little worn and certainly weren't all that bright. "And great teeth and talons. The better to make spells from. You three and the swans will probably just end up in some sort of witch's brew. Or a wizard stew. They do like cooking people alive."

"I'm not going to be anyone's soup," I said. "Or stew."

"Many a rabbit has said that," Brax replied. "I'm just being the grown-up in the group and letting you know what lies ahead. So steel your tiny little mortal guts."

"Well, thanks for that cheery news," Thord said. "Do you have any suggestion on how we can prevent ending up in a pot?"

He glanced left and right. "Well, we can't turn back—our

guardians will prevent that and I have a feeling that if I fry these few ravens, they will just call the rest of their stinky brethren. So we have to meet this council. Thord, it's probably best if you say nothing while we talk to them. You clench your jaw and look—well, not intimidating—just look like you're not a soup bone."

"Great advice," Thord replied, though his answer came through gritted teeth.

"In fact, it might be best if I do all the talking," Brax added.

"Why?" I asked.

"Because wizards don't harbor a grudge against we innocent dragons."

"And they have a grudge against the three of us?" I asked.

"Just think for a moment, Carmen. Think of your occupation."

"Yes, we're assassins, I know." Then I realized what he was suggesting. "Oh, they see us as representing the assassins who helped the emperor round up the wizards."

"Yes, I'm afraid you've all been tarnished by that brush," Brax said. "So don't be surprised if they want to sacrifice one or two of you. These magical mortals have long angry memories."

"But that's not fair," Megan said. "We hadn't even graduated when the wizards and witches were all hunted down."

"Wizards are very wise, but they don't always play fair," he said. "And they do so love getting revenge. So it's agreed, I will do the talking."

We grew quiet. The emerald, rolling land continued below us. Was this still Sartoria, the fief that Blacktooth controlled? Or had we already strayed onto another wizard's domain? Our short conversation with Blacktooth indicated that each wizard or witch had their own fief. I didn't imagine any of them were much friendlier than the witch.

We passed a village built on a large bridge over a river. On either side of the village, dwarfing the buildings, were giant watermills that were likely used to grind grain. The villagers were tiny in the distance, even when I squinted through my dragon eye. We weren't tiny from their vantage point, because many of them filed out onto the bridge to stare upwards. I guess we made quite the sight.

"There must have been regular mortals who came with the wizards and witches," Thord said.

"Or there were already villages here before the wizards arrived," Megan suggested.

"Oh, that's a good point, Meg," Thord said.

I'd never heard him use a short version of her name before and I expected Megan to correct him with a sharp word or a sharp crossbow bolt, but her only response was a smile and a wink.

She winked at him? What was going on?

Stop kicking my side! Brax shot this request into my head.

I'm not! I shot back, then looked down at my rebel leg. *I mean, sorry. Must have been a cramp.*

I took a few deep breaths and concentrated on the distance, as if by staring alone I could see our destination.

We passed over a large lake and the landscape beyond it was white. I assumed it was some sort of salt plains, but with each sweep of Brax's wings the air grew colder, and very suddenly we were flying over snow and ice with the occasional stone peak sticking into the air—a very forbidding sight. The whiteness ran along in a clear line to the north and south, as if it followed a map's boundaries. On either side of that line, the landscape was green. From what I knew of the colder lands, they were either far in the north or south, not plopped right in the middle of a land mass. And yet here this grim landscape sat. I could just make out a small palace with sharp toothlike towers made of ice.

“There dwells a wizard with a cold, cold heart,” Brax said. “Be glad we didn’t land there first. What type of man would choose ice for a home?”

"It might be a woman," I said.

"No. Women aren't that stupid."

That was about as close to a compliment as Brax would give. So I pretended he was telling me I wasn't stupid.

The ravens guided us along the edge of the winter fief. It now became clear that the fief to the north was a desert. It boggled my mind that the two types of landscapes could exist so close to each other. Did snow ever creep over and fall on the desert?

In time we left the desert and the ice behind and flew directly over another fief that was only the tops of thick trees, covered with leaves and vines. There was so much moisture in the air that soon all of us were dripping, even the ravens. We couldn’t fly over the rainforest fast enough. In the center of it all was a stone obelisk that sat a hundred feet above the trees. Someone had carved it into the shape of a giant ape.

“Well, you can’t say wizards and witches aren’t creative,” Brax said. “This Azadiq seems like the perfect place for them. Perhaps being hunted by the emperor was the greatest thing to happen to their kind.”

“Being hunted by the emperor was good for them?” Megan said. “Maybe you shouldn’t do the talking for us—we’ll all be soup in a few heartbeats.”

“I am just making an observation,” Brax said. “I’m wise enough to not share it with the council.”

“I find it all very frightening,” I admitted.

“Why is that?” Thord asked from the opposite side. It was one of the first times he’d said anything directly to me since we’d left Drachia.

I pointed at the jungle. “Imagine the power it takes a wizard to shape the very land to your will.”

“Oh, so they can grow a few vines,” Brax said. "Big deal." But his words weren't spoken with as much bravado as I was used to from him.

We were soon above another desert plain of red sand that was so dry every last bit of moisture was sucked out of our skin. I started to long for another glass of mint tea, preferably cooled by ice chips. The sun seemed like it was leaning right over the flat and empty landscape—whatever gods made that great ball of fire in the sky were trying their best to melt us. There was not a single plant or sign of life. It was such a barren place even scorpions would find it uncomfortable. The only break from the sand was large red stones that had been arranged in strange circular patterns. It made me queasy to look at them too long—like I might fall into a trance and leap off Brax toward one of them.

Several minutes later, I spotted our destination. At the very center of the fief was a perfectly round chasm that descended into darkness. In the middle of it was a flat circular floor of rock that appeared to be levitating. Circling the outside of that floating floor were obelisks that looked as if they’d been plucked up by a giant and formed into a circle. Or maybe a real giant had done it. In my limited reading about magic, I had learned that circles were the most powerful symbol in spell-casting. This platform was a place where magic could be amplified. Each obelisk pointed into the sky.

The ravens were taking us straight there. “I have a

feeling we are arriving at the Gorzed Circle," Brax said. "I for one find it wholly unattractive."

The ravens circled around the place, leaving an opening for us to land. I first thought the platform was deserted, but then saw that standing still next to each of the stones was a wizard or witch, faces hidden by hoods.

"I don't like this," Megan said. "It seems off, somehow."

"Yes," Brax said. "I agree with Megan for once. It looks a little like they are all prepared for, oh, I don't know, a ritual sacrifice. I'm just pulling that out of my thought bag of bad endings."

There was something about how they were positioned in perfect relation with each other. As if they were part of a complicated and ancient pattern. Again, I knew they drew power from patterns.

The ravens wanted us to land right where a circle of runes had been etched into the stone. They might represent a thousand spells.

"I will add my voice to not liking it," I said. "Thord?"

"Oh, I'm with all three of you," he answered. "There are at least twenty spell wielders there that I can see. Who knows how many are invisible or disguised as stones. I'm halfway thinking we should make a run for it."

"There's the problem," Brax said. "We could run. We might even outdistance the ravens, but where do we go? Back to Drachia? I can't fly that far without a day's rest and at least a goat lunch."

"So we don't have a choice," Thord said.

"We always have a choice," Megan said. "We can die fighting to get away. Or die there."

"Or get what we came for," I added. "Maybe this is all a show. You said yourself wizards are egotistical. They're just showing us their powers to intimidate us. What would they benefit from killing all of us?"

"They might just do it for fun," Brax said.

"You're not helping!" I smacked his back, which I was sure he didn't even feel.

A shadow moved away from one of the stones. It was a woman in the same robes as the others who strode toward the center of the circle. There was something familiar about her gait—I'd seen her walk before—but before I could place it, she threw back her hood, revealing gray hair and a shadow of a mouth.

It was Blacktooth. "How in Belaz's name did she get here before us?" I asked.

"She's a witch," Brax said smartly. "They're all show-offs."

Blacktooth was gesturing at the circle, and shouting as if she were an angry mother. But her words didn't travel up to us.

"I suppose if she wanted us dead she would have just poisoned us," Megan said.

"That's true," Brax replied. "Let me make this decision for all of us, because there really is only one." He descended, and so did I because I was on his back.

Brax?

As I said, we don't have a choice.

Megan and Thord guided their swans on either side and we landed softly in the middle of the circle of runes.

"It's about time," Blacktooth said. Then she raised a hand.

It was a signal that I hoped would mean that the other witches and wizards would come forward, maybe with their own hands extended in a sign of peace. It would be ideal if they were holding plates of steaming food.

But I was wrong. In a blink a blue bolt of lightning lashed out like a whip from the runes in the ground. Brax was the first to let out a cry of warning, but he didn't get to finish whatever he was saying—the energy instantly wrapped itself around his wings, all his limbs, and his mouth and then slammed him to the ground and knocked me off his back. The two swans were bound the same way.

Thord, Megan and I landed on our feet and, following the dictates of hundreds of hours of training, we took up back-to-back positions, squaring off against our circle of enemies.

6

RED

"You forgot to ask me for continuous protection." Blacktooth's smile was as wide and sinister as it had been every other time I'd seen it. "Though I guaranteed safe passage—I didn't guarantee what would happen after that passage."

Sparks flew as Brax scraped his talons into the stone and rose, trying to break the lightning bonds. Grunting and roaring between clenched teeth, he nearly made it back to his full height, then was slammed into the stone.

They are too strong, he sent to me. *I will wait and gather strength.*

You do that, I replied, then I turned to Blacktooth who looked like she was about to comment on my communication with Brax.

"You betrayed us," I spat. "You lied!"

"I only omitted details," she said.

"It's the same thing!" Megan pointed her small crossbow toward Blacktooth. "I should put a bolt through your heart."

"Oh, do I really have to do this?" She rolled her eyes, then made a motion with her staff. Both Megan's crossbow and Thord's short sword burst into flames. They shouted in pain and dropped their weapons.

My daggers did become enveloped by fire, but they didn't grow hotter, so I kept a tight grip. Scales rose across my hands, protecting me from the heat. Blacktooth wagged a finger at me. "That is curious," she said. "Very curious." Then she flicked a finger and two lightning whips came out of the stone and snapped against my bare wrists. A charge of power zipped through my skin, and I dropped the daggers. "That's better!"

We three assassins continued to stand back to back. Brax had stopped his writhing and the swans, such intelligent beasts, became still and watched us and our enemies for cues.

Blacktooth breathed deep, the sound of snot gurgling up her nose, and then cleared her throat. "It is very curious to have three assassins land on the great land of Azadiq. It is a secret place and we want to keep it that way."

"Just tell us what your intentions are," Megan said.

"My intentions?" Blacktooth put a hand to her chest as if she were innocent. "Oh, you think I am the leader of this gathering? Oh, how delicious! No, Snot-nose."

"Takes one to know one," Megan said.

Blacktooth narrowed her eyes so they became two burning orbs. "Be careful with your words! I am the closest thing you have to an ally—for I am the only one who has had some conversation with you, simple as it was. But let me now introduce the high consul."

All the wizards and witches, who had been standing back near the obelisks, walked slowly toward us from every direction, their features still hidden in the shadows of their hoods. It wasn't until they got closer that they, one by one, pulled back their hoods and revealed many male and female faces of different colors, skin types and ages, some surprisingly plain, some eye-catchingly ugly and others so beautiful I wondered if they'd cast a charisma spell. They had one thing in common: They all looked angry.

"This is not good," Thord whispered.

"Are you going to interrogate us?" I asked Blacktooth.

"Oh, no, not me! I'm too soft for that work. Allow me to introduce Red. You'll like Red. You'll find her very, very interesting." Blacktooth backed away, revealing a scrunched-over, smallish figure. Her exposed hand, which was gripping a walking stick, was shriveled up to the point of looking like bones. She leaned on the staff and struggled, inch by inch, forward. And when she finally reached us, she looked up. Her skin was papery thin, her flesh withered, and her hair a scraggly gray. She looked so old that she may have been here to watch as the lands were first formed by the gods. Her eyes were a blazing blue, though, and she had one streak of red hair in the center of her skull.

"By the laws of Azadiq, I declare that you are all charged with betrayal and sentenced to death." Her voice was steady and crackled with command. "We shall reduce the dragon to useful parts. And we will add the swans to our menagerie of flying creatures."

"What?" Megan said. "You will kill us without a trial? For no reason at all."

Red banged her staff against the stone floor and the platform seemed to shake. "We have plenty of reasons. The first being that you have broken our laws by landing on Azadiq. The second law you broke just by existing: any assassin who comes within sight of a witch or wizard will be executed. It was the first law our council decreed. An imminently fair law."

"What sort of laws do you have if the accused are not

even allowed to defend themselves?" Thord asked. He had been particularly interested in the legal systems of various countries. "Even the despot emperor Sargon has the pretence of judges and courts and trials. Surely you are more civilized than him."

"Don't speak of being civilized, child!" Red shouted, and the words were so powerful I had to take a step back. "Traitor! Betrayer! Assassins have no rights to a trial. Each of you is the excrement of false truths."

"I assume you are talking about how our comrades aided the Empire," Thord said. He was surprisingly calm before this witch. I tried to stand straighter. "They were only doing their jobs."

"ONLY DOING THEIR JOBS," Red repeated. Her words were almost a physical force hitting us with each syllable. She was small, but it was as if she were drawing from the deep wells of darkness below her, from the sky, moving worlds with her words. "Only children hide behind such excuses. Your masters and your comrades hunted us down one by one and brought us to the emperor for whatever nefarious ending he had planned in the white tower." I knew that ending: he had eaten the heart of each captured wizard or witch and gained their powers. I decided this wasn't a good time to share that information. "Enough prevarication! There were agreements between our guilds, and your kind broke them for greed. And for that you and all your brethren are always sentenced to immediate execution."

She made a motion and each of the wizards behind her whispered words that rang in some sharp, unfamiliar language. Words of power. Words of magic being repeated by a group of wizards and witches.

"I have this feeling something horrible is about to happen," Megan whispered. "It's been nice knowing you."

"Yes it has, Megan," Thord said.

"What about me?" I said. "Has it been nice knowing me?" I meant it to sound like a joke. Alas, it didn't.

Thord opened his mouth to reply, but was drowned out by a horrible roaring noise.

Cracks had appeared in the air between us and the council. A glowing mist seeped out of those cracks, curling like a hundred smoky tentacles reaching toward us.

They have opened the paths between worlds, Brax informed me.

For what?

Hungry Ones.

What's that?

But he didn't answer. It became clear what a Hungry One was when lanky, thin creatures twice as tall as normal men stepped out of those cracks. They had wide obsidian eyes and malformed faces with mouths that were a circle of teeth. Each of their long arms were stone blades.

They stepped into our world, sniffed once, and loped in our direction.

7

HUNGRY ONES

"Wait!" I said. "You don't need to do this." But the wizards and witches responded by stepping back and fanning out to get a better view of the outcome of their summoning and, I assume, to avoid being splattered by any blood that was about to be spilled. Brax and the swans twisted and fought against their bonds, the energy crackling around them—but they didn't break free.

Run. Run if you can, he sent to me. But there was nowhere to run—the creatures were coming from all directions. I leapt forward, snapped up my daggers and turned to hand one to Megan because her crossbow had been reduced to ashes. "I've been dying to try one of these!" she said. Thord grabbed his sword from the ground, gripping tight even though it must still be hot from the flames.

The first creature came at me swinging a stone arm. I ducked and the blow swooshed just above my head as I shoved the blade in its chest. The thing collapsed into a pile of wriggling worms. I let out a small sigh of relief—at least the Uriken blades were powerful enough to defend us.

But that gave only a moment's respite as another creature stepped in, its mouth—a ring of teeth—opening and closing. Its blow came so fast that I couldn't move in time, but Thord pushed me down so that the stone blade missed both of us. Megan shoved her dagger into the thing's head and the creature crumbled into a collection of dead flies.

"This is easy!" she said. Then one of the Hungry Ones caught the top of her head with a stone arm. I thought she'd be decapitated. The blow looked horribly hard, but when she fell her head was still on her shoulders. Thord yanked her out of the way of the next strike and I stabbed the monster, making it fall into a pile of dead moths. Megan got to her feet. There was a red line of blood along her forehead.

"Your head must be made of stone," I said.

"And yet I have more brains than you," she answered through gritted teeth.

Several of the lanky creatures were within striking range, and they rained down a flurry of blows, so it became a constant act to dodge and deflect those stone blades—and it was almost impossible to strike back. Behind them, the swans hissed but couldn't come to our aid and Brax continued to fight against his bonds—there was no help for us.

The most awful part was the wet sounds the things made as they moved their mouths, hungering to eat us—to suck out our brains or slurp on our intestines. The sound alone would drive me mad.

"More keep coming out of the openings," Thord said. "Bigger creatures! Soon the numbers will be too many for us to keep at bay."

He was correct. Each new Hungry One that arrived was larger and more twisted in shape. The next wave of creatures had several arms each and looked more like insects than the others. One was only a large, toothed, blind head on a long neck that reached out tentacles from the other world.

That thing charged through, uncoiling, smashing others out of the way in its desperation to reach us. Then, despite being blind, it sniffed and smelled until it located us and raised its massive maw of a face and drew in a breath.

I guessed what would come next. Either fire, or acid, or something worse.

I pushed Megan and Thord behind me and spread my arms.

The thing breathed out, a white flame, so horribly cold that the creatures beside it froze and the blast hit us full on.

At the same moment, the scales popped up on my skin. I closed my mouth and my eyes and felt the cold. It burned, it threatened to turn me to ice, but with my eyes closed I was protected, and continued to shield my friends.

"What's all over you?" Thord asked.

I couldn't open my mouth to tell him to shut up. I didn't want my tongue to freeze. The glacial freeze grew slightly warmer and I risked opening my dragon eye. The mouth was rearing back and snapping forward, coming to devour us. It looked to be large enough to swallow me whole. It obviously preferred its food frozen.

I leapt up as it drew back and met the thing in the air, stabbing it below the gaping maw, pushing upwards. My blade went deep and cut into what I hoped was the brain cavity. The creature shook, and I fell back, just able to pull my blade out of that wound. The massive mouth exhaled once more and then fell to one side and shattered along the length of the ground.

The scales retreated from my skin.

“How in the seven hells did you do block that blast?” Megan said. Both of them were gaping at me like I was the monster.

"You—you grew scales," Thord said. "Scales."

"Get it together," I shouted. "Both of you. We have work to do."

Now that the giant mouth had fallen, there was room for the other Hungry Ones to come charging in. I did get a glance through the crowd of creatures to see Red watching intently, her face set. She seemed neither pleased nor saddened by what was happening.

“Stop this!” I shouted at her. “Stop this attack!”

Thord shoved me aside so that a blow missed me. He stabbed the creature with his sword, and it collapsed.

“They don’t want to talk,” he said. “Keep your mind on the fight.”

But I didn't keep my mind on the fight—a desperate thought had occurred to me.

Somehow my brain remembered that these wizards and witches knew nothing about the events in Ellos. So, in an eye blink, I came up with what I believed was a reasoned argument: “There’s no point in killing us!” I shouted. “Red, there is no point! The assassin’s guild is dead. It’s destroyed forever. The Red Assassin Fortress has fallen.”

After hearing that last sentence, Red raised her hand and the creatures suddenly stopped and backed away, their mouths opening and closing as they each emitted a whining, disappointed sound. One by one they stepped back into the openings in the air and vanished. I lowered my blade. So did Thord and Megan.

“Explain,” Red said. “What’s this about a dead assassin’s guild?”

I wiped the sweat from my forehead. “The emperor

Sargon declared war on the assassins," I said, keeping my voice steady while trying not to show how winded I was. "His forces attacked the Red Fortress and every single assassin—except we three—has died. The guild is broken. The school destroyed."

"All assassins are dead?" she repeated; her gravelly voice held a tone of triumph and a pinch of glee. "All of them? Even Banderius—the greatest of the wizard hunters?"

"Yes, even Banderius," I said. "Though Banderius wasn't killed by any Immortal." I gestured toward Brax who was doing his best to look big, despite being bound by lightning. "He killed him."

"Burnt him to a crisp," Thord added with a bit of pride —almost as if he liked Brax. "He did it right after Banderius stabbed me." Thord didn't mention that he was using Banderius's sword.

"Banderius is dead!" Red's grin showed that her teeth were perfect. Which, in a mouth so old, was disconcerting. She turned to the others and raised her withered arms. "Banderius is dead! This is the most glorious news!"

The wizards and witches broke into such great applause you'd think they'd just reached the ending of a famous play. Their clapping echoed around us, and with that applause and laughter I felt something rise in me: hope. Hope that we might survive.

Red turned back to us. She was so happy she didn't need to lean as hard on her staff. "You have brought us great tidings. The guild is destroyed! Our enemies have suffered and been brought low—a fitting end for the backstabbing traitors."

I chose not to mention that many a great maestru had died.

"You say only three of you remain?" she said, and a chill trickled down my spine. "Every other assassin is dead?"

"Yes," Megan said. "We are the last."

Of course, none of us mentioned Maestru Beatrix, who was in the Avenus Library. But perhaps that wasn't a lie of omission. She might consider herself more of a librarian than an assassin these days.

Red crinkled a finger at me. It looked so old I thought it might snap off when she bent it. "They train your kind to lie, but I choose to believe you because the news is so wonderful and blessed." She drew in a rattling breath. "So to complete the absolute destruction of our enemies, we just have to kill you. Our whole nation has sworn to destroy every single cretin who has taken the oath of the assassin."

"It was a nice try," Thord whispered. "But I think we're done for."

He was right. All I'd won were a few more breaths. Judging by the glee in Red's eyes, we would soon be fighting for our lives again.

I clutched the dagger. I glanced at Brax, who was staring at me, then moved his eye as if looking at his foot. His bonds! Maybe with this ancient dagger I could cut that lightning leash and we could fight our way out of here. I would just have to get there. I imagined the gathered wizards could poke me full of holes with magical bolts or fireballs before I made it halfway to Brax, but I had to try.

I took a deep, quiet breath and loosened my leg muscles, ready to leap.

"You will break your law, if you kill us," Megan said.

"She's right," Thord agreed. "She's right!"

I stood up straight. What in Belaz were they on about?

"What do you mean by that?" Red's tone was suspicious.

"And if you are delaying me with a lie, I will pull out your entrails one by one with a knitting needle."

I had no doubt she could do it.

"You have all sworn to destroy every single assassin who has taken the red oath," Megan said. "Well, the Immortals attacked the Keep of the Red Assassins on graduation night. Not one of us students swore the assassin's oath. So your law doesn't apply to us."

Red stared at her for several moments. The old woman's eyes were of such a dark color they seemed to be all pupil. That withering gaze was tinged with cruelty and...

... and she laughed. It was a crackly, wheezy cough of a thing, but it *was* a laugh. "You are a gifted speaker," she said. "And you are correct. If you have sworn no oath, then you cannot break it and we should not kill you—at least for that reason. You have snatched your lives from the very jaws of justice. Congratulations." She didn't sound congratulatory. In fact, she looked like an old cat that had just had a dangling mouse taken away from it.

I breathed out a sigh. I wanted to clap Megan on the back, but felt that showing such joy might not be received well. "Now," I said. "We came all this way for a reason. We—"

Red held up her hand. "No, child. We are not done. Even if you haven't sworn an oath, you were trained to the cusp of becoming a full-blooded assassin. You have been corrupted by their teachings."

"Corrupted?" I said and Megan elbowed me.

"Yes, corrupted," Red continued. "You have escaped on a technicality, but I want a sign of good faith. You wear assassin cloaks. I demand you remove them and renounce your teachings."

None of us moved.

"You must do this to live," Red added. She clicked her fingers together, making a small, crackling sound. "Otherwise I will have no other choice but to consider you to be assassins and execute you."

I thought of Maestru Alesius and of all the other maestrus. Could I turn my back on our teachings to survive? What would he say? Already his disappointed face was rising in my memory.

Megan and Thord were having the same thoughts. But before I could whisper anything to either of them, Megan dropped her cloak. "We cannot die for people who are long dead," she said, loud enough for Red to hear. "It would be completely stupid."

But neither Thord nor I moved.

And then Thord got down on his knees and dropped his cloak. I was standing alone.

"Carmen," he whispered. "Get down. This is no time to be stubborn."

He was right. Megan was right. I hadn't sworn an oath. But could I turn my back on my assassin life? The maestrus had raised me in the fortress. That lifestyle was as much in my blood as anything. I had defended their ideals. I was an assassin to the core. "No," I said, finally. "No. I cannot."

"Then it looks like one of you will die," Red said. "Since the dragon killed Banderius, we'll let the dragon live."

"Would you betray your teachers?" I asked her. "Would you turn your back on those who passed their wisdom down to you?"

"I earned my wisdom," she answered. "And I ate the heart of my master, but he deserved that. You have chosen your side. You will die."

With a speed that belied her age, she took a step forward and poked the staff right below my collarbone.

And her aim is what saved my life. For the staff hit the soulstone and suddenly in both my head and, I knew with certainty, in every other head there, a female voice shouted, *If you kill any of them then all of Drachia will descend and tear you wizards and witches and all mortals on this ugly land to pieces and burn this country down to its bones.*

8

NO ONE

Red staggered back two steps, then stabbed her staff in the ground for support. "What?" she asked. "What is it you wear?"

"Oh," I said. "This?" I drew the soulstone out from under my shirt. "This stone contains the sister to the king of all Drachia." I was as shocked as anyone that Brenna had spoken to us. "Her name is Princess Brenna Andorium," I added, though her voice had sounded nothing like a typical princess. Her anger still echoed in my ears. "I would suggest not upsetting her any further."

"Brenna," Brax said. "It was Brenna." He whispered this, clearly in shock. "Speak again, Brenna. Speak!"

But she didn't say a word. Instead, in the silence that followed, it was I who opened my mouth: "You haven't asked me why we are here."

"W-why have you come to our land?" Red asked. She was still shaking a little, and not just from her age. She continued to stare at the stone as if it might explode.

"Brenna is the reason," I said, tapping the soulstone. "And we have one other request which I will ask later." I knew it was important to take as much control as possible of the situation.

Red continued to lean on the staff, holding it out in front of her like a shield. "And what is it you want for this dragon princess?"

"First," I gestured toward Brax, "I ask kindly that you release Brax. He is the brother to the king."

Oh, you're thinking quick on your feet, Brax said, *and sounding all dramatic. Just don't call me a prince!*

"He is Prince Braxorius Andorium," I added. "So if you harm one scale on the prince's hide, all hellfire will rain down on you. And I mean that literally."

I said not to call me a prince! he sent to me.

If the name fits.

Now that I had found my voice, my training was coming back to me—Maestru Alesius himself had taught me how to use my voice to soothe an enemy or to wield it as a weapon. Today, it was a weapon: "I would suggest that keeping a member of the royal family bound will not reflect well on all of you wizards and witches. And though you are powerful and wise," I continued, "I doubt you could hold off the overwhelming strength of the dragon armies. They are mighty. As mighty as the heavens themselves."

Don't get too dramatic, Brax warned inside my head.

I was speaking as if I had some influence over these mighty dragon armies. I smartly skipped the part where they'd just chosen a new king and were, at this moment, probably putting down several rebellions. But there was no way for my audience to know that. And, as Maestru Alesius always said, knowledge is power. I was enjoying the guarded respect that I now saw in the eyes of the council. Even Blacktooth looked impressed. I could tell by the way she was gritting her black teeth.

Red had straightened her spine—well, as straight as her old spine would get. She snapped her fingers and the bonds holding both Brax and the swans vanished with a crackle. The swans made a perturbed series of honks and hisses, suggesting in their own way they might poke an eye or two from the gathered wizards. Brax just stretched and unfurled his wings, which made him appear rather impressive—though many of his ribs were showing and his scales lacked luster. The journey had taken a toll on his strength, but the wizards wouldn't know that.

"Is this all true, dragon?" Red asked.

"It is true," Brax said. "These youths have been telling the truth since the moment we landed. I burned Banderius to a crisp. It is also true I am the brother of Kon Andorium, king of all dragons. And my sister just gave you a rather serious warning. And yes, we are here seeking aid for her."

"Well, well." Red spared a glance at the stone around my neck. "Such old, old magic on that chain around your neck. Even I don't have much knowledge about it."

"A dragon mage, Vecterix, sent us." I paused but no sign of recognition appeared in her strange dark eyes. "He instructed us to fly here and find a man who is gifted at bringing back the dead. A man who has no name."

Red laughed. "None of us has a name, at least not one that we share with other living beings—that's why we are all still alive. As for raising the dead." She gestured at the gathered wizards and witches around her. "All have meddled with that little art with varying levels of success. Take your pick."

Varying levels of success wasn't a resounding endorsement. It was the first time I was able to get a clear look at the gathered mages—you tend not to focus too closely on your surroundings when your life is threatened. Some appeared frail and old, though I guessed their magic was still powerful. There weren't as many as I had first thought—fewer than fifty. And, since they didn't seem to want to kill us at this very moment, they did look a bit friendlier. The difficulty was that they also were shaking their heads to indicate they had little knowledge about the necromancer arts.

"What is it you expect this raiser of the dead to do?" Red asked.

"Though I have the soul of Brenna Andorium here," I said, "her body is encased in stone in the Hall of Ancestors in the royal keep at Dreki. We want to find someone who knows enough of the elder arts to bring her back to life."

Red inched closer and reached out to touch the soulstone again with her gnarled fingers. She made a soft noise as if in feeling it, she had learned something about its power. "This is so very interesting," she said. "Such possibilities. Condensing a soul—all that a person is—down to this stone vessel would take more power than I can imagine."

"But can you help us?" I asked with a tinge of anger, trying to hide the fact I was feeling desperate.

"No," she answered. "This is beyond me. The old magic users forgot more than we ever knew. This binding power is from the first magic—when the world was young. The strongest of the magics."

"But Vecterix can't be wrong," I said. "There has to be someone here who knows what to do. Otherwise why would the mage dragon command us to come?" It dawned on me that Vecterix had been in a state of mind where he couldn't tell the present from the past from the possible futures. Had he been wrong? "Is there anyone here who recognizes the symbols on this soulstone?" My voice cracked.

"May I look?" A man had worked his way forward, gently moving through the other wizards. He was slightly portly, brown-skinned, and mostly bald—except for two puffs of white hair just above his ears. "I am Goran and I have, on occasion, had the pleasure of raising the dead."

"And were you successful in doing that?" Brax asked.

"Mostly," Goran said, and then he turned to me. "May I hold the item?"

Of all the wizards I'd met, he seemed the most trustworthy, but I had been charged with the carrying and protection of Brenna in this form. I glanced at Brax and he nodded his permission.

I'll bite off his head and spit out his brains if he tries to steal her, he said inside my mind.

Thanks for that image.

I lifted the chain from my neck, feeling a weight come off me and a sense of sadness as I handed her—it—over to the wizard. He examined the stone, lifting it into the air and looking with one eye. "It is perfect," he said. "So very perfect. And I believe I've seen a few of these markings in the Saga of Exdoria. I have an odd library, even for a wizard. It includes several dragon manuscripts."

"Which manuscripts?" Brax asked.

"The Saga of Exdoria," he said. "And the Compendium of Zanius."

Brax raised an eyebrow, an expression which I still found disconcerting. Of all the dragons I'd met he had the most control over his facial features. "Long have I hunted those sources. I would love to read them."

"That can be arranged, my friend," Goran said, looking across at Brax.

He seemed to mean those words of friendship. And then he motioned toward Thord, me and Megan. "I invite all of you to the fief of Algaria. We could sup and exchange wisdom and try to find the secret of this soulstone together."

"I would very much like that," Brax said. He sounded more gentle than I'd heard him.

The wizard Goran handed the stone back to me. It was warm and I remembered a saying that Maestru Beatrix had often used, "Warm hands, warm heart."

"The invite is pending the decision of the council," Goran said, bowing slightly and stepping back.

Red shuffled forward, lifted her staff and pointed at me, though not in a threatening way. "You said you have another request. Would you be so kind as to share it with us?"

I was about to answer when Megan pushed to the front. "Yes, we do have another very important request. And there is only one way to ask it."

And to my great shock, Megan kneeled before Red and all the gathered mages. And, after a moment of hesitation, Thord joined her. I felt silly and didn't know what to do, but Megan shot a frown at me and that convinced me I should kneel also. I got down on my knees. The stone floor felt extra hard.

"Oh, great and powerful wielders of magic," Megan began, and she kept any sarcasm from dripping down her words. In fact she sounded humble, which was not a normal tone for her. "We come from the land of Ellos, a land that you helped shape and form into a place of comfort. It is your home. It is where all of you were born. As you have heard before, there is war in our land. The Emperor Sargon seeks to subjugate all the realms beneath his sandaled feet." She was getting a little flowery for my taste, but wizard types liked flowery language and I had no idea that Megan could get so descriptive. "Sargon has gained his throne by killing his brother and his nephew but he is also a great wizard himself now, and, if his own confession is to be believed, he gained that power by dining on the hearts of the wizards and witches he locked up in the white tower."

I shivered when I thought of that place next to the emperor's palace. Even just seeing it from outside was enough to frighten me. I didn't want to imagine the horrors that had happened beyond its gate. The gathered council's faces were stone cold with fury.

"He consumed your brothers; your sisters in magic. Your comrades. They have all met an ignoble and undeserved end, and they deserve to be avenged. The remaining realms have gathered armies to fight him, but they are falling one by one. Soon all of Ellos will be under his yoke." She made her voice even louder—in fact, I daresay it was a stirring speech. "And so I ask you, every one of you to forgive we assassins, to forgive the consuls and the kings, the courtiers who betrayed you, and to return with us as an army of witches and wizards. An army that would balance the scales of justice and defeat the pretender Sargon and return Ellos to the land it was meant to be. A land of peace. A home for all its citizens. We can only do this with you at our side. I beseech you to join the cause of right and goodness and free Ellos from this tyranny."

A long silence followed. No wizard stepped up or spoke until Red said, "It is true that Ellos was the land in which we were born, but it is no longer our home. We are wizards and witches and we are individuals, and no patch of land defines or owns us. We stand alone in our powers. Alone in our thoughts. Here we have each created our own fiefs. Lands that reflect us. We are also ardent individualists. It is only when we meet as a group that we make decisions for the whole land. Otherwise there are no kings. No queens. No overlords. Just wizards and witches, living their lives and seeking not to interfere with their brothers and sisters in magic. So that means that each wizard and witch standing here must look into his or her heart and decide if they would like to aid our former home of Ellos."

Still kneeling, I glanced around at the men and women gathered there. The old ones likely wouldn't come, but some younger ones—who were maybe only in their third decade of life—would have the fire needed for the fight. A youthful wizard with oddly gray hair caught my eye, but when he saw I was looking at him he gently shook his head. Several of the witches took a step back as if our words might infect them with a horrible illness.

"Are there any at all, who would aid us?" Megan's voice cracked.

Again we were met by silence. A raven cawed in the distance.

"The wounds are too deep," Red said to Megan. Her voice was soft, as if explaining the death of a pet to a child. "And the bonds that tied us to Ellos have been broken. That is what betrayal does."

"There is no one brave enough?" Megan shouted. She got to her feet and we followed her lead. "No one?"

Again a cold silence met her exclamation, and her words echoed off the surrounding rocks so it seemed as if they were speaking back. Mocking her. She had gripped her hands so tightly that they were now white-knuckled fists. There were lines on her forehead from her gritting her teeth.

"I will aid you," a male voice said far in the back of the council. A few of the wizards and witches turned, looks of surprise on their faces. I couldn't see who was speaking—there were too many tall wizard-types in the way—but the crowd began moving out of his way. A man came through, slipping with agility between the wizards and witches. He still wore his hood. He had come from the back, where I assumed the very youngest were standing.

"I will aid you," he repeated when he was standing before us. Then he gently pulled back his hood.

It was my brother Corwin. Alive. A patch over his eye. "I will," he said. "This I promise."

9

NOT A REPTILE

Thord had his sword out first, and Megan drew back, lifting my dagger in one hand. I could only stand there in shock, my mouth agape.

It was Brax who reacted faster than all of us. He leapt forward and shot an arm between Megan and me, aiming directly at Corwin, his talons out. I wasn't certain whether he was meaning to kill him there and then.

And I didn't find out, for in that moment Corwin threw a small glass ball skyward that burst with brightness, and he vanished as if he hadn't been standing there at all.

"That was a very curious display of sudden violence." Red's voice was hard and angry, her eyes narrowed so they were half hidden by wrinkles. Her staff glowed with energy. The other wizards and witches had brought their own staffs and wands to bear, and the air crackled with so much magic my hair rose.

"Yes," said Goran, the wizard who had been talking books with Brax only moments earlier. He hadn't lifted a finger. "That was a very, very curious display. It is almost as if you know my apprentice."

"Your apprentice?" Megan said. "Why would you have a snake as an apprentice?"

I slowly looked left and right, expecting Corwin to come out of the darkness, blade in hand. I even glanced up, in case he somehow had risen above us and was dropping right now. But he was gone.

"Snake," Goran said. "That is an interesting choice of words. It suggests an evil aspect to him. A darkness. A slipperiness. Assuming one believes the stories about snakes and does not see them as another of nature's wondrous creatures."

"Yes, he's a snake!" Thord spat the words. "Times ten."

"Well," Goran said, calmly. "He is no snake, nor is he a reptile of any sort. I see him as a lamb."

The wizard had been fooled. Only moments ago I'd thought he was intelligent, now I looked for signs of him being a simpleton—but wisdom gleamed in his eyes.

"Where is he?" I asked. I had sheathed my dagger but kept my hands on the hilt.

"Yes, show us the mortal," Brax demanded. "Show his face." Brax was right beside me, his nostrils flared as he sniffed for a scent of Corwin. I felt a lot more powerful when he was backing me up.

"Do you promise not to skewer, burn or strike him with blunt objects?" Goran asked.

"That's a lot to ask," Brax said. "We have a nasty history with that one."

"Then first, let us explore that history," Goran said. "Since he is my apprentice, I promise your safety from him and from me and all around us." He glanced around to be certain of this and Red nodded. "Do you promise not to harm him until after we have discussed this so-called *nasty* history?"

"Yes," Megan said. "We promise that." Thord, Brax and I nodded.

"Then, apprentice, show thyself," Goran said with obvious pride in his student and a bit of flourish. Every wizard was a showman at heart.

Corwin appeared before us in exactly the place he'd been standing only moments before. He looked from me to Megan and Thord and finally to Brax. His face was calm; there was none of the cockiness imprinted there that I'd grown up with. It was not like Corwin to not show pride—after all, he'd just vanished and reappeared again before Brax could grab him. I had no idea how that trick worked. "I am not your enemy," he said. It was my brother's voice—a voice I still sometimes heard at night, and that I both longed to listen to and feared in my very heart.

Here was the brother who had booted me over the wall at the Red Fortress. The brother who had killed my classmates and destroyed an order of assassins that had existed for over two thousand years.

And he didn't have the slightest bit of recognition in his eyes. He had always been a consummate actor, perfect at playing his role. He could be the soft-hearted brother or friend when it served his purposes. He'd fooled the maestrus as to his true nature, but now he truly looked as if he didn't recognize us at all.

Especially me.

"What game are you playing, Corwin?" Thord grunted. He still had his hand on the hilt of his sword, squeezing it so tight his forearm flexed. "What cruel game is this?"

"Was that my name?" he asked. His question was gentle and curious. "Is Corwin what you called me?"

"We called you much worse than that," Megan said. She was holding my dagger pointed at the ground, but she could have it at his throat in a heartbeat. If he didn't vanish, that was. "Traitor. Viper. Murderer. Those are the names we reserve for you."

He watched her carefully as she spoke, but didn't respond to any of the insults she spat out. "The name Corwin means nothing to me," he said. "It is unfamiliar and I have no memory of being a traitor. I find those accusations very curious."

The corporthium pill I had used appeared to have worked exactly as designed. If what he said was true, he had no memories of our past. But I had to test that—he could still be acting.

"There was another name I called you," I said. "It was brother."

Again, no reaction. He stared at me for several seconds, searching my face. It was so strange and frightening to have his eyes—eye, that is, since we'd taken his left orb—looking at me again. "We have similar features. Your hair is the same. Your bone structure is the same and the color of one of your eyes is the same color as mine. Not your other eye. It's a serpent's eye. It is possible we were—are—siblings, but I have no memory of you. What is your name again?"

I hesitated. The wizards could wield power using names. Should I give it to him? What would he do with it? But it wasn't like it was a secret—there were many of the wizards and witches here who already knew it.

"It is Carmen Dore," I said. "And you were Corwin Dore. My brother."

He rubbed his chin. It was not a gesture Corwin ever used. "And do you know why I am the way I am now?" he asked.

"No," Megan said, before I could answer. "No, we don't."

"Oh." He looked as if he believed her. Perhaps he didn't

recognize guile. He'd always been so good at catching others in a lie, mainly because he was the best at telling untruths. "If I knew how I came to be in this condition, I might be able to peel back some of the layers in my mind. The mysteries. Where do I come from?"

"From Ellos," I said. "It's a land to—"

"I do know what and where Ellos is," he cut me off, but not in a mean way. Again each sentence was measured. "I even know its history, but I do not have any memory of being there. In fact the only memory I have begins right here in Azadiq. When I first landed in Goran's fief. Are you certain you can't tell me why I am the way I am today?" This time he was looking directly at me. "Do you know where my memories went?"

"Uh. No," I said. "I don't know. I'm not sure anyway. It might be just a bump on the head. That's all."

You are such a horrible liar, Brax said inside my mind.

Shut up! You're not helping.

"When did you last see me?" he asked.

"Uh... I'm not certain," I answered. Gods, I *was* horrible at lying. But if he didn't have his memories and he was a different person, why would I want him to learn to be his old self again?

"We saw you at the palace of Emperor Sargon, at his side," Megan said.

Corwin had no reaction to this, but Goran did. "The emperor's side?" he said. "Now that is also very, very interesting."

"No, it is not interesting," my brother said and for the first time his tone was slightly angry. "It is frustrating. Even more so because something that big, that important, you would think I would remember it."

"It's good that you don't," I said. "It's a really good thing, Corwin."

He gave me another measuring glance. "Please don't call me that."

"Call you what?" I said.

"Corwin," he answered. "That is not my name."

"Then what is it?" Brax asked.

"I am known as Nameless," my brother answered. "So I insist that you call me that. I am Nameless."

10

YEA OR NAY

"I think it best if we discuss names and the past over mulled cider at my home." The wizard Goran pointed over his shoulder in what I assumed was the direction of his fief. "And some roast beast. You all look like you could use a good meal. It will be a civilized discussion, and these puzzles are perhaps best solved without such a large audience measuring every word."

Red tapped the bottom of her staff against the stone ground, and the gathered crowd fell immediately silent. "Do you, Goran of the fief Algaria, promise to—"

"They should not leave this sacred ground!" a thin, bald wizard shouted. His pale skin looked as rubbery as an eel's and his eyes were shaped wide and unnaturally large which, combined with his beak nose, made him look like an owl.

I would never want to be on the receiving end of the angry glare Red gave him. But when she spoke her words were calm: "Please explain your outburst, Nekor. And do be sure to bring forth a reasoned argument."

"Look at them!" He pointed at us. His fingers were twice the normal length, and I couldn't stop staring at them.

"They are weak—beaten and crawling to us for aid. If these three and this dragon return to Ellos, the emperor will break them and they'll give up the secret of this land to save their hides. The next thing you know Sargon will be here looking for new lands to conquer and more enchanted hearts to eat."

"He's right! He's right!" a woman shouted from the back of the crowd. Several others spoke out, in guttural agreement. "Hear, hear!"

Brax stirred his wings, and the swans did so at the same time, all three of them rising to their most impressive heights.

"We wouldn't betray you," Megan shouted with enough force she sent a spray of spittle with the words. "We only requested your help to defeat him. We would not speak a word of this land."

"You are an infant," Nekor said. And this time he directed one of those longish fingers right at her. "You don't even have twenty years under your belt. Here's what will happen: you will be caught and tortured. As strong as you assassins pretend to be, you cannot withstand the pain a wizard emperor will inflict. You will offer up any secret to be released from it. You would betray even your closest loves." He pointed at Thord. "You would even betray him."

Did he mean Thord was one of her closest loves? What magic spell told him that?

"I wouldn't," Megan said. The confidence in her voice impressed me. "*We* wouldn't. I give you my oath. All of us would swear to this."

"Oh, little red-haired doll!" This time it was Blacktooth who spoke. "There is no keeping an assassin's oath in the face of magical torture. We users of the dark arts know pain. But let's say the gods of luck are on your side and you somehow pull off a victory—what is to stop you from coming here with an army of Avenians a year from now? Or smelly, stocky Wodenites in their legendary boats wielding their cold, cold iron? You lesser mortals want our magic. You always have."

"So you cannot let them leave this island." Nekor had turned his back to us and was addressing the council, waving his long arms. "If we will not execute them, we should at the very least keep them safe from themselves and keep the secret of our land safe. They should be bound to this land."

Red drew in a deep breath that rattled in her lungs. "We value personal freedom above all things. Would you imprison these fellow mortals?"

"And this dragon, too, I assume," Brax growled. The swans hissed. It was almost like they were following his lead.

"Azadiq is not a prison." Nekor's voice had become calm. "It is more beautiful and has more potential than any other land. These magicless mortals could have long and fulfilling lives here. The price for that is they could never leave."

"That only makes it a larger prison," Red said.

"Well, they—"

"Oh, shut it, Nekor!" Red interrupted. He opened his eyes even wider, as if he'd been slapped. "You would argue with the sun until it stopped burning. We will put it to a vote." She turned so she addressed all the witches and wizards. "To you, the gathered council, I present this question: Do we take away the individual rights of these guests and force them to live among us for the rest of their lives?"

I blinked several times. Was my whole future in the hands of this staring, angry crowd? Thord put his hand on my shoulder. I turned, surprised to discover it was Megan.

"We shall hear from the yeas first." Red shouted the next words like she was commanding an army: "Speak now."

"Yea!" It was like a thunder, one word that normally should sound happy. But now it doomed us to stay here on Azadiq.

Red nodded and waited for silence. "And we shall hear from the nays. Speak now!"

I held my breath. Not one wizard or witch opened a mouth to shout. My heart thudded. Once. Twice. Then—

"NAY!"

It was loud. Loud enough to echo off the stones around us.

"Was that a larger number of nays?" Thord whispered. "Was it enough?"

"The nays have it!" Red shouted.

To my surprise not one member of the council let out a complaint, though Nekor turned his back and walked into the crowd. Blacktooth grinned at us and winked. It had all been an aggravating game for her.

"Goran of Algaria," Red said, her voice formal. "Do you take them under your protection and your watch?"

"Yes, I do," he said. "I will protect them and watch over them to be certain they are respectful guests of Azadiq." It seemed like a lot since he didn't know us. "Will you have me as your protector?" he asked. No one answered right away. Nameless was watching our reaction—measuring things the same way Corwin always had, but he didn't seem to gather all of that information like he was gathering arrows for a bow. He was only gaining knowledge.

"You would promise the safekeeping of a dragon?" Brax said.

Goran didn't even pause. "Especially a dragon. They are the wisest amongst all living, sentient creatures."

I like this wizard! Brax said.

"And, just to let you know, my sheep are not as precious as Blacktooth's. They are bred for eating."

He's brilliant! Brax added.

"Well, I am sold," Brax said aloud. "What about you others?"

I nodded, my eyes still on Nameless. My brother looked at each of us and smiled.

It wasn't a grin of guile. He appeared genuinely happy.

"We accept you as our guardian," Thord said at the same time as Megan.

"Then please take your foresworn guests and depart." Red punctuated her words by tapping her staff. "For our council meeting is not finished. We have sewage disposal to discuss. I'm certain you'll be saddened to miss that."

"Incredibly saddened," Goran said. He gestured toward the sky, and seeing what he meant, we all mounted up. The wizard then tossed a glowing ball into the air that levitated about ten yards above us. "Follow that bauble," he said. "It will lead you to my home. Don't stop to smell the flowers or the dung along the way." And then he affectionately patted Nameless on the back, and the two of them walked directly into an obelisk.

They were no longer there. They had simply ambled into what looked to be solid stone. "I'd like to know how that works," Megan said.

"I think it's best to go now," Brax said. There were several wizards staring at us, and not with happy smiles. Their hands were gripped tightly on their magic staffs. We took to the air.

The floating bauble began to zip ahead at a good clip, and we followed. I swear I could feel the stares of the angry wizards and witches for the next several leagues.

11

SECRETS AND POWERS

"That isn't Corwin," I said, when we were far enough away from the Gorzed Circle. We were heading northeast and a prairie now stretched below us, with cows dotted here and there and clumped in herds. Not a fence or a barn was in sight. "It wasn't like him at all."

"Oh, that is Corwin," Brax replied. "He looks the same and he moves the same. But the glint of a killer no longer shines in his eye."

"Why would Corwin help us?" Megan asked. Both she and Thord had brought their swans close enough to have a discussion.

I eyed the bauble which was flying twenty yards ahead. I guessed it wouldn't somehow send our voices to Goran, but I still spoke just loud enough for the others to hear. "We will find out."

"The other question is: do we want his help?" Thord said. "You know where his help has led us in the past."

Brax took a moment to yawn before saying, "Well, the safest thing is to kill him."

"We can't do that," I said.

"We won't, you mean," he replied. "And I knew you'd have that reaction. You're so sentimental and foolish enough to believe in good outcomes. What I should have said was the wisest course of action would be to let him come with us, then dump him off in the middle of the ocean."

"And why would we do that?" I said.

"It's obvious, Carmen, and I worry that so soon you are already blinded by emotion, though you have two eyes. One day Nameless may remember his old self, and that old self is not someone we ever want to see again."

"Maybe he's changed," I said.

"Bah!" Brax turned his head enough to give me a glare. "Don't dream of the brother you never had. Look at reality: he is a trained assassin who has now been apprenticed to a wizard. I cannot imagine any mortal more dangerous than that."

I didn't know what to say. He spoke truth.

"It is odd," Megan said. "If I was meeting this new Corwin for the first time, I might even have liked him. He seemed... innocent."

"Innocent?" Thord said. "The scar from my gut wound says different. He's the one who commanded Banderius to stab me."

"It's not like I don't have my own scars," Megan answered.

"He has cut all of us," I said. Though my cut was my eye, and if he hadn't done that I wouldn't be looking through a dragon's eye right now. So I was a little conflicted about that. "But innocent is the right word."

"Innocent for now," Brax said. "Mark my words: an evil sleeps inside him."

"You can't be certain," I said. He had begun gliding so

that it was easier to hear him. The swans also spread their wings.

"It is better to expect it," he replied. "How long has it been since we tied him to that swan and released him to his fate?"

"It seems like a hundred years," I said.

"It really isn't that long," Brax continued. "It is not much more than a fortnight."

"It has to be more than that!" Thord said.

I was tempted to agree with him because so much had happened: the crossing of Bitterwaters, being imprisoned in Dreki, fighting at the Althing. Not to mention the emperor taking over most of Ellos.

"Brax is right," Megan said. "We sent him here just over a fortnight ago. And remember, Corwin would have been flying for several of those days just to get here."

Brax looked back at me with his one good eye. "And yet in his brief time here he has learned how to turn himself invisible. What other tricks does he have up his sleeve? Perhaps an affinity with magic runs in the blood."

"What does that mean?" Thord asked.

"Oh, Brax thinks I'm good with magic," I said. "Because I can unlock a few locks with a spell."

"And there are other... umm ... magical occurrences," Brax added.

"Yes, there are," I answered, gruffly. I gripped the spike in his back more tightly. I would rather be pinching him.

"What are they?" Megan said. "Is it your skin? I mean today it burst out in pimples."

"Pimples!" I shouted so loud that all of Azadiq might have heard me. "Those weren't pimples! They were scales. And they saved us from that... that cold fire blasted at us by the Hungry One. You two would be dead if I didn't have those scales."

"So that was what those were," Thord said. "You have scales under your skin." Was it my imagination that he uttered this with a pinch of disgust?

"Thord and I know nothing about your new, umm, scales," Megan said. "Did these weird protrusions help you fight that dragon one on one? Back when you were in Drachia. The dragon the slave said you killed."

"Did Dyn blab to everyone in the palace!" I said. That man couldn't keep a secret if they tattooed it to his back.

"He said you took the full blast of a dragon," Thord said. "I thought he imagined that—he seemed to be an imaginative fellow. My guess is those... those scales helped you." Again, he had difficulty saying the word.

"You must tell us about anything that has changed within you," Megan said. "Secrets are not good between us."

"Fine!" I spat the word out. I didn't want to tell them anything. I hadn't quite come to terms with all the changes myself yet, and I didn't understand them. "When I fought that Hvitur dragon, Darius, he blasted me with flames and those scales came out to protect me."

"So you're fireproof?" Megan said. "I thought my eyes were deceiving me."

"Yes, I am fireproof. But I don't seem to be able to control when it happens. Oh, and I'm stronger than I was."

"Stronger?" Thord said. "How much stronger?"

"You two should arm wrestle," Brax said.

Thord put up his hands as if I were about to jump over to his swan and wrestle him. "No thanks," he said. "Though that does explain how you were able to lift the door at the end of the tunnel in Gudheim. All by yourself."

"Is there anything else?" Megan asked.

"Well..." I began, then bit my tongue.

Tell them, Brax said. *It'll rattle their tiny brains. This will be fun to watch.*

"Brax and I can talk mind to mind."

"What!" Megan said. "What does that even mean?"

"He can send his thoughts directly to me," I answered.

"That's very, very strange," Thord said.

"Strange?" I glared at him and he nudged his bird a bit further away. I guess having pop-up scales and extra strength and mind-to-mind talking with a dragon was too much for him. "You wanted to know my secrets."

"It's really interesting," Megan said. "And silent communication is great for coordinating tactics." She put a hand to her forehead. "I will send a thought to you."

I waited a moment before answering, "I'm not getting a thing."

"Good," Megan answered. "Because I was lamenting about how much your hair needed washing."

"What!"

"And that is why you children don't get to talk mind to mind," Brax said. "You're not intelligent enough. In fact, Carmen can just barely make it work. It's like a god talking to an ant."

"Ugh," I said. "I suppose you see yourself as the god."

"You said it, not me." He gave a fake humble shrug which threw us off course a little. "Anyway, now you two know our secrets. Please remember there has been sheep and other food promised, so let's not waste too much energy discussing these sundry revelations until we have full stomachs."

The other two spread out a bit and Brax began to flap his wings, keeping pace with the glowing orb. The land below us had changed without me noticing: it was a system of rivers and small islands, as if the wizard or witch had formed the land into a thousand waterways. There were villages built on tall posts. What sort of villagers would live here, and what sort of master was the wizard? It was a green land below us; maybe winter never iced those rivers. Perhaps it was a heavenly place to live.

She is alive, Brax said.

I knew who he was talking about at once. His sister Brenna had spoken through the soulstone.

Yes, she really is there. The soulstone felt warm under my tunic. Was that my imagination?

Has she spoken before? Brax asked this almost pleadingly. *To you?*

No, I said. *I was as surprised as you were.*

She is here. She is with us. A few wingbeats later he added, *I hope she isn't still angry at me.*

I'm sure she isn't, I thought and at the same moment remembered how powerful she had sounded. And the tone was not that of someone you wanted to be angry at you.

Brax didn't reply.

12

MOVING DUST

We traveled for several more agonizing hours. I realized Brax and the swans were getting close to exhaustion, but that never-tiring, never-pausing globe guided us forwards. Plus, we couldn't land because any part of this magical country might be jammed full of wizard-made traps.

We passed over one fief that was a green, flat and moving landscape. It took time for me to recognize that it was a constantly shifting collection of vines.

"My gut tells me that Nekor the creepy-eyed wizard lives there," Brax said. "He was slithery and that looks like a slithery fief. I am certain that each of these fiefs is a reflection of its mistress or master."

"Let's go a little higher," I said. We did, and the others followed. The bauble also moved up.

In time, a coastline became visible. We had flown from one end of the land of Azadiq to the other. "Despite Blacktooth's claims," I said, "the entire land of Azadiq isn't as large as Ellos."

"No, it isn't," Brax said. His voice was a little hoarse. "And that's a good thing. I can't fly much further and a coast must mean we will land soon. Unless Goran lives on some distant island, in which case you'll be doing a bit of swimming."

As if on cue, the globe dipped down toward the earth. We followed, getting closer and closer to a gentle and normal landscape. There was grass, rocks and trees, small hills and myriad paths—no burning lava pits or poisonous gases. It would be a comforting place to take a walk.

Or to eat twenty roasted turkeys. I was getting that hungry. Also, I spotted a flock of wild turkeys near one hill.

The wizard Goran's home was a simple round house made of orange bricks, and surrounded by paths that led to a chicken coop, a small wooden barn and several fenced-in areas for cows and pigs. It looked comfy and wasn't in the slightest bit ostentatious. In other words, it hadn't been built to impress.

"He's a bloody farmer," Brax said. "Thord, this should seem like home to you. Go beg him to let you shovel manure."

Thord shot an angry glance at Brax. Obviously, the trip had slowly squeezed out every last bit of his good humour. He even reached toward his sword hilt as if he were about to challenge Brax to a duel. But then Thord did something surprising—he gave a loud sniff and said, "It does smell like home. It's a beautiful, welcoming scent of sheep excrement. It's good for your heart and good for your soil."

Brax laughed and I joined in. Maybe it was a saying Thord's father had often said.

The globe guided us to a patch of grass next to the home and vanished. We landed. The bricks and roof were weathered, making it look as if the home had been here for a hundred years.

Next to the house was a sight that gave me a chill: a series of cages that contained dead bodies of a variety of animals. There weren't any human remains that I could see. The breeze brought a smell of decay. Of death.

"This bodes ill," Brax said.

"It smells ill, too," Megan added.

There was a pile of dark rags next to the cages. Why Goran needed so many rags, I couldn't guess. But then the rags moved.

Naga and Bolt hissed and made a warbling sound deep in their throats. I knew that noise, though they rarely made it—they were deathly afraid. The animals that had been trained by Maestru Arvid to fear nothing, were suddenly consumed by terror. They backed a step or two away, pulling against their reins.

For it was not a pile of rags. Two gray, pupil-less eyes blinked and the rags rose until they took the outline of wings. And with that movement the smell, that horrible smell of death, was closer now. Brax rose, drawing in a breath in case he needed to burn whatever it was to ashes.

Then the shape became clear—it was a ragged black swan, part of its skull showing. Its beak glittered as if someone had sharpened it. And there were white rib bones revealed along its chest.

"Is that Corwin's swan?" I asked.

At the sound of my voice it let out a hissing, angry blast of dried air and then raised its head higher and glared from me to Brax to my friends. The other swans were now pulling as hard as they could on their reins, while Megan and Thord whispered calming words and glanced over their shoulders at the thing.

"It's part of his swan, at least," Brax said. "The bird has seen better days."

The thing raised its head even higher, as if it were about to strike. I put a hand on my dagger.

The door to the house opened. “Friends!” Goran strode out of his home with Nameless a few steps behind him. I was aware that I now used ‘Nameless’ when I thought of him. He was that different than Corwin. “Friends, welcome! Pay no mind to Dust, she’s wary of strangers, that’s all. Well, and to be truthful, she’s wary of the living in general.”

Goran stopped in front of us, but Nameless crossed over to the swan with his hand raised. He got close enough to stroke its head. The creature gave two short hisses—I swear they were aimed directly at me—then nuzzled up so that its neck was resting on Nameless’s shoulder. How could he stand to be so close to the thing?

“Is it alive?” Megan asked.

“Dust is alive in her own way,” Goran replied. “Though her inner nature has been altered by going to the spirit world and coming back. Let us just say she’s not the same as she was before and leave it at that.”

“Do we have to fear it?” I asked.

“Not as long as Nameless is near. She remembers her master. Even death did not break their bond.”

Nameless whispered and the swan settled down, though she glared at us with those dull, dead eyes. Given a chance, she would joyously peck out our eyes or snap off a finger and gobble it down. As if in answer to that image, Nameless reached into a smaller cage, brought out a live mouse and dangled it in front of the beast. She took it in one bite.

I turned away, not wanting to watch the mouse work its way down the swan’s throat. When I turned back, Nameless was only a few feet away from me. It was as if he had appeared there.

"Now that Dust is settled," Goran said. He didn't even smile at his pun, though there was a bit of a twinkle in his eye. "I just want to repeat my welcome. I am so eager to converse with you and I am certain Nameless is, too." Nameless did not smile or nod. "And, as we all know, talk is best done over food. I can tell that you are all in need of a solid meal." He elbowed Thord gently. "With at least two or three helpings."

"A meal would be wonderful," Thord said.

"I'll take the extra helpings," Megan added. She was licking her dry lips. Even with dry lips she still looked attractive.

"Good. Good." Goran turned to Nameless. "Please fix our dinner."

"Yes, my master," Nameless said. There was no bitterness or sarcasm in his words. Corwin had always spat out the name *Maestru* as if he were better than each and every one of our teachers. Nameless went back inside the brick house.

"You are safe here," Goran said. "I want you to think of this as your home. You can make yourselves comfortable and soon we will sup, and in our land the sharing of a meal is the bonding of friendship."

"So that's why Blacktooth wouldn't feed us," Thord said.

"She didn't offer strangers food?" Goran said. "Well, that doesn't surprise me. She wouldn't want to bond. And, to be honest, she's not the kindest witch."

"That's an understatement," I said.

"Well, we are as far away from her fief as one can be." Goran tapped the side of his skull. "So let's not let her visit us in our thoughts. Please, have a seat." He gestured toward a circle of large stones on the other side of his house. They were shaped perfectly for sitting. I chose one that was at an angle, allowing me to lean slightly. If they could speak, my legs would have cried out in joy at not having to stand or ride. Thord chose a stone across from me, Megan to one side and Brax settled himself to the other side. "I am curious about your backgrounds," Goran said. "And about the soulstone, too. But I have a first question for all of you, and I do hope you don't see it as impertinent."

"What is it?" Brax asked.

"Why do you want to return to Ellos?" He moved an open hand in an arc, gesturing at each of us. "You are assassins and you are a dragon. From what I understand, you have no more of your comrades remaining. You perhaps have family who still live there, but I imagine all of you have been long enough from your family that the familial bonds are broken." He looked at me, his gray eyes showing a sense of interest. "Except perhaps you. It has not been that long since your bonds were broken with your brother." He waited for an answer, but I bit my tongue. I didn't know if the bonds were broken. I was in such an odd state of mind right now. After all, at this very moment, my brother was fixing me dinner. But he wasn't my brother.

"No, it hasn't been that long," I said, finally.

"I only want to go to Ellos because I have promised to help Carmen," Brax said. "I have no other reason to return to the mortal realms. I wasn't treated well there."

"Let us hope, from this moment forward, that we treat you better in the wizarding realm," Goran said. "And you three? Why return?"

"I have family," Thord said. "The emperor has conquered Woden so I don't know if they're alive, but I can't abandon them."

"I have no reason to go back," Megan answered. "But I really, really don't like to leave things undone."

"Sometimes doing the thing you've left undone will undo you." Goran pinched his jaw in thought. "And you," he said to me. "Your family is here."

"I also don't like leaving things undone," I said.

"What she means," Brax shook a talon in my direction, "is Carmen is someone who believes in her tiny mortal heart that injustice should always be set to right. It's a sickness."

Goran gave a flicker of a smile at this. "Such foundational beliefs are important—otherwise we would have no laws. I..." He held up his hand. "Ah, dinner is served. Please help yourselves to our limited bounty."

And with that, Nameless returned bearing a tray that looked too heavy for him to carry. He must have been aided by a spell, for it was a bounteous mountain of food. He set the tray on the low stone table between us, revealing an array of roasted hens, purple carrots—was the color magic? —boiled potatoes, long green beans and in the center a roasted pig with an apple in its mouth. This tray was enough to feed a troop of soldiers. My mouth watered, my stomach grumbled, but I held myself still. And so did Megan and Thord. Brax was eyeing the pig, slaver dripping down his lips, but he held back, too.

"Ah," Goran said. "Not one of you has lifted a finger, though I can see ravenous hunger is in your eyes and hear it in your stomachs. And it's not politeness that holds you back: it's the assassin training. I know that you fear being poisoned. What a way to live." He lifted a chicken leg, a carrot, and a piece of mutton. He took quick bites of each—large bites so that if there was any poison, he would get a substantial quantity of it. "See—we did not poison it. And I am not offended that you waited. It is your nature. One should never be offended by another's nature."

He gestured with the chicken leg. “Eat up, my friends. This meal will cement our bonds of friendship. And once we are done, we’ll talk about the weather, our favorite books, and about saving all of Ellos and bringing a dragon sister back to life.”

13

A SERIES OF QUESTIONS

My brother was a good cook. The Trellish hen and vegetables had been perfectly spiced—not too salty, and not too much thyme. Nameless watched us with a smile, not one of guile, but of pleasure. "I told you the hen was the right choice," he said to Goran. "Hen is always the right choice."

The wizard laughed a happy laugh that came from deep in his chest. "Yes, my apprentice, it was a wise choice." The hens had been delicious. They were only bones now—in fact, Thord was peeling the meat off the last one with his teeth.

I didn't get a chance to try the pork because Brax had scooped up the pig with a talon and shoved the whole thing into his mouth, crunching it in his bone-breaking way.

"The apple is a nice touch," Brax said. His teeth were jammed with meat. Another pig appeared, and Brax ate that. "This is real food, isn't it?" he asked. "I will not be hungry an hour later, will I?"

"It is as real as you or I," Goran said. Wizards were fond of sounding mysterious. I moved on to a bowl of purple carrots and potatoes, aware that it would not be good to eat too much after such a long time without a proper meal. But it was hard to stop.

"Well, I am curious—and I'm certain my guests are curious, too—about one thing," Goran said, and he leveled his gaze on Nameless. "I am wondering why you promised to help them with their fight?"

Nameless glanced toward me, then looked at Thord and Megan but didn't answer the question.

"Are they familiar to you, is that why you spoke?" Goran said.

"These people are not familiar to me," Nameless said. "Even now after spending this short time with them, they remain strangers—nothing they do is familiar or reminds me of a past life. When I pledged my aid, I was speaking from my heart because they were people in need of help and I could provide it."

"That is very magnanimous of you." Goran shook a carrot at his apprentice. "Though, may I add that you volunteered without my permission?"

"I am so sorry, Master." Nameless lowered his head and put out his hands like a supplicant. He spoke his next words with genuine regret. "I beg your forgiveness and ask for your patience and I will take back my pledge of aid, if you command. Their words overwhelmingly compelled me; compelled me to do something good."

My eyes widened slightly. Doing something good was a thought Corwin had never entertained.

"Ah, I have trained a soft-hearted wizard," Goran said with another of his deep chuckles. "They're going to kick me out of the mean wizard club." He patted Nameless's hands and my brother raised his head, looking relieved. "I forgive you, apprentice. And never forsake your word—words are all we're made of." The wizard then gestured toward us. "Well, as your promise is to them, I propose this: the dragon and I shall go for a walk together and leave you alone to discuss your service to their cause. I would like to learn of Brax's sister and that soulstone and provide whatever resurrection advice I can—though I wish I could get the advice of my own master and teacher."

"Who taught you?" Thord asked.

"It was the wizard Boqin, the master of death."

The name didn't mean anything to me, but I hadn't studied the witches and wizards carefully in school.

"Had he truly mastered death?" Megan asked.

The question brought a grin to Goran's face. He was such a friendly, kind man. Why couldn't all wizards be this way? Or all mortals. "We do like our dramatic names," he said. "And our drama, for that matter."

"Did he die?" I asked.

The smile slipped away. "That's the hardest question to answer. He—he was captured by Banderius, through deception and a sleeping powder—and they took Boqin to the white tower. If the accounts of Sargon's appetite are true, then my master is dead and his powers reside in the emperor." He breathed in through his nostrils and grew quiet in contemplation. Here he was, a wizard whose master had been taken by an assassin, and still he had fed us dinner and treated us as guests. "The strange thing is that I cannot convince myself that my master is dead. He had traversed the paths between life and death so many times they were as familiar to him as the veins on the back of his hands. If anyone could stand up to the emperor, Boqin could. Plus, if my master was dead I would know. He would have sent me a dove message." I wanted to ask what that was, but the sadness imprinted on Goran's face stopped me. "It doesn't matter. We are here, and we are in the now. Nameless, make yourself familiar with these three if you are going to travel with them."

"I will, Master," Nameless said.

Goran patted Brax on the shoulder. He obviously had no fear of the dragon. "What say you, Braxas Andorium. Would you honor me with a stroll through my fief?"

Is this safe? I asked Brax thought to thought. *Should we split up?*

It's safe. As powerful as he is, if he wanted us destroyed it would have been when all the wizards and witches were together. I'll chomp his head off if he does anything.

You said that last time.

Well, then I'll chomp off his arms. It's hard to hold a magic staff without arms.

Again, thanks for the image.

"Shall I assume by your silence you are not interested?" Goran asked. He didn't seem to sense that Brax and I could talk mind to mind.

"I am absolutely interested," Brax replied. He pushed away from the table. "Let us go for a stroll, wizard. And leave the mewling children to chat."

And with that final comment, he and Goran walked away from us, down a wooded path.

We were all silent for several moments as if no one, including me, knew exactly what to say or where to start. Nameless looked from me to Megan and then to Thord. His gaze was curious and gentle, and he began by asking me a question that I hadn't expected.

"Do our parents live?" he asked.

I shook my head. "They died shortly after we were born. It was a plague."

He nodded, not showing any emotion at this news. "And do we have any other family?"

"Not that I am aware of," I said. I had only known of my parents, but the records were all burned or stolen from the Red Assassin Keep, due to the actions of the man in front of me.

"Then you are my only family and I am honored by that. Am I to understand that all three of us were classmates?"

"Yes, we were classmates," Megan said. "But not friends."

"Ah, I see," Nameless said. "Forgive me for this curiosity about my other self, but he is a stranger to me, too. And the more I know before we go to Ellos, the better."

"I'm still uncertain we should travel with you," Thord said. He was tightening his jaw, doing his best to make his face look stony and cold. It was, honestly, a bit of a handsome look for him.

"That is understandable," Nameless said. "Even though I am no longer Corwin, obviously his nature and actions have instilled a powerful hatred in all three of you. I would ask forgiveness, but his actions were not my actions. I only ask for an understanding of the state I am in now."

"Or you're faking all of this." Megan pointed a fork at him. She knew how to kill him about twenty different ways with that fork. "I wouldn't put it past you."

Nameless rubbed his chin, and in that moment I thought of the many times Corwin had rubbed his chin in thought. "Perhaps, with enough guile and acting, I could fool you three. But I could not fool the great wizard Goran. You do not fool someone with a mind like that."

"Unless he's in on the trickery," I said. I hadn't meant to say it out loud, but both Megan and Thord nodded in agreement. Nameless held my gaze for a few moments with that same searching look. He didn't mind thinking before speaking—another reason to believe he wasn't Corwin. My brother had always been so quick to show how smart he was. If he wasn't cutting with blades he was cutting with words.

"Yes, you are right," Nameless said. "This could be a complicated charade with Goran as the puppet master of it all, but it is very unlikely. We had no idea you would be arriving. And yet, maybe, since the enmity between assassins and wizards runs deep, he would use me as a prize card in his deck, so to speak. So it is a fair supposition." Nameless was completely a creature of logic and very little emotion. We had taken more than his eye.

"I have another question." He rubbed at the patch over his eye. How many times had I scratched at my own eye patch because of him? "Which of you blinded me?" he asked. He was looking directly at me.

Thord and Megan and I exchanged glances. "It was none of us," Thord said.

Nameless nodded. "I would have thought it would be you, despite the kind nature you have displayed so far." He hadn't moved his gaze from me. "I see by the scars that you once lost your eye and had it replaced by... by, well, the eye you have now. So perhaps this Corwin was responsible for you being blinded."

I bunched my hands into fists. He was a quick thinker. Or he remembered more than he let on. "I didn't blind you."

"Then the dragon did it," he said. "Yes, the scars are wider than a blade and likely made by a talon. That makes sense because he is a creature of honor and duty. Perhaps he was trying to balance out the crimes of Corwin."

"You are as smart as Corwin was," Megan said. There was both wariness and a bit of wonder in the tone of her voice.

"I hope that's a compliment," Nameless replied. "I am endlessly curious. Why was I blinded and tied to a swan and sent away?"

"I..." I started to say; the words were about to tumble out. "I—"

"That is not something we will tell you now," Thord said. He had raised his voice to be loud enough to drown out anything I was about to say. "We were once enemies. Who knows what you will do with any information we give you. Just let it be known we sent you here and spared your life when we had no reason to spare it. And that we would blind and banish you again, or worse, in a heartbeat if you ever betray us."

If Corwin had heard those words spoken with such ferocity from Thord, he would have responded with a sarcastic clapping of his hands. Instead, Nameless drew in a breath and spoke evenly, "I am sorry that my request has wrought such anger in you. I am sorry that the person I once was caused you such pain. I will work, in whatever way I can to sooth those wounds. I am not Corwin, but I am in his body and I understand your dislike of my presence. Please, let us discuss the blinding no further." He stood slowly and bowed to us. "I have been a horrible host. You have traveled far, and I see the weariness in your eyes and in the way you hold yourselves. I will prepare your beds for you. It is what my master would expect, and it is an honor to have such guests. You deserve rest." He bowed once more to us, again without a pinch of sarcasm, and walked toward the orange brick home.

When he was inside and the three of us were alone, Megan looked at me and Thord and said, "I like this new Corwin. I really, really hope he doesn't kill us in our sleep."

14

A DOOR OPENS

The cot inside the wizard's home was made of clouds. Not literally, though that would be impressive, but the moment I lay down on it, I felt such a sense of peace and ease that I was suspicious they had cast a comfort spell upon it. The quilt had a relaxing tulip scent, as though the smell itself could keep the rest of the world at bay.

If there was a spell, it wasn't perfect: it didn't block out Megan's snore, nor did it muffle Thord's snuffling inhalations. I had agreed to keep first watch, because... well, we were assassins in the home of two wizards. Both of my friends had fallen asleep only moments after their heads hit their pillows. Megan's hair had grown out and the dye had faded so it was again that familiar eye-catching red. And Thord, well, his hair was longer too. And tangly. I wondered what it would be like to run my fingers through it.

Concentrate! I told myself. Stay focused. Be vigilant!

There was only one person in the room I should keep a watch on: Nameless was in the far corner, sitting on a pillow with his arms crossed and eye closed. With my dragon eye, I could see that he was breathing very slowly. I did not know if he usually slept sitting on a pillow, or if he was in some deep meditation or summoning up a spell that would destroy the three of us.

The interior of Goran's home was surprisingly bare. I had expected a collection of bones, jars jammed with spell ingredients or skulls used as candleholders; instead there were rows and rows of neatly shelved books on one wall, a fireplace in the center where a chimney came down, and a small oak desk against the far wall. And, of course, the three cots we were currently using.

There was a mirror on the wall near my cot so that if I turned I could see my reflection. The first time I did that, my heart nearly stopped. I had seen myself several times since Brax had first put his eye in my socket, but something had shifted. I looked older. Stronger. Weary.

And intimidating.

That was the biggest change. Of course, there would be change: I had killed a Hvitur dragon, fought a mage dragon (with Brax's help), and faced a pack of wizards. Those events had marked me. Add to that the strange dragon's blood now running through my veins, making me grow scales and giving me strength.

Was this what others saw when they looked at me? Obviously, it was. If I went back in time and walked into my room at the Red Fortress to see my younger self, she wouldn't recognize me. Maybe even Maestru Alesius would wonder who in the seven Hades I was.

I wondered that, too.

It was well past midnight now, and Brax had been gone for hours, which made a little tentacle of fear grow in my head: had he somehow been tricked into a trap? But that was mostly paranoia because the moon was full and the air was still warm in the fief of Algaria, so it was a good night to walk. And I was certain I would have heard any commotion caused by an attack on Brax. Or he would have shot a thought my way, like a warning arrow.

A cock crowed outside, even though it was dark. This was followed by a hiss, then the cawing of a magpie, and then an odd and lasting silence. Perhaps the wizard's birds were confused by the moon. Normally they would crow and caw at the rising sun—at least that was how it worked on Ellos.

Nameless had not stirred for over an hour.

He looked so much like my brother. Yes, he *was* my brother, but I found that I kept staring at his face, looking for—I don't know—an understanding of what had happened to him.

And of where Corwin had gone.

The eye patch he wore was very much like the one I'd worn. In some ways I felt like I was looking at my past, at who I used to be. He didn't seem to be hampered by the lost eye in that he didn't run into walls or spill drinks when he poured. In fact, he had adapted to that painful change rather quickly. It was as if he'd been wearing that patch for years.

His good eye opened and he stared directly at me.

I shuddered, feeling guilt at staring, and opened my mouth to say so, but he put a finger to his lips.

Then he turned his head slowly toward the door, as if he didn't want to alert anyone with a sharp movement.

I did the same, my heart now beating slightly faster. The door was open. How had that happened without me hearing? It was a failure of my training. But there hadn't even been a squeaking hinge.

Someone stood in the door, sniffing. The shape was undefined, as if my eyes had gone blurry and couldn't focus on a single aspect. There were shadows that seemed to move and a smoky substance emanating from the visitor's clothes —which were made of rags. Or moss, I couldn't tell. I blinked several times, and the person standing in the door became clear.

It was Red, the leader of the council. The ancient witch did not announce herself, but she continued to slowly scan the room. The smoky substance drifting off of her reached the crackling fire in the hearth and the flame grew duller.

I was tempted to call out and let her know where we were. She had promised us safety, and in a way we were under her watch. And so she might be here to warn us of danger.

Red took a step into the room and the door swung silently closed behind her. The flames grew even dimmer, as if her presence were slowly snuffing the fire. Her face looked friendly, trustworthy, and glowed slightly in the dark. She was here to help, that certainty grew in my head. She was a friend. She was someone I should inherently trust.

She looked toward me, our gazes locked, and I felt a sudden need to rise and move closer. She was here to save me. To save us. She was a mother and would hold me and keep me warm from the cold world. She was *my* mother. The one I'd never known. She could fill that space and make me whole, and no one would ever hurt me again.

Red raised her hand and gestured, and I rose from my cot.

The assassin side of my mind, trained to measure every detail, knew something was wrong. A fact was missing. Even just looking at her, I listed the things that were different: she had been bent-backed when we'd met her and forced to lean on her staff. And here she was standing before us, tall and straight and without a staff. She even looked younger.

She mouthed words that I was certain would soothe me if I could hear them properly. I only had to get closer to her. Now the rest of the cabin had vanished and her glowing, friendly face became the only thing I could focus on. There was such gentleness in her dark, dark eyes. Such perfection. I wondered if this was what my mother had looked like.

I took a step and another, and with each movement I felt warmer and calmer and more whole. My eyes were so trained on her that I couldn't see Nameless anymore, and my friends were behind me on the cots. It didn't matter. We would all be safe in her embrace. Forever protected.

A third step. A fourth.

Her lips were still moving as she whispered just below my hearing. My feet shuffled with each of those words.

I put up my hands to hold her.

And something shot out of her cloak with the speed of a whip. It hit my forehead and stuck there—a line directly between her and me.

In a small part of my mind, so very far away, I felt fear. For this was not safety. The whip-like thing had penetrated into my skull and it was pulling at who I was. It was like a very thin wire, and my thoughts were tumbling out into that line.

But she was Red. She was my mother. And I took another step, eyes open.

Sleep. Sleep. Sleep forever, a voice said in my head, making my eyelids heavy. They closed. My feet kept sliding me toward her.

Then—a heartbeat later—the room grew very bright, so bright it blinded me even through my eyelids. Nameless shouted, "Begone, foul spirit!"

I opened my eyes. The hearth had become as hot and glowing as a forge at an armory. The heat blasted us and still that line pulled at my thoughts and I edged closer and closer to her.

But it was not Red. It was not my mother. For this woman before me had scales and what looked to be spiders running across her face, and what I'd thought was an open mouth were moving webs.

"Up, assassins!" Nameless cried. "To arms. Your sister in steel is in need."

There was a commotion behind me and two more of the lines—webs—shot out and there was a struggling followed by silence. A fourth strand shot toward Nameless, but it never grew tight, a sign it had missed.

She wanted me to hold her and I knew now that to be in her arms was death, that those webs and spiders would envelop me and consume everything that I was.

"Your blade." Nameless's voice was a distant whisper. "Carmen, use your blade!"

I strained to reach down to my daggers, to get my fingers on them, but my hand would not move. The daggers were a thousand leagues away from me, and I was now only inches from her and I could smell the horrid, dead stench of her breath. Maggots slithered inside that mouth-shaped web.

Then my blade was out, it was moving through the air, slicing upwards through the webs. But it wasn't in my hand.

Nameless had it.

The moment he cut the strand of web connected to my head, the vision of the thing in front of me became even clearer. She—it—was truly ugly. She didn't even slightly look like Red, or even like a mortal—it was a collection of insects and webs woven in her shape.

"Strike now," Nameless said, for he was struggling with several of the webs. "Strike now, Carmen!"

I grabbed my second dagger, yanked it out of its sheath and drove it into the heart of the thing.

If it had a heart, that is.

The creature let out a horrible hissing scream, then it fell down and burst into thousands and thousands of spiders skittering across the floor and out the crack at the bottom of the door. In a few moments all that remained were a few wiggling webs.

I turned. Thord and Megan had plucked the wire-thin webs from their heads. Thord threw his away, disgusted. Megan stared at hers.

Nameless offered my dagger back to me handle first. I took it, but didn't put it away.

"What was that thing?" I asked. "What was it?"

"One moment," he said. Then he clapped his hands together and a white glowing bird appeared and flew through the wall of the wizard's home. "I had to alert my master."

I swallowed. He had learned so much magic in such a short time—exactly how powerful was he? He also had just saved our lives.

"You asked what attacked you," Nameless said. "Well, it was two things." His voice was calm. "It was a munculus; a creature made from the will of a wizard. And it was also a sign that if you do not leave Azadiq immediately, you will be dead."

15

A STAR FALLS

"Who sent it?" I asked. "Was it Red?"

"Is that who you saw?" Nameless had grabbed a broom and was sweeping up the dead spiders as if it were a normal house-cleaning day. "I saw my master Goran."

"And I saw Maestru Beatrix," both Megan and Thord said at the same time.

"It was a very powerful summoning," Nameless said. He threw a dustbin full of spiders into the fire and they crackled and snapped and looked briefly alive, which made my heart jitter a bit. "The munculus reflects someone you trust within moments of seeing it. So, I guess you trust Red."

"Trust her?" I said. "I don't even really know her. But did she send it?"

Nameless shook his head. "No. She would not send it because she gave her word that you were safe, and she hasn't broken her word in her three hundred years of life. It was another wizard or two or three, for these are not easy summonings. And it's clear they want you three dead."

"Just because we're assassins?" Megan asked.

"That's one reason. But most likely they want to keep the

secret of this land safe—wizards are rather secretive, as I'm sure you've noticed." Nameless leaned on the broom. The calmness in his voice was almost aggravating, like he was discussing a mathematical equation. "Whoever summoned this munculus decided it was necessary to go against the decision of the council. You must remember that my fellow wizards and witches watched as their leaders, the best of them, were taken one by one on the emperor's orders. By assassins' blades. By trickery and by force. And those who weren't murdered outright had their hands bound and staffs broken, and then were transported in wicker cages to the white tower. So the last thing these wizards want is the emperor or anyone from Ellos discovering that they have found a paradise. We are powerful, but we are not a multitude. And we—they—are playing it safe by killing you. Their guess is that the dragon would probably get angry but just go home." He said all this without emotion.

"We foiled them," Thord said. "Well, you stopped them, I mean. But we're safe now."

"No, you are in more danger." Nameless put the broom in the corner. "Because they know the munculus failed, and soon they will send something bigger to be certain of your death. They also know that they have gone against a council decision and will be punished for that and, well, there's no use being punished for something you failed at. So they will be extra desperate."

The door swung open and the three of us put our hands on our weapons, but it was Goran, sweeping in. "At peace, at peace!" he said and a moment later Brax stuck his head in the door, because it was not wide enough for him to go any further.

Are you unharmed? he sent.

Yes. Yes. But where have you been?

That is better answered later.

Goran did not have a calm look on his face—in fact his upper lip was twisted with anger. He whispered several words and pointed upwards at the ceiling and then all around the house.

"The munculus is completely gone," he said. "Good work, Nameless. Now tell me what happened."

Nameless gave his account without showing any emotion or worry. When he was finished, Goran turned to us and bowed. "You have my most sincere apologies. This happened under my watch, in my home and in the center of my power. I was too trusting of my kind and in the binding power of the council. We are perhaps overly obsessed with being individualists, we wizards and witches. The ones who launched this attack will be punished. But Nameless's conclusions are correct. You will have to leave now because a second attack will follow on this one's heels. It would be better to be in the air and far away before it arrives. There is not a moment to spare."

A few minutes later the swans were saddled and Thord and Megan climbed on. Naga and Bolt squawked their anger at having to fly so soon, and Brax just let out a low, wordless grumble as I climbed onto his back. "How much did you eat?" he whispered. "My spine is going to break."

"Oh hush," I replied. "There's nothing sadder than a whining dragon."

Nameless had helped stuff our knapsacks and saddlebags with food and water and then he had mounted his swan, Dust—that odd creature that obviously still loved him. I didn't know how he could stand to be so close to something that looked dead.

Goran brought two books up to Brax and me. "These are the books we spoke of on our walk. They should be of use to you in your quest to bring Brenna back." He stuffed them into the knapsack I had strapped to Brax's back, pushing hard to make them fit alongside the food. "You may borrow them as long as you promise to return them to me. There is much to be learned of the old magics. I wish we had hours to learn more together."

"As do I, Goran," Brax said, and his voice was warm with friendship. "One day, if all is well, I will return to continue our discussion and to bring back your books."

Goran patted his shoulder. I nearly dropped my jaw and felt a pinch of jealousy. Had Brax made another human friend? Well, Goran was a wizard, so I wasn't certain he was entirely mortal.

Goran then strode over to Nameless. The swan gave the wizard a gray-eyed look then turned away. Nameless was straight-backed as he gave his saddle belt a final tightening.

"And you are certain, my apprentice, that this is the right course for you?" Goran put a hand on his shoulder. "I still have much to teach you."

"It is what is in my heart, Master," Nameless said. "When I promised my aid to these visitors, it was coming from the very center of my being."

Goran nodded. "We must always do what resides in our hearts. I release you from my bonds and no longer call you apprentice. I do hope you are able to find yourself. Or, should I say, the self you were meant to be. And may you discover a name, too. You cannot be Nameless forever."

"I will do that, my master." Then Nameless shook his head. "I mean Goran of Algaria. I appreciate your aid and teachings. And—"

Goran lifted his hand, and I wondered if he was already tired of Nameless's list of the things he'd done for him.

"Silence," the wizard said, and the word carried across

his whole yard so that even the animals in his pens and the creatures of the night fell silent. Not even a cricket dared to make a peep. I clamped my mouth shut in reaction, and the swans held their beaks tight.

A high-pitched whistle grew in the distance and Goran glanced up at the dark sky. More whistling and hissing followed this first noise, and then something in the sky grew brighter than the stars. "Starfire!" Goran said. "Brace yourselves!" He raised his arms and a glowing shield of light appeared above us. One star fell from the heavens and struck the shield with such force that Goran was knocked to his knees. I felt heat and was momentarily blinded, but when my sight came back, we were all fine. Another falling star struck the roof of his home and it exploded into flames.

"Fly! I cannot hold them much longer. Head over the waters and away from any of the fiefs, that is where their magic is strongest. Get as far out to sea as possible." Another burning ball hit the livestock pen, breaking down fences and scattering sheep. "Nameless knows the way to Ellos! You must follow him. Begone!" Goran began spinning his staff in a circle, making the shield wider and higher.

Nameless swung himself up onto Dust and, with a running start, his swan took to the air. Brax flexed his wings and followed, with our companions only a few wingbeats behind. We flew low under Goran's shield, which followed us as another ball of starfire burst only a few yards away. I was smart enough to cover my eyes this time, holding tight to Brax's back. Then the stars came down in twos and threes. Goran's whole fiefdom would burn.

"We can't leave him," I said as Nameless led us further and further along.

"They will halt the attack when we are gone," he

shouted. "The best thing for him and for us is to leave with great haste."

And soon we were over a short beach and out in the open water, but the shield no longer could be stretched that far. The stars burst around us, causing the swans' feathers to singe, or they plunged into the water, briefly illuminating the deeps. Nameless led us at breakneck speed over the waves and fewer and fewer stars burst, until they stopped completely.

There was time for one glance backward. The home and farmyard were ablaze, and Goran was now casting a spell that looked like a raincloud forming. And then we were too far to see properly, even with my dragon eye.

"Don't slow down," Nameless shouted. "Stay close!"

And we followed the one who used to be my brother over dark waters.

16

A STREAM IN TIME

Our swans and Brax struggled to keep pace with Nameless. His swan—for something that had once been dead or was still dead—could travel at a great speed and didn't seem to tire. We'd had very little rest and after a short time at this pace, even Brax was getting winded.

"Slow down," I shouted as Nameless outdistanced us. "Slow down!"

He turned and whispered a word and Dust did slow. Her wings didn't look airworthy, and yet they clearly kept him aloft.

"I only wanted to be as far away as fast as possible," he explained when he was close enough. "We will turn to the east in a short while. That way lies Ellos."

He was closer now and the death smell of his bird stronger, so I breathed through my mouth. "Do you know the distance? How many days of travel?"

"I was not awake the last time I traveled." He spoke without sounding bitter—he was only sharing a fact. "But it was far enough that it tested the very limits of my swan when she was in her previous state. We have no choice, of course. Azadiq is no longer a safe haven for us."

"Then we will hope our slight bit of respite was enough," Brax said. "Though I could have used a nap, at least."

"I will make it easier," Nameless said. He turned Dust sharply so we were heading east. Directly ahead the first red rays of the sun were lighting the sky. "And now, if I remember the words, this little spell will make our travel a breeze." He paused. "Forgive me for that pun, it is one of Goran's favorites."

He whispered in a language that sounded like Oldtongue and then made a gesture at the sky. A moment later a breeze came up from behind us and began pushing us forward. Both Thord and Megan flew closer, but their swans wouldn't let them get near Dust. They crowded to the left of Brax.

"The stupid swans seem to like me now," he said.

"Don't let it go to your head," Megan answered. "It's because you don't stink. At least not too badly."

"Someday, Megan of the red hair," Brax said, "I will snack on your toes. One by one."

"I'm certain they will taste good," she replied.

"This will be a long flight if you two wield verbal barbs the whole way," I said. I turned to Nameless. "How did you do that?"

"The wind summoning? Oh, it is a rather simple spell that my master—that the wizard Goran taught me."

"And what other spells do you know?" Brax asked.

"I know nothing," Nameless said. Then he laughed, which was close enough to Corwin's laugh to send a slight chill down my neck. "At least that is what Goran would say to me repeatedly. If you are asking my skill level as a wizard? Well, I was only at the beginning of my studies."

"But you turned yourself invisible," Thord said.

"Not exactly. I just hid myself from your eyes."

"Isn't that what being invisible is?" Brax didn't try to hide the exasperation from his voice. "Or is this wizarding mumbo jumbo to make it all sound fancy and mysterious."

"True invisibility means you can't be seen by anyone." He absently stroked the feathers on his bird's back. "Every one of those wizards could still see me because they have trained their eyes not to be fooled. I used misdirection to fool you. You remember, I tossed a glass ball into the air? That distracted your eyes long enough for me to perform the spell. That said, I am adept at not being seen. Goran said it was my assassin skills. And he did once compliment me in saying that I was a natural when it came to magic. Perhaps I should have never become an assassin in that other life I had."

I didn't want to picture what Corwin would have been like with the power of a wizard in his hands. Maybe all of Ellos would be in flames. "It may be best that you weren't," I said, not meaning to say it aloud.

"Yes, that Corwin you speak of sounds like he let power rule him." Nameless shook his finger in the air. "But you were asking how I know so much magic in what seems a short time. In weeks, I have learned months' and perhaps years' worth of skills. That is due to Goran. He is a wonderful teacher. And he has a stream that slows time."

"Slows time?" Megan asked. "What does that mean?"

"When he taught me we would stand in that stream, and time would slow around us so that lessons that were many hours long happened in that stream, but when we stepped out of the stream only minutes had passed. He perhaps suspected that there was danger coming our way, so he had chosen that method of instruction. He was worried too about the dreams I would have."

"Dreams?" The hand resting on my leg tightened into a fist.

"Oh, nothing too deep. They were dreams of the past, that is all. Goran is a worrier, but he has seen many reasons to worry."

"He showed me the stream," Brax said. "I dipped my toe in it. And in that time we spoke for an hour."

"Yes, that is how it works," Nameless replied. "It left one with cold feet."

"Cold feet?" I asked. "You mean you were afraid to do it?"

"No." His laugh was gentle. "Literally cold feet. It was not wise to stand in the stream for too long. And one should never lie down in it."

"Because you would be trapped in time?" I asked.

"No. You would drown. It is still water." He said this with no sarcasm. "But that is why I learned so quickly. Many, many hours of cold feet and long lessons. But, as you can see, I am only an apprentice. I don't even have a staff. We carve our own from wormwood or ash trees and invest our powers, our selves into it. And our secret name."

"So we have half a wizard as our secret weapon against an empire," Brax said. "Perhaps it's best if we all dive straight into the ocean now. At least the fish will get a good meal."

"Brax!" I said. "Don't belittle the gifts he's offering us."

"The dragon is correct," Nameless said. "My abilities, meager as they are, will not tip the balance against your—our—enemies. I can only offer to be a small piece of a larger battle."

"Well, we appreciate it," I said. "Don't we, Brax?"

"Yes, absolutely," he said without enthusiasm. "Having

one more body for our enemies to aim at means the chances of me dying go down slightly."

"He does have a way with words," Nameless said. "I do like this dragon."

"Well, that's an odd feeling to have for the creature who blinded you," Brax said. "But you mortals are a strange bunch. I also wonder if we have been talking too much and not looking around enough."

"Why would you say that?" I said.

"Because I believe we are being followed," he answered.

17

A SMALL PIECE OF SKY

"What is it you see?" I snapped my head left and right and looked behind us.

"Ah, even with one eye, I have better sight than you," Brax said.

"Just tell us what you saw!" I nearly shouted this.

"A little piece of blackness is following us." He pointed a talon behind us and to our left. "There, just below the moon a part of the black sky is moving our way."

I looked where he had indicated and squinted my dragon eye. The moon grew closer, the stars brighter. "There's nothing there," I said. "Wait..."

For he was right—a small section of the sky had shifted slightly, and those lines of darkness were moving up and down and up and down. Like wings.

"It's a raven," I said.

"I have an aversion to ravens," Thord said.

"We all do now," Megan added.

"I will return," Nameless shouted, then he pulled on his reins and circled up in the air above us until he was flying in the opposite direction, aiming directly at the black spot.

"If there is one raven," Brax said, "methinks there will be many more—another pestilence of ravens."

A light flashed behind us and moments later, Nameless returned to say, "It was a bone raven. One of Blacktooth's horde—she can easily wield magic above water and far away from her place of power."

"And was there only one raven?" I asked.

"I cast about but could see no other pursuers," Nameless said. "Blacktooth and her partners are very motivated to stop us."

"And they know exactly where we are," Megan said. She was forcing Naga to stay close to us. The swan kept glancing over at Dust in fear.

"That is also true," Nameless said. "But the other rebellious wizards and witches cannot help her much, as their magic is bound to the land or invested in their staffs. Her magic is unbound and alive in those bone ravens. She is them and they are her."

That statement made me shiver, because I had not liked those ravens at all. And that meant a part of her was as dead and cold as they were.

"Well, I suggest we change direction," Thord said.

"The Wodenite brat is right." Brax jumped in before Thord could say another word. "She will expect us to fly straight and she will intend to intercept us somewhere up ahead. I don't want to dance with a horde of those bone ravens out in the open."

"That is a wise suggestion, Thord and Brax," Nameless said. He was way more clever than my brother because he knew using both their names would compliment them both. "Though any change of direction will make our flight to Ellos longer and perhaps lead to overextending our reserves of food and strength."

"The ravens will tear us to shreds for certain," Thord said. "I'd rather fly a little further out and avoid them."

"I will take your advice," Nameless said. "My bird will not tire, but all of yours will. So it is more of a risk for you."

"I say we change direction," I said. And the others nodded.

"Then let us go southwest," Nameless said.

"You want to backtrack?" Megan asked.

"Yes, Blacktooth will not expect that. And—"

"Traitor apprentice," a voice said. "Betrayer of witches and wizards, you will pay for your transgressions with your blood."

With that announcement a cloud of ravens came shooting down from the darkness above, flapping into the shape of their mistress, Blacktooth. Each of them cawed through her raspy voice. "For the rest of you, I want you to know that what I do is not personal. It is necessary surgery—you should have been excised from this land the moment you arrived. Alas, curiosity got the better of me. Now it is up to me to correct the mistakes of the council. They have so soon forgotten the lessons of Ellos. I do not. I will see your bones and brains scattered on the bottom of the ocean."

"She isn't the friendliest of witches, is she?" Megan said. Her voice didn't even quaver.

The birds lowered their beaks, breaking out of her shape and into an arrow formation. And then they rushed forward—their dead eyes trained on us.

They hit us like a flock of winged arrows, and it was all I could do to knock them away with my dagger. But there were too many, their beaks as sharp as blades slicing my skin. Where were the scales I so badly needed? The ravens that hit Brax in the chest and arms bounced off, but others went for his eye, his weakest point, and soon he was flying blind, his good eye closed. Others flew into his wings, cutting the softer stretched skin there.

Megan screamed and swung her dagger and Thord had already vanished in a cloud of stinking rotten death.

A bird gouged my cheek and I batted it away, only to be struck by another beak and a third. A sharp talon ripped across my knuckles and I nearly dropped my dagger. It would not do to lose one of these prizes above the ocean.

"Can you see the others?" Brax shouted. "Are they in front of us?"

"I can't see anyone." I swung again and again, but the swirling maelstrom of feathers and dust and sharpened beaks kept closing in on me. "I can't see them."

"I have to keep my eye closed," he said. "I will feel momentarily bad if I hit anyone."

He opened his mouth and blasted out a swath of flame. It caught the birds directly in front of us and they burst into fire and almost immediately became ashes. The flame was so hot it brought out sweat on my forehead. At first I thought they would be even more dangerous—burning ravens—but they disintegrated.

"When I said I can't see our companions," I said, "I meant I couldn't see them at all."

"Oh, well, I hope I didn't fry any of your friends," he said. He sucked in another breath, and soon more flames were clearing the way of ravens. We pushed through into open air and I could breathe again.

"I maybe have one more good blast in me," Brax said. "Then we'll be in trouble all over again."

The birds behind us were a huge cloud of wings and beaks. Somewhere in there were my friends, if they hadn't already fallen to their deaths. A light glowed in the center, bright enough to make me cover my eyes, and then Nameless and Dust burst through, knocking the ravens out of the way. I glimpsed Megan in that horde; she looked to be clinging to her swan's neck.

Nameless swooped down. "We should split up," Brax said. "At least that means only half of this stinking flock will follow each of us."

"No," Nameless said. He was bleeding above his good eye and had to blink to keep it clear. "Water is what we need."

"Water," I said. "Water?"

"Water will destroy them," he said. "It will weigh them down."

"Well, it's too bad we don't have a hundred thousand waterskins," Brax said. "Can't you just conjure up a rainstorm?"

"I don't have that knowledge." Then Nameless pointed at the endless waves below us.

"I don't float," Brax said.

"Neither does Dust," Nameless replied. "But your friends are in that pile and will soon be shredded."

The ravens were swirling around.

"We have to save them, Brax," I said.

Brax turned to look directly at me. "I hate it when you do that."

"When I do what?"

"Make me feel like it's my duty," he said. "I can't even remember their names." He let out a sigh. "Let's get this over with."

"We must get the horde to follow us." Nameless flew back toward the mass of ravens. We arced through the sky so we were a few wing flaps behind him. Nameless pulled up a short distance from the swirling mass of death and shouted, “Blacktooth, you are a horrible witch. You are pointless and your powers are weak.”

Only a handful of the ravens stopped and looked at us, and it gave me a chill to think she was looking through those eyes. But the rest continued to buzz around in a swirling mass. I got a momentary glimpse of Thord, swinging his sword, but it was clear he barely had enough strength to cut through the ravens circling around him.

“Were you trying to insult Blacktooth?” Brax said. “Is that your plan?”

“Yes,” Nameless said. “I want to draw them away.”

“Well, you’re about as gifted as Carmen is at insults. You’re obviously brother and sister. What a sad showing.” Brax then snorted in a breath through his nostrils and shouted in his deepest, most sarcastic voice. “Blacktooth, many are the magical creatures and witches and wizards I have met, and you are no more than a pimple on the buttocks of their talent. You are an oozing wound of stupidity. You are a pretender hack who has only birds for brains. And your teeth are ugly.”

The ravens stopped as one and swirled to face us.

“See, that’s how it’s done,” Brax said and, if we hadn’t been in the air, I’m sure he would have taken a bow.

Then, we fled.

18

FOLLOW MY LEAD

I didn't have time to see if Thord and Megan were saved for we were flying in unison, so close that the smell of Dust filled my nostrils, but it was not as bad as the stink of the dead ravens, who were gaining on us.

"Pieces and parts is all you will be," they cawed. "And shredded entrails!"

"Well, you've made her really, really mad," I shouted.

"Is it my fault I'm so good at my job?" Brax said, and then he shouted: "Did you hear that, Blacktoot? Your threats are laughable."

"Did you just call her Blacktoot?" I said.

"Yeah, I know, it was an infantile thing to say. But it sure felt good."

In one way it was the wrong thing to say. Because Blacktooth's anger and her need for revenge was lending strength and power to the ravens; at first we were outdistancing them, but they closed in quickly, their cawing and crackling of bones filling the sky behind us. Each time I turned back they were getting closer and closer.

"Stay near me," Nameless said. "And follow my lead."

"You better know what you're doing, wizardling," Brax said. "I don't make a habit of trusting mortals."

"Die, you maggots!" the ravens shouted, and I imagined Blacktooth somewhere outside her house shouting these words. "Die a thousand thousand deaths, you excrement."

"Excrement!" Brax said. "Now she's gone too far." But his tone was jovial.

The cackling, cawing mass of wings and razor-sharp beaks hit us—slicing into my shoulder and my back and pecking at Brax's scales with such hard beaks that they made sparks.

The pecks to my head hurt the most. The ravens would crack open my skull and snack on my brain. I batted them away only to have double the number land again.

"Dive!" Nameless commanded. His voice cut through the caws and crunching beaks. "Dive now!"

And then he dove straight down and Brax followed. The birds were right on us as we plunged like two comets.

Hold tight! Brax said in my head.

I am!

We hit the water at full speed, carving into it. The force of impact was so strong that my grip broke and I was thrown from his back, and only by pure luck did I reach out and wrap my arms around his tail, willing every last bit of strength into my fingers. My eyes burned with salt, my nose and throat were full of water. Deeper and deeper we went. Under the water it was darker, so all I could do was hold on and pray to Belaz and any gods and goddesses of the water. I'd forgotten their names in the madness.

We didn't seem to be stopping and I wondered if we'd plunge right to the bottom, but then I felt his wings brushing me and knew that he was forcing his frame upwards, gaining speed as we climbed toward the surface.

We broke out of the water at an angle and his back feet dragged in the waves, but with effort and each giant sweep of his wings we went higher and higher, the ocean dripping off of us. The water dripping off our—his—wings, reflecting the moon.

I wriggled my way up to my usual position on his back.

"Do you still have the books?" Brax shouted.

"The what?"

"Your knapsack. Is it still on your back and are the books intact?"

"That's the first thing you ask me?" I said. "Not… are you well? Do your peck wounds burn with sea salt? Are you missing another eye? Nothing like that?"

"Just answer the question!" he snapped.

I patted behind me, felt the shape of the knapsack. The books were still inside. "Yes. Whether they're soaked through, I don't know."

"Good," he said. "Now let's finish off these bone ravens. Only after that can we talk about your aches and minor pains."

The moon was bright enough to reveal a mass of black ravens, looking like an oil stain—caught in the waves. They were slowly sizzling and sinking, but a voice repeated, "You'll pay, you killed my children, you'll pay. I'll gather myself together, wing and bone and feather, and hunt you down," Blacktooth said through the last collection of crows, struggling to keep their forms in the salt water. "I will destroy you."

"No," Brax said. "Let those dead raven ears convey this message to you: what will happen, witch, is that I will summon my brother and his army and come to your tiny little fief and we will burn your gardens, your gates, your bird pens and your house to the ground. And then we will turn on you and burn you from head to toe. Slowly. We will not touch the hair on another wizard or witch. So prepare yourself for our reckoning."

The last raven opened its mouth but no words came out, and it sank with a hiss and vanished.

"Will you really do that?" I asked.

"For a witch?" He laughed. "Not worth the effort. But she doesn't know that—she'll spend the rest of her days looking fearfully at the skies."

There was no sign of Nameless. I spotted Megan and Thord in the distance coming toward us.

"Corwin," I shouted. "Corwin, where are you!"

"You meant to shout to Nameless, of course," Brax said. "One could easily mix up the two." He swooped lower over the water and then circled the area again, but it was getting harder to see where the ravens had been.

A head burst above the water. "Here!" Nameless cried out. "Here! Dust cannot rise from the water." The bird was moving its wings under the waves but couldn't rise up. It squawked a harsh, frustrated noise.

"Oh, I need to shut that thing up," Brax said.

Brax dived and his talons dug into the back of the bird and lifted both it and the rider into the air until they were high above the water. "Just a bit further," Nameless said. "And we will be dry enough."

"Your dead bird is not light," Brax said. "And neither are you." But he forced himself to go higher and higher in the air, straining his wings. Dust snapped at Brax, even though Nameless was making soothing sounds. "Get that thing under control!" Brax said.

"Release us," Nameless said. "We are dry."

Brax released him and they plummeted about a hundred feet, far enough I thought they'd hit water again, then Dust spread out his wings and they turned through the air and joined us.

Both Thord and Megan arrived. Megan looked horrid. Her face was covered with welts and scratches. “I still have both my eyes, at least,” she said.

Which made me wonder if Thord had lost one because he approached covering one eye. “It’s not gone,” he said. “We already have enough people in the ‘one eye’ club. But they did their best to poke it out.”

“It’s a nice eye, it would be a shame to lose it,” I said.

Megan rolled her eyes at that. Thord might even have blushed, but it was hard to see because his face was blotchy with wounds.

There was no place to rest. So we shared our soggy food, drank from our waterskins and then we flew slowly to the east, each of us tending to our wounds in the best way we could.

PART 8: BURNING EMPIRE

1

AN ENDLESS OCEAN

I was beginning to believe that Ellos didn't exist.

As each day passed the horizon remained the same in either direction. It was water, water everywhere. I started to wonder if my whole life before this had been a dream.

None of us had had a decent rest on Azadiq, especially Brax. The swans had at least been able to sleep for a few hours. The four flying beasts were doing all the work—all we riders had to do was hold on and do our best to stay awake. Our V formation and the occasional wind spell from Nameless were helpful to cut down on the amount of energy needed to fly, but it was still tiring to stay aloft. Three of the winged creatures were visibly growing more and more exhausted—the two living swans and Brax. In fact, he complained less and less, which was a bad sign.

Dust, being dead or near dead, didn't tire at all. She might fly until the sun and all the stars had fallen from the heavens.

The food we had slowly dwindled. Brax's stomach rumbled below me, sounding like gastric thunder. "I will eat

Thord or Megan," he whispered. "Which one would you miss more?"

Thord's face popped up in my head, and I blushed.

"You won't be eating anyone." My voice was hoarse and my skin was dry, too—the scales that came out were not the dragon kind, but the grotesque flakes that formed when I hadn't had a proper drink for far too long. "We're almost there. Just a bit further."

"You said that several million wing flaps ago."

Our waterskins were empty and the only way to get water was when we encountered a rain shower and would fly through it, our mouths open. Thord caught what liquid he could in a cooking pan he had in his haversack and shared the meager spoils with us.

Just when I thought I'd faint from hunger, we came across a flock of ducks. "This is a favorable meeting," Brax said. "We must be near land."

"They are traveling toward Azadiq," Nameless replied with no emotion. I almost longed for my brother's anger or sarcasm. "So either they are migrating to that land or they have been summoned. Ducks can travel an impressive distance."

"So that means we aren't anywhere near Ellos?" Thord asked.

"Not exactly," Nameless replied. He looked thinner and seemed to spend most of his time meditating. "The presence of the ducks can't be used as a measure of how far away land is. I wish I had better news."

"They are good news, either way," Brax said, "as long as you three get underneath that flock and hold out your arms."

Before anyone could ask why, and without warning me, he gave a few sweeps of his wings, and rose into the air until he was at the same level as the ducks. A few of them turned their long necks to look at us, then began pumping their wings faster.

"What is your plan?" I asked.

Brax's answer was to let out a blast of fire that knocked several smoking ducks from the air and into the hands of my companions, who juggled the burning bodies until the flames went out. Brax snapped up a few flapping and honking ducks before they dispersed in several directions. Their thin bones, designed for flight, made small crunching noises as he chewed them.

He then swooped down to our crew, and Megan tossed a roasted duck over to me. Well, roasted makes it sound like it was cooked properly. I don't recommend eating duck that way, with the feathers baked in, but they had trained us assassins to eat anything from insects to fried rats to poisonous mushrooms. So it wasn't the worst meal I'd ever had.

"You're a surprisingly excellent cook," Thord said, waving a charred leg of duck at Brax. "My compliments to the chef."

"You will never get on my good side." A few charred feathers flew out of his mouth with each word. "But thanks. Don't choke on the duck."

I hadn't seen Nameless eat any of the duck. Maybe, as a wizard apprentice, he was fasting. He and Dust were the oddest pair in all of creation.

As food filled my stomach, hope filled my heart. We would make it to Ellos. I again believed it was possible but when the hours passed into night and then, many wing flaps later, into morning, that hope faded. The ocean was always the same—beautiful and endless.

Then, when I was just about to doze off, Brax shouted out, "Yo! Ahead."

I squinted at the distance. A boat was on the horizon, one small sail cutting a white line against the sky.

"A fisherman," Nameless said. "And it is not a boat meant for a long ocean voyage. This is excellent news."

We gathered speed, getting closer. The boat was far too small to land on and the fisherman stared up at us, one cupped hand shading his eyes from the sun. And, even from this distance, it was clear he didn't like the look of three black swans and a dragon flapping toward him. He rushed to the rudder and began turning his craft toward what I assumed was the direction of land.

"I'm too tired to eat him or his catch," Brax said. "At least the boat means we are near Ellos."

His words proved to be true, for we caught our first sight of land a few hours later, and though the view of the rocky coast was welcome, it also brought a bit of fear into my heart. For there were several towers on that coast that looked out over the water.

"We don't want to land there," I said. "That's the southwest corner of the Akkad Empire."

"Your ability to state the obvious is noted," Brax said. He sniffed and tried to snort out flames to accent his words, but couldn't summon the fire. I wondered if an exhausted dragon might not be able to make flames at all.

"Carmen is right," Nameless said. "Being spotted by soldiers would not be wise. One fisherman seeing us is a mirage. A fisherman and a few soldiers, that is confirmation that we exist. We are a meager threat to the emperor, but we still want to be a surprise for him."

And so we flew away from shore and continued in an easterly direction—that would take us to Avenus. If the city hadn't been burnt to the ground, that is. We kept our distance from any ships we saw, staying far enough away that we would appear to be oddly shaped birds. My hands had long ago grown so tired that holding on was almost impossible. And though Brax could adjust his angle to keep me in place, he might not do that now that he was in such a sour mood. Or he was exhausted enough that he wouldn't notice me slipping from his back.

I glanced at Thord and Megan. They looked thinner. Their birds seemed to be becoming only feathers and bones —reminding me of the bone ravens. Thord gave me a meager wave and I returned it with a nod.

A small trail of smoke appeared ahead of us on the water, even though there was no land visible. When we got closer it became evident there were several ships in the middle of a skirmish.

"Those are Avenian triremes fighting Akkadian asitu warships," Thord said. He sounded proud of his marine knowledge. "Does that mean the emperor controls all of Ellos except Avenus?"

"That's entirely possible," Megan said. "And he may soon control the sea, judging by the outcome of this battle."

The lone remaining Avenian ship was burning and listing to one side, and it would soon sink. There were men scrambling to take off their armor before leaping overboard. "We could swoop in and save them," I said.

Nameless raised a hand. "I caution against that. The Akkadian ships cannot be allowed to see us, and I don't think we could sink them all in our current condition. We are a more powerful weapon if we are kept as a secret."

"And the Akkadians may have ballistae on their boats," Brax added. "Not ones big enough to bring me down, but a bolt through a swan and it and the rider would be dead. None of you are strong enough to take on a wet lamb, let alone twelve ships full of battle-hardened Immortals."

"Then," Nameless said. "If there are no other opinions on this matter, we should stay out of sight of the Akkadians." No one else said anything.

Nameless was the first to turn, guiding his bird away from the distant battle. He didn't look back. Brax followed, but I couldn't help but watch. The ship was nearly below the water, and those men would soon drown. Thord and Megan were the last to join our formation. It was clear from the grim looks on their faces that they, too, didn't like leaving a battle unfought.

I can feel your sadness, Brax sent the thought to me. *It is understandable. But that is the unforgiving logic of war. Hard choices have to be made.*

I know, I sent back. *The logic doesn't make the choice any easier.*

Pray choices like that never become easy.

We traveled in silence in V formation. Nameless summoned another breeze to move us along. It was several hours later that Brax first spotted the corner of the island of Avenus. No one said anything, but I felt a sense of relief as we passed from endless ocean over land. We were near safety now.

Well, perhaps not safety. For in the distance was the city of Avenus itself, but all around the walls were tents and makeshift huts and masses of people who seemed to mill around. The clouds hid us from their eyes. I first thought it was an army gathered there, but it was too disorganized and ragged.

"They are refugees," Megan said. "They have been driven here by the war. Adding to the burden on Avenus."

Thord took the lead and guided us toward the massive hills that overlooked the city. It was dusk, and we came out of the clouds and into the cover of the trees quite quickly, hoping no nearby farmers or hunters would spot us. The small forest we landed in was familiar because Brax and I had once hidden there—the day I was reunited with Thord and Megan. It already seemed a much simpler time. Our only job then was to survive attempted assassination by one of the emperor's minions. Now we had to somehow turn the tide of war.

The moment we touched down, I slid off my dragon and stood, my legs shaking from not holding weight for days. Brax collapsed slowly onto his side and the swans, two seconds after Megan and Thord were on the ground, slid their heads under their wings, stood on one foot and promptly fell asleep. Dust did none of those things: instead she nuzzled at Nameless as my brother pulled what looked to be a dead mouse from his pocket. She snapped it up, and the crunching echoed in the trees.

Even as tired as I was, that creature still gave me chills.

"We will need to sleep," Thord said. "Then I suggest Megan and I go down to the city in the morning to find Maestru Beatrix and contact the Avenians. They will be pleased to know that aid has arrived."

"I'm sure they'll be overwhelmed with joy," Brax said. He didn't even bother to open his eye. "Perhaps don't mention that Nameless was once the right-hand murderer for the emperor. Oh, and pray that no one recognizes him."

"I must state again that the person who did those actions was not me," Nameless said. "But I am cognizant that my presence may constitute a perceived threat. At least people will be distracted by the fact I have an eye patch and may not recognize me. I will take the first watch."

"No," Thord said. "That won't be happening. You're not in my *someone to trust book* yet."

"Understood." Nameless opened his hands in a gesture

of friendliness. It seemed nothing would offend him. "Though I want to contribute, if you feel safer I will stand back."

"I'll take the first watch," I said. "I feel peppy." My voice was so ragged they probably could barely hear me. "Now sleep, all of you. Sleep."

Brax fell asleep in less than a minute, and soon the others had found a resting place. Nameless slept further away from the fire and nearer to Dust. I watched Nameless, expecting his eye would snap open and he would catch me staring. My brother was here, right here, and yet he was far away. He moved several times and muttered in his slumber, his dreams causing him to grimace. Soon his muttering faded, and his face grew calm.

It was the only actual emotion I'd seen from him since I'd met this alternative version of my brother.

I looked up into the air and found I could see a few stars through the leaves. I wondered if the gods truly watched us from up there. Or were they too busy in their heavenly homes?

When Thord relieved me from my watch, I went happily into the dark kingdom of slumber.

2

THE DARKEST DREAMS

In the morning, looking ragged and tired, Thord and Megan walked down to Avenus, leaving the three of us and the swans hiding in the forest. Hiding mostly because we didn't want a Scythian dragon to be flying about scaring the population. Our situation was made worse when Brax announced, "Well, I'm taking to the sky."

"You're what?" I said. "The whole point is to hide."

"I'm too hungry!" He ground his teeth together. "I flew from Azadiq to Avenus carrying a dead weight on my back—sorry, I mean my dear Carmen. If I get nothing to eat in the next few minutes I will have to choose between you and your brother."

"I'm comfortable with the dragon leaving," Nameless said. "He would not endanger us needlessly. He has a good heart and is kind to the people he loves. He must truly have great hunger."

Brax smiled, showing his teeth. His gums looked pale. "Your brother is so much wiser than he used to be. Besides, it is foggy in the valley behind us and there are only a few sheep farmers. I will easily find a meal without making any

Avenians soil their togas." Then he put a paw on Nameless's shoulder. "And, good heart or no good heart, if you harm Carmen in any way I will turn you into a great big pile of redness."

"As I said"—Nameless actually patted Brax's paw—"he is kind to the people he loves."

Brax lifted his paw, looked as if he were about to say something else, then rolled his eye and shook his head. He swept into the air a heartbeat later, bursting through the branches, and then swooped low over the forest and was gone.

A silence followed his departure. The swans hadn't raised their heads from their wings, that was how tired they were, though each was resting on its opposite leg. Dust sat watching me now, looking like she wanted to bite off my nose. Or my whole head.

"Do you not fear Brax?" I asked.

"Of course," Nameless said. "He is a fearsome beast, the wisest and most dangerous breed of dragons, and he has many reasons to not trust me. Plus, he removed my eye. It is natural and logical to fear him."

"But you don't tremble in front of him. Not even a trickle of sweat."

Nameless shrugged. "That wouldn't accomplish anything."

"Do you feel any emotion at all?" I asked. Because just looking at him, at the handsome face of my brother with one half scarred by a dragon's talon, gave me sorrow. I wondered if he had ever looked at my missing eye with sorrow.

"I feel some emotion. But my training allows me to not let it overtake my thought processes." He looked directly at me. "I am uncertain it will always be that way."

The admission made a little chill run along my back. "What do you mean?"

"I think..." He swallowed and a shadow of emotion passed over his face. By the gods, he could actually feel something! "I think some of my memories have returned. I am having nightmares."

Without meaning to, I put my hand to my dagger hilt. "What sort of nightmares?"

"In these night terrors that have visited me, I am in a fortress and there are others like you."

"Other assassins, you mean?" I asked this quietly.

"Yes. And they are all dead. And..." Nameless swallowed and blinked several times. "And I am the only one standing and I am happy. No, not just happy—ecstatic to be the only survivor. And worse than that, I am proud because somehow I knowingly caused all the destruction."

I leaned back against a tree, getting a little further away from him. "That's more than a dream. I don't know exactly how dreams work or where they come from, but that's a reflection of what happened the night the Red Assassin School was destroyed. You betrayed your oaths and your teachings and let the Immortals into our... our home."

His eye was unreadable.

"And many, many people died," I continued. "Including our classmates. Our maestrus. Our friends."

Nameless nodded slightly. His face had grown pale. Was it wrong that I was a little pleased to again see a flicker of emotion? "I believe I'm beginning to understand why there is no trust between you, your friends and me. That is a horrible event."

"Yes," I whispered. An image of the dead classmates flashed in my eye. "Yes, it was."

"And that is why you tied me to that swan and sent me

away." He put a hand to his chin, rubbing it. "Why didn't you kill me?"

"Ending your life would have been the safest thing to do," I admitted.

"But you erased my memory instead."

"Yes, with a corporthium pill."

He stared at me for several moments until I had to look away. "It was an act of mercy," he said, finally. "An act of mercy after all the destruction Corwin had caused. You took the harder moral path and I thank you for it."

Never in my life did I expect my brother to thank me for strapping him to a swan, removing his eye and his memories, and sending him west. "It was a hard thing to do to my flesh and blood. But you had committed so many horrible crimes."

"It wasn't me," he said. "I am Nameless. But that... that other me. That Corwin. I don't know how to put this—the pill didn't kill him—he is still here." He pointed at his forehead. "And here, too." He gestured toward his heart.

My stomach filled with ice. "What do you mean?"

"I have had versions of those nightmares since I woke up on the back of Dust in Azadiq. Master Goran said to fight against them. But it is like Corwin is there waiting for me. In those nightmares, I do the terrible things Corwin did over and over again."

The tree I was leaning on was biting into my back, I pressed so hard against it. "And you feel guilt for it?"

"Yes." Then he breathed in as if steeling himself to tell the truth. "No. Not always. Sometimes I feel an overwhelming satisfaction. It is as if those actions, those horrible actions are what I was meant to do."

"What you are meant to do?" I blurted.

He shook his head. "No. Not me. I, Nameless, don't want

to do them. But in those nightmares I become Corwin. And now that you've told me his name, the dreams are getting more powerful. The sense that he is there just outside my awareness. Waiting for me to... to slip up and let him in."

I should put a dagger through his heart, I thought. I couldn't imagine Corwin back in our world again, wielding the power of a wizard and an assassin.

"But since we've met," he continued. "Since I know your name and your face, I have felt closer to you. I've grown to trust you, Carmen. A part of me knows you are my blood, and I should put myself in your hands. Without reservation. I feel that we were meant to meet again, and that I must toss away that past completely."

"Can you do that?" I asked.

"That's the thing." He let out a sigh. "I don't know. Even Goran wasn't certain where my past had gone. Is it possible to erase it like words written on sand? Or is it forever etched in stone that cannot be ground down?"

"And is that why you're not showing emotions?" I asked.

"Yes." He pointed a finger at me. "You are very quick. Very empathetic. I want to stay clear. I want my mind to remain my own. Anger clouds it." He put his hand out, and I flinched but allowed him to touch my shoulder. "I am sorry for what I've done," he said. "I am sorry for what *he* has done. This other side of me. Please forgive me. And please forgive him."

"I—I do," I said and put my hand over his. It was warm. "But, I must tell the others about your plight."

Nameless shook his head. "No. I fear they would never trust me."

"They distrust you already."

He continued shaking his head. "It would be worse. Give me a chance to find the answer and to find balance."

"I don't know. I—"

"Please, Carmen. Swear it." Desperation leaked into his voice—an emotion! "We are the same blood. Please swear it, sister!"

I swallowed. "I swear I will give you a chance."

He let out a sigh and said, "I will repay this debt a thousand—"

A dead rabbit interrupted him.

It fell from the sky and landed between us, making me jump up. Nameless backed away, too, and Dust let out a loud hiss.

Then branches snapped above us as Brax came, rather inelegantly, down from above, so that leaves and twigs rained in my hair and along my shoulders.

"Like a cat for its master, I brought you some nice, fresh lunch," the dragon said once he'd landed. "Did I interrupt anything?"

"No," Nameless and I replied at the same time.

This made Brax give us a doubtful look. It was made ominous by the fact sheep's blood was streaking his snout. "Already you are giving the same answer at the same time like the twins you are. I am uncertain this is a good sign." Then, as if to accent his statement, he let out a blast of fire.

It lit a pile of twigs next to us. "There!" he said. "You'll have to skin the hopper and cook it. I'm not doing that for you. I'm not your mother"

I drew my dagger and began preparing our meal.

3

SHADOWS IN THE FOG

In the midafternoon, four shapes appeared in the fog. They were moving quietly, but stepped on a few twigs and coughed to warn us they were approaching. Brax didn't even lift his head from his nap and Nameless said, without explaining how he knew, "Thord and Megan have returned."

And, as if his words had summoned them, the two came out of the mist. They had both washed their faces—they might have been forced to before talking to any of the Avenian politicians. The Avenians were known to be a very clean society—the joke was they went through a bar of goat's milk soap a day. Thord had run a comb through his locks and Megan had tied her red hair back. The days of travel had turned my hair into knots, but that was the least of my worries.

"We have news," Thord said. "So much news."

"And two guests," Nameless added. "Will you be introducing them?"

"Yes, we also brought guests." Megan gestured, and the first to come out of the fog was Maestru Beatrix. She stepped directly over to me and gave me a hug, not seeming to care that I hadn't bathed in—well, I didn't want to count the days—not since Drachia. I probably smelled like a dead racoon. Maestru Beatrix then turned to Nameless and looked him over. "I am told that they call you Nameless, though I remember you with a different name."

"That is my name now," he said. He reached out a hand. She hesitated—I was certain her memories of that horrible graduation night were flashing through her mind—but she took his hand and shook it.

"It is good to meet this new version of you," she said, her voice firm. "I have one more guest to introduce."

The fourth person stepped into the light. The man was tall, wide-shouldered and wearing a long, ragged cloak, the hood pulled up to hide any facial features. His hands were gloved.

From behind that hood two piercing eyes stared at me, then at Nameless and at Brax, who had opened his eye and narrowed it. I wondered if this was another assassin, but this man had not traveled as silently as the others, so he wasn't displaying any of that training.

"Well, who is our guest?" Brax let out a long, exasperated breath. "The tension is making my teeth ache. Who needs to hide in a cloak in the peaceful, book-friendly land of Avenus?"

The man pulled back the hood, and it shocked me to discover that I had misread all the signs. It was a tall, imperious woman looking down at us. I knew her face because I had seen it once before at a banquet at the emperor's palace. On the night we'd tried to assassinate Sargon.

"You recognize me," she said to me. That night she'd been in a stunning blue toga, dressed in the finery of her status to impress the emperor and all the other gathered guests. She'd had a small laurel of bronze leaves on her head. Now she was in an old hunting cloak with her dark hair held back by a simple knotted black rag. "I was told by my ambassador we were in the same room several weeks ago."

"You're Archon Thena," I said. "One of the two archons who lead Avenus."

"Yes, your studies served you well." Her eyes narrowed slightly. "I am the only archon, alas, since my dear fellow archon Perkan has died in a recent sea battle. He drove back the Akkad boats who were attempting a landing but succumbed to his wounds."

"I am sorry to hear that," I said.

"There will be time for mourning later," she replied. I knew the Avenians had elected the two archons to share power, and now she would be the sole leader of Avenus until the next election. I had memorized their political structure in class—well, truthfully, they had forced us to remember the politics and the players in every corner of Ellos.

Brax sniffed. "And why are we blessed with the presence of the most powerful woman on Avenus? Why are you dressed in rags, wearing pads on your shoulders and standing in the forest above your fair city?"

"I wanted to see you all with my own eyes." She pointed at Brax. "Especially you."

Brax put a paw to his chest. His talons caught the light. "Me? Little ol' me?"

"You aren't little." She put her hands on her hips and that seemed to make her stand even taller. "Though I am told there are dragons who are much bigger. But I wanted to see this living, breathing weapon for myself."

"Weapon?" He snorted out a tiny flame—he always was a bit of a show-off. "Oh, how insulting to be reduced to a set of talons and teeth and flames. I'm a dragon—I have feelings." He said this last line with some drama.

"I'm learning that," Archon Thena said coldly. "And you are not at your best—you look ragged."

"It was a lengthy flight to get here," he answered. "Too long of a flight to be belittled by you."

"It was not belittlement, only an observation of your battle readiness. I have no time to worry about anyone's hurt feelings." She glanced from Brax to me and the others. "And to answer your question, I came here in disguise because I don't want anyone, even my most trusted comrades, to know that you exist." She pointed at me for some reason. "That any of you exist."

"And what would your reasons be for keeping us secret?" Nameless asked. He was looking at her with his head slightly turned so that only the side of his face with the patch over his eye was visible. He'd done this on purpose, I was certain.

"You are the one recent arrival I was told the least about," she said. So neither Megan nor Thord had let her know his original name. That was good. I wasn't certain how Archon Thena would respond to having Corwin only feet away from her. "What I do know is that you have the intriguing name of Nameless. That sounds like something an all-too-clever wizard would choose. Is it true that you have some wizarding skill?"

"Aye," he said. "I do. But I am only an apprentice."

"And why do you hide your face from me?" She didn't miss much, I realized. One didn't survive in her position without noticing details. "Show me what you look like."

He turned slightly so that the other side of his face was visible.

"Traitor!" the archon shouted. "I recognize you. I have

been betrayed!" She raised a hand. "Tell me why I shouldn't have you all killed at this very moment?"

"We haven't betrayed you." Maestru Beatrix's voice was calm.

"There is no one out there to kill us," Thord said. "We came alone."

Archon Thena shook her head, but her gaze didn't once leave Nameless. "A troop of my Elite archers surround us."

Megan shook her head. "That's not true. We would know if they trailed us."

Thena made a hand motion and an arrow thudded into the tree next to Megan.

"I stand corrected," Megan said. To her credit, she didn't even blink. "We were followed. I am ashamed to not have noticed and apologize to my fellow assassins for my error."

"The Elites are my personal guard," Thena said. "They are trained since birth, so you would not hear them. Assassins aren't the only ones with hunting skills. And they are in large enough numbers to overwhelm you mortals and keep the dragon at bay." She still glared at Nameless, who only returned her gaze with a stare of calm determination. "Why is that evil viper here in my woods? And why shouldn't I have him eviscerated and left to die here?"

"Because," I said. "We did not intend this as a trick, and he would not be here if we didn't believe he could help."

"Help?" Archon Thena said. "He only helps himself." She still held her hand up and I was keenly aware that somewhere just out of sight, a multitude of bows was pointing at us.

"You can lower your arm, Archon," Maestru Beatrix said. "If you trust me in anything, trust me in this. We would not put you in harm's way. It was I who proposed to these other two that we should keep Nameless's background from you. I was certain you wouldn't come if you knew who waited up here."

"That is true," Archon Thena said. Her hand didn't show a sign of shaking. "My gut is telling me to kill you all. Allies who keep such secrets are not true allies."

"He is here," Maestru Beatrix said, looking from Nameless to Thena, "because I have concluded, after I received a report from Akkad itself, that Nameless is the key to victory against the emperor. More so than even the mighty dragon."

"The key to victory?" Archon Thena's hand wavered slightly. "This I have to hear." She opened her hand, then closed it into a fist and I heard at least thirty footsteps as her Elites retreated slightly. They had wanted us to hear that. Not one of them was visible, though. "Begin your explanation and make it good."

And so we each told a part of our story, and then Maestru Beatrix let us all know her plan.

4

A LIST

I started the story by telling how we had captured and blinded Corwin. I didn't look at Nameless as I retold that part of the tale. We then spoke about our time in Drachia and the journey to and from Azadiq. Even mentioning the land of wizards and witches felt like a betrayal, but what could the leader of one city on an island surrounded by an Akkadian army do with that information?

"Well, so that is why you are missing an eye," Archon Thena said to Nameless. "And there is a land of dragons! I assumed that was all an imaginative ale-inspired tale told by Northerners. I am pleased to hear the wizards discovered a home—it assuages some of my guilt for not giving them safe harbor here—it was a political impossibility. Of course, I now wish I had them all in my arsenal." She tapped her chin. Her fingernails were short and as ragged as a farm worker's. "A land of dragons," she mused. "Do you suppose they—"

"There is no chance they will aid you," Brax interrupted. "Believe me, the concerns of the mortals are the last thing on my brother's mind. I'm the only dragon you have."

"Then you will be enough." She stretched slightly, which I read as a sign of her growing comfort. "Your caustic wit alone might make the emperor's forces fold."

"I shall take that as a compliment," Brax said.

"I have a question." Archon Thena continued to stare at Brax. She had a very steady gaze that took measure of all the slightest details. "I am told by these two assassins that you are on the side of my cause—my cause being to stop the onslaught of Emperor Sargon. Why?"

"I go where she goes." Brax gestured in my direction like he was shooing away a fly. "And she goes where I go. To put it bluntly, because this matters to her, it matters to me."

Thena's gaze lingered on me and, particularly, my dragon eye. "I did not expect to learn about such a powerful bond between mortal and dragon. As far as my limited knowledge goes, this is unheard of."

"No," I said. "Once thousands of years ago we had much stronger ties with the dragons—all of us mortals did. I learned about those ties from a mage dragon."

Thena raised an eyebrow. "A mage dragon, how very interesting."

"He's dead, so he can't be added to your arsenal," Brax said.

"Ah, you have read my mind." Archon Thena smiled, and I was struck by how her face balanced both beauty and power. "And how I wish the ties between the dragon and mortal realms were strong now, but like so many better things in the past, they are broken and we are, at present, facing an emperor who wields the most powerful magic to appear in generations." She jabbed a finger to the north. "Sargon and his forces have brought Woden, Trusk and Eshya down. Trella has opened its gates and disbanded its armies and now the emperor sits in his golden wagon on the opposite shore from Avenus gathering his troops, waiting with all four kingdoms under his feet. There is a full regiment of Immortals and at least fifty thousand Akkadian soldiers and, within a day or two, the barges and warships will have amassed to the point they will easily be able to cross in force. Bit by bit they are picking apart our navy. Our only advantage is being better on the water and in the field than any army, but there are so few of us. We can only field five thousand hoplites."

"Those are sobering numbers," Thord said. "Will your walls not hold him out of the city?"

"For a few hours, perhaps. But he has a vast collection of catapults and battering rams. And messengers from other battles suggest he can guide the catapulted stones through the air with his spells. He will make quick work of our walls." She said all this without bitterness or fear. "And I am certain that since we did not surrender Sargon will raze this island as a lesson to future generations. He'll also do it because he's the type of despot who enjoys that sort of thing."

"Why not flee?" I asked. "I know the Avenians are renowned for their bravery, but also for their logic."

"Yes, fleeing is the most logical thing to do," Thena said softly. "I have considered it. But all of our vessels are defending the strait. And there is nowhere to go. Even this newly discovered land of Azadiq is too far." She drew in a breath. "So we must fight and we must hope. And so I am turning to you strangers for help. Please tell me, Nameless, that you have a thousand spells dancing on the edge of your fingertips and on the tip of your tongue a thousand black curses."

"I only know a handful of spells." His voice was as blunt as always.

"That is a shame. I guess one works with what one has. It's what my father used to say." Archon Thena pointed at Nameless. "You do seem different. Though, I only saw you once in the emperor's palace. Let us just say you exuded power and conceit. It was an ugly sight."

"I can only imagine," Nameless said.

"No, you can do more than imagine." Maestru Beatrix stepped closer so that she was in between Nameless and the archon. "You can remember."

"What do you mean?" he asked.

"I have read about resurrecting past remembrances and I am certain you can have your memories—Corwin's memories—returned to you, and with those memories you'll find the way to defeat the emperor."

"This is your plan?" Archon Thena said. "It is madness! We cannot unleash Corwin on the world again."

"I'm in total agreement," Thord said. Megan was also nodding her head. I swallowed, uncertain what to think. Nameless was standing as still as possible, his face unreadable and calm. I'd seen that face twist into a grimace while he was having nightmares about his past.

Maestru Beatrix put her hand on the archon's shoulder. "My friend, I have no intention of unleashing Corwin on the world. His memories could be returned, but not Corwin himself. I'm modestly certain that's how it would work."

"Modestly certain?" Archon Thena shook her head. "That's not good enough. I prefer absolute certainty in matters like this."

"First off," Maestru Beatrix said. "How could it make our situation worse? We already have an emperor poised to sweep over our land and destroy our city." I noted that the maestru had called it "her" land. This was her home now. And perhaps she'd been born in Avenus. "The limited reading I've done indicates that Nameless would remain, but he'd be able to remember the emperor's weaknesses—something we can use to turn the tide of war."

"And how would one accomplish this great returning of memories?" Brax asked. "We have told Nameless about our binding and blinding him and he has accepted it without a ruffle of his feathers. But, to my knowledge, he doesn't actually remember it. His mindset might be quite different if he can recall the actual events."

"I can't promise that my plan is perfect," Maestru Beatrix said. "Or even safe. There is always the chance that we bring Corwin back along with his memories, and believe me, I never want to see him again." She spared a glance at Nameless. "Sorry to put it that way."

"It is an understandable and rational statement," Nameless said. "I, too, don't want to see this Corwin."

"But we are at an impasse," Maestru Beatrix continued. "Sargon will be here in a day or two. There is only time for a great risk and a very small hope."

"And how does this man get his memory back?" Archon Thena asked.

Maestru Beatrix took a calming breath before answering. "He goes to the White Tower at the emperor's palace in Akkadium."

Mentioning that prison made a chill go down my back. I had looked at that tower from outside and never wanted to get any closer.

"You want him to go to the very center of Emperor Sargon's power?" I said, failing to keep the incredulity out of my voice. "To the place where Sargon executed every last wizard and witch he was able to capture. He... he ate their hearts."

"I didn't say it would be easy," Maestru Beatrix said. "Nor do I know if it will work. Nameless could come back as Corwin or he could lose his mind altogether. But the wizard Boqin was taken into that White Tower, and I know that he never came out."

"Well, maybe he ended up inside Sargon." Brax tapped his lips with a talon. "The emperor did have the aforementioned habit of consuming spell wielders."

"The wizard Boqin, you say?" Nameless had tilted his head to one side, a look that Corwin used to give when he was surprised. "My master's master is still alive?"

"Yes, Boqin is alive," Maestru Beatrix said. "Or he was alive. This is information I've learned through the librarians of Akkad. There was a record copied that listed Boqin as a living asset. Every other wizard or witch taken to that tower has an X beside their names. Empires do keep records on everything, including the living and the dead. But this record is over a month old."

"This is such excellent news." Nameless stood taller and Dust edged a little closer, as though sharing his excitement. "My master Goran believed his master might still be alive. But surviving in that prison for years appeared impossible."

"It is a listing on a paper," Maestru Beatrix said. "It is not proof. But it is hope."

"The wizard Boqin was a kind and moral wizard," Nameless said. "My master viewed him with the utmost respect. If he is still alive, he could aid us—both in getting my memories back and in the fight. He was gifted at returning the dead to life but also in transferring their memories to their loved ones."

"This is news we are forced to cling to," Archon Thena

said. She turned to Nameless. "There isn't time to deliberate about what could go wrong. A trip to Akkadium and back will take at least two days, if not longer. Every minute matters now. So I have only one question: what say you, Nameless?"

"I will go to the White Tower," he replied without hesitation. "And I will rescue my master's master."

5

A PERSONAL REASON

"You don't have to do this," I said. "There may be another path to victory. We have only just arrived in Avenus."

"No." His eye, the mirror reflection of mine, was a pool of calmness. "Those memories—Corwin's memories—could be a powerful weapon to use against the emperor. Everything Maestru Beatrix said is true, and it matches with what my master Goran has told me. The great Boqin was not one to be easily destroyed. They displayed him in the victory square, then took him to the tower, still alive. He would be the final beating heart in that tower."

"I hate to ask grotesque questions," Brax said. "But what would stop Sargon from dining on Boqin?"

"There are laws to these rituals," Nameless replied. "Even as barbaric as the eating of hearts sounds. A wizard has to surrender his power into his heart for the consumption to work. That wizard or witch has to be broken completely. But the hardest wizard to break is the wizard who already knows death inside and out. There is good reason to believe that Boqin is alive. Especially now that he is listed as a survivor."

"But we should get more proof," I said. "You can't just charge in there and magically release him. How many Immortals remain at Akkadium? Is Scyllia at the emperor's side or does she guard his capitol?"

Nameless crossed his arms. "There is no time to gather information. Archon Thena has explained that. And we need to discover some secret weakness of the emperor to defeat him. A habit. A fear. A hole in his magical armor. Something that only Corwin would know. I don't know it."

"But I don't want you to go," I said, shaking my head. I nearly added: *I just got you back.* But that was not completely true because I'd never had this version of him before.

"You'll be coming with me," he replied as if it were already common knowledge.

"What?" I and Brax said at the same time. The word echoed in the trees, loud enough that the hidden Elites would have heard it.

"It is the logical course of action," Nameless explained with such calmness that I wanted to slap him. "Brax is healthier and faster than the swans. Dust never tires. We are the only ones who can get there with the utmost speed and return before the emperor has taken Avenus."

"You can't go alone with him." Thord put his hand on my shoulder and squeezed it a little too tightly. "That would be foolish! You would have no one to watch your back."

"I can watch my own back." I shrugged off his hand.

"Back-watching aside," Archon Thena moved so that she was in the center of our little group, "the wizard apprentice is correct. Judging by their ragged appearance, the other two swans are at least a week away from being pushed that hard. I cannot speak of the dragon's stamina."

"I am the king of stamina," Brax said. "Whatever that means. But the truth is I fly much faster than the swans. It's just the laws of flight." The swans both squawked and he laughed.

"But you have a personal reason to go, too," Nameless said. He was looking at Brax.

"I do?"

"Yes. Boqin may be able to answer questions about bringing your sister back to life. Of any wizard, he understood the paths to walk between death and life and back again. He had a vast knowledge on the topic."

"That sounds like an interesting conversation," Brax admitted. "It's a shame it has to take place in the middle of a White Tower surrounded by the emperor's guards."

"We can have no further prevarication," Archon Thena said. She was such a tall woman and intimidating in the way her eyes looked right through me. "You must decide now. You will need to leave in the next few hours if you are to be any help at all."

"I don't like the idea of flying so hard, so soon," Brax said. "I've only had a sheep and a few ducks in the last several days."

"Your meals will be taken care of," Thena promised. She gestured to Megan and Thord. "And the two of you are needed here. I have plans, newly formed, for you."

"We can't leave Carmen with him!" Thord pointed at Nameless.

Megan put her hand on his arm. "We are all going to have to take risks. And I am certain Carmen and Brax together can handle themselves. If Nameless should go all Corwin on them, well, he couldn't bring down a dragon on his own. And you know how angry Carmen gets if you make fun of her hair."

"What are you talking about?" I said. "I don't get angry about that!"

"I believe you just proved my point." Megan's smile was thin.

Thord's gaze didn't leave me. "Will you go?" he asked.

"Yes," I said and there was certainty in my voice. "Yes, though I agree with everything you've said. There isn't a straightforward choice for any of us. I have no desire to return to the emperor's palace, but at least I will go with Nameless at my side and not against me. And with the emperor in the field far away from Akkadium, it is the safest time to break into his White Tower."

Brax cleared his throat. "Well, I guess we're going." He rolled his good eye. "No one seems to care about the opinion of one little dragon, but, like a mindless mistreated work-horse, I'll carry the waif there and I'll break the skinny one's neck if his old self shows up."

"I am learning to appreciate the dragon's sense of humor," Nameless said.

Brax squeezed the talons on his right paw together, digging into the ground. "That part wasn't a joke."

And then he looked over at me. *Don't forget you have my sister hanging around your neck,* he thought to me.

I never will.

If Boqin the wizard still somehow lives, then perhaps we'll find an answer there. I long to hear her voice again.

"Then it is agreed," Archon Thena said. She grabbed my hand and held it tight. I wasn't sure why she chose me for such a gesture, maybe only because I was standing closest to her. The archon's palm was warm and her grip firm, and she looked me directly in the eyes. "I am honored to have all of you on our side. When this is finished I will make what payment or fulfill what wishes I can." She let go of my hand and turned to the others. "Food will be brought to you within the hour. By dark, I expect the mission to the White

Tower to begin and I will have orders for Megan and Thord. I take my leave of you. May the gods and goddesses shower their blessings upon you."

She bowed. A king or emperor would never bow, but an archon would. For, despite her power, she was still a citizen representative of her people. We bowed back and even Brax tilted his head slightly, and then Thena stepped into the fog and was gone. I assumed her Elites went with her but heard no sound of their passage.

"I wonder what kind of food they'll send?" Brax said. "I hope not all of it is cooked. I am not a fan of cooked food."

"I'm certain it will be perfectly edible," Maestru Beatrix said. "I want to say, because there was no time at the beginning, how happy I am to see all of you again. I am proud of what you've accomplished in the time since we last laid eyes on each other, and your maestrus would be proud, too." I couldn't help but think of Maestru Alesius. Nameless said nothing, but nodded. "And I am pleased to have an acquaintance with a dragon of such fine repute, Brax. I am told you are a reader. Perhaps some day, when this is done, you can visit my library."

"Well, that would be something of a sight," Brax said. "The citizens scattering as a dragon lands on top of the fabled Avenus Library. Librarians rarely like having fire-breathing creatures around their books, but if that day comes I'll gladly visit and be extra careful with my flames."

She smiled at this. "I shall take my leave. For I have become the archon's council in all things sneaky. I do suggest that you rest until the food arrives."

She hugged the three of us, shook Nameless's hand and waved to Brax. A moment later she was gone.

Thord volunteered to be on watch. I pressed my back against Brax and promptly fell into darkness. I don't know if

I even dreamed. It was the sounds of soldiers leaving the food that woke Brax first, and he nudged me.

I went out to see three carts with a variety of boxes, barrels and jars. There were even two sets of brown peasant's clothing which looked to be Akkadian in make—disguises for our journey. The soldiers who had dropped this bounty off were gone, and I could only imagine what they thought of leaving such a fine meal in the middle of a forest. One cart had live lambs and turkeys in the back. "Oh, they thought of me!" Brax licked his lips. "This is wonderful."

I didn't watch what he did next. Instead, with Thord's help, we brought our food deeper into the wood, so we were not visible to any spies. The meals were still warm, and included fish, chicken, ham, grapes, olives, figs and cheese. There were also jars of fresh water for our waterskins and saddlebags stuffed with dried fruit and meat for the journey. There was even a sesame honey candy that I would remember for the rest of my days. Maybe things tasted better right before a dash into danger and death.

Brax came back to our hiding place and I was glad to see he'd wiped his mouth. Only a few feathers clung to his face. There were no sounds of the farm animals, so I assumed they were all inside him.

"Well, the sun will set this hour," he said. "It is time to ready ourselves for a hellbent-for-leather flight."

I packed the least amount of supplies necessary. It felt like I was preparing for a one-way trip.

6

A WALK UNDER THE STARS

"I am going to stretch my legs, before we go on a mad dash," I announced. The feeling—the need to be alone—had come over me quickly. It had been so long since I was by myself and given a chance to sort through my frazzled thoughts. If even for a few moments.

"Well, don't dillydally," Brax barked. "We have to infiltrate the capital of the most powerful empire in all the mortal lands. I'm really looking forward to that."

"I'll be back," I said.

Nameless gave me a small wave, then returned his attention to the piece of wood he was carving with a dagger. He'd cut a branch from a white ash tree. He'd explained that he needed to invest some of his power into it—to make it a magical staff. I hoped the white color would reflect the pureness of his heart.

I turned away from the rest of them and followed a deer path. In time I came across a meadow, and I stood in the center. Since Nameless had first appeared, I half-expected the stars to have shifted in the sky, but when I looked up, I saw the constellations were in their familiar places. They were immune to the movements on our world and made brighter by the fact there was no moon. They twinkled in a mocking way. I would soon fly under those stars with my brother who was also a stranger at my side.

On top of that, I was about to part with Thord and Megan. I thought of that day, which already seemed years ago, when I went looking for the swan egg to get enough points to pass my classes. All I had worried about then was whether I would graduate. Now that fortress—my home—had been sacked by Immortals, my school destroyed, and that same emperor who'd ordered the destruction was lurking across the water.

There was never a simple time in my life. Being left with my brother on the doorstep of the Red Keep was not the lot of most mortals. Even as children there was never time for Corwin and me to play: there was work for us to do, pails to fill with slop, dishes to clean and blades to sharpen. Not once did I ever see other children; as far as I had been concerned they were mythical creatures. I wondered how that fact had affected me. The first time I saw children was when the youngest of the recruits arrived, and they were really young men and women—twelve years old. Maybe I was always acting older than my true age.

I put my hand on Brenna's soulstone. I wasn't completely alone because she was resting just above my heart. Perhaps I was the first mortal to carry around a sleeping dragon. She had spoken so loudly and clearly to the wizards and witches that her voice still echoed in my head. So much power and confidence. And not a peep from her since.

What happened if I died and she was lost forever? But I had been charged with carrying her, and I would not let her slip from my neck so easily.

A twig cracked behind me, and I tensed but didn't spin. The loud way it was broken indicated the person wanted me to hear the noise. I turned, expecting to see Nameless.

But it was Thord.

"I am sorry to bother you." He was rubbing his hands together, a nervous tic. "I know you wanted to clear your head."

I swallowed. "There is a lot to think about these days. Too much for my tiny brain."

"Your brain is not tiny," he said. "And like you, I feel as if we have been caught up in a tidal wave of madness and confusion. You would think spending all that time flying—with nothing to do other than point the swan forward—would settle my mind. Too much has happened in far too short of a time."

"That's right." I adjusted a lock of hair behind my ear. Was surprised how oily it felt. "We trained for all those years but no one gave us a single class on fighting off dragons, dead ravens, or heart-eating emperors. I feel as if I have aged to be... well, as old as Maestru Beatrix."

He laughed. How I missed hearing a laugh about a simple joke. "I'm sure it would offend Maestru Beatrix to hear you call her old."

I clasped my hands together, pretending to beg. "That's right! Please, please never mention my insulting comment."

"I won't." He clenched his fists as if he were swearing a very serious oath. In fact, everything about him seemed extra serious. He gestured toward the heavens. "At least it's a pleasant night for flying. No clouds. No moon. You will be able to slip unseen across borders."

"Are you here to talk about the weather?" I asked.

"No."

"Then why did you seek me out?" The question came out sharper than I'd intended it to.

He scratched at the side of his jaw. "Well, I felt compelled to."

"Are you going to warn me about Nameless again?"

Thord shook his head and smiled. His lips were thin and pale. "No. You are too stubborn to listen to my warnings. And I was starting to sound like an old amma warning her grandkid about sinkholes. It's not a good tone of voice for an assassin."

"Are you still an assassin?" I asked.

His jaw muscles tightened. "What do you mean?"

"Well, you were willing to forsake your oath before the council of wizards and witches."

"Does that bother you?" His reply was on the edge of being snappy. "Of course, it would. You were always so rigid in your thinking."

"Rigid?" I crossed my arms. Had he come here to insult me?

"Perfect, is what I meant to say." The way he said it didn't sound like a compliment. "But if you must know, in that moment, the words of Maestru Arvid came to me. He often told me that 'one should never die on the altar of idealism.' He was a very pragmatic man." Thord narrowed his eyes and gave me an unfriendly look. "I'm uncertain why you're judging me."

"I'm not judging you," I said.

"You can tell yourself that. Besides, none of us took the Red Oath." He huffed out a breath. "I'm not here to argue, Carmen. I am here to tell you something I've been meaning to say since, well, since I first saw you after our school was destroyed. In Avenus."

My heart beat faster. I had no idea what he wanted to say. But I wished for something, didn't I?

"You are different." He said this with what might be a pinch of awe.

"I look different? That's what you wanted to say to me?"

"Yes." He nodded. His blue eyes were unwavering. "When I look at you—well, I don't know how to say it. But your other eye—"

"My dragon eye you mean."

"Yes, your dragon eye—it looks right through me."

I frowned. "You've come to tell me about how strange my eye is? Thanks a lot."

"Don't be offended. It's just different, that's all. Everything is different about you. You are becoming something else."

My skin itched when he said this, and I couldn't help thinking of how the scales could rise on my skin. How wounds healed faster, and sometimes I saw flashes of the future. "Does that frighten you?" I asked. I hadn't meant for my voice to sound so strangled. So defensive.

"No. No. No." But he spoke rather quickly, like he was trying to convince himself of that fact. "I'm just curious—really, that's it. I wonder where the changes end."

"I'm not changing on the inside." I pointed at my heart. "At the core." But even as I said that, I didn't know if it was true.

"Good," he said. "Perhaps none of us will change at the core."

Those words drifted in the air for several seconds, and we both looked up at the sky. I wanted to prove that I wasn't that different. We were looking at the same stars. Although, my dragon eye revealed the magic that surrounded every one of them. I was tempted to take his hand. To just hold on to something. I reached out and—

Where are you?

I shuddered. Brax's voice was so loud, I was certain that Thord could hear it.

Just walking. That's all. Just walking.

Well, stop walking and run back. It's time to go.

Is everything good? I asked.

No. All of Ellos is on fire. Therefore, we must fly. No sense delaying it.

I am on my way.

But I shuddered again. For this time Thord had put a hand on my shoulder. "We're a good team," he said, and when I gave him an odd look he added: "All three of us. Me. You. And Megan."

"Yes, we are." I patted his hand. "But you mean four, if you count Brax."

"Oh, yeah, Brax, too," he said. "I kind of think of him as part of you. If that makes any sense."

"Don't mention that to him. He'd snap your arms like twigs."

Thord chuckled again. It was such a rich, natural sound. "I won't mention it."

"Well, it is time for us to go our own ways," I said.

"You be very careful."

"What was that word again you used for grandma? Oh yeah, *amma*. Thanks, *amma*. You be careful, too."

But he grinned, and we walked together to the clearing where the others were waiting. Brax grimaced when he saw Thord was with me.

Oh, for crying out loud, he sent to me. *Don't tell me you kissed him.*

No! I shot back, wishing my thought was a fireball hitting right between his eyes. Well, right beside his one good eye.

Nameless was already on his swan and Megan had her hand in a sack, apparently packing something. She glanced from me to Thord and frowned.

She then walked up to me and opened her hands, revealing a collection of tiny jars and small leather bags. "I took the time to gather a few potions and powders when we were in Avenus. Nothing special, but they might come in handy during your mission."

"These are great. Thank you." I slipped the materials into my assassin cloak's pockets.

"We'll communicate by spellbird," Megan said. "Keep us informed of everything, watch your back and don't get your head chopped off."

"I'll try not to," I said. "If I get decapitated, I will shout in your direction with my last shout." She laughed, and then we hugged. Assassins liked jokes about death. It didn't feel right to hug Thord in front of everyone, so I just waved to him and climbed onto Brax's back.

It was such a natural feeling now to be on my perch—a place where I belonged. He spread his wings and without a backward glance, we took to the night sky.

The stars continued to mock me.

7

WINDSPEAK

We flew north, first passing near Avenus itself and looking down on the last free city in all of Ellos. The parapets of the long, thick wall were jammed with troops, their armor catching the starlight. And beyond them, stretched to either side of the main road, were tents and other makeshift lodging for all the citizens who had left the smaller, unprotected towns and ports. When the enemy came, these frightened citizens would be let into the city, flooding it with people and making any war effort even more complicated.

We continued toward Avenus Strait. "We won't get too close," Brax said. "But I want an idea of what we're up against."

"That is good planning," Nameless agreed. "Always take the measure of your enemy."

That sounded like a saying they had taught us in assassin school, and I tried to see if there had been any change in him. But he still looked like Nameless, not the cynical Corwin. Maybe that had also been a wizard's saying.

He clutched the white ash branch—it wasn't much longer than a baton, but it glowed with power.

We stayed very high so we would be impossible to spot from the ground. There was a chance that Emperor Sargon was using birds as his eyes, but we were flying at a height that should even hide us from them. Scyllia or some Immortals might patrol on swans, but Brax and I would see them first with our dragon eyes.

Avenus Strait was on fire. "Those are Avenian triremes, fishing boats and barges with massive torches lit to shine a light on the oncoming force," Nameless said. "In case Sargon tries to cross at night."

I had come to that conclusion, but it was proof he was my brother—he still had to explain things to me like I was younger. We didn't know which of us was firstborn. Our parents hadn't left a note detailing our order of birth, and we'd never get the chance to ask them. He had always assumed he was the eldest.

As we crossed over the strait something truly frightening gripped my heart, threatening to make it stop in my chest. For the lit campfires and forges of a vast and powerful army were glowing all along the Trellian shore. That sense of horrible foreboding made the back of my neck cold. Doom and hopelessness raised their heads in my thoughts. For the gathered army, even though it was spread out, also had a great depth, the lights going far into the hills. We could never beat that army. *Give up*, a voice was saying like a drumbeat in my head, *give up give up give up.*

Nameless laughed. It didn't sound like Corwin because there was no mockery in its tones.

"What's so funny?" I asked. I was feeling like I might vomit—which I was certain would get Brax all riled up. I wanted to shout at him to turn back. He was shaking underneath me.

"It's an ancient, simple and potent spell," Nameless said. "A dread hex has been cast over the whole army, drifting across the waters. Even the most unpracticed of apprentices could counter it—but all the wizards and witches are gone." Nameless spoke a strange word and the dread vanished from my skull. I looked down at the armies in the distance and felt fear but not that unnatural, overpowering foreboding. "That's better, I assume."

"Yes," I said. "Much, much better."

"It is better," Brax growled. "But I have seen enough." He turned his wings so we flew west over the open water and then pushed his powerful muscles, making us gain speed. It almost seemed as if we were fleeing.

"I will admit to experiencing just a pinch of hopelessness for our cause," Brax said after several minutes. "It's like the first time I saw you and calculated the chances you'd be able to get me out of the cave."

"But that worked out," I said.

"I know. Otherwise, I would be beyond hopeless now. And that's not just the shadow of the gloom spell speaking."

"Dread hex," Nameless corrected. "It was a dread hex."

Brax snorted a few flames out of his nostrils. It was a sign he was getting some strength back. "You know, my little assassin wizard friend, you'll have a much longer life if you don't correct me."

"Understood," Nameless replied. I glanced over at Nameless, who was staying just beyond Brax's wings so we could talk. "My apologies. I shall not correct you again." He said this without sarcasm. Even I would have rubbed the mistake into Brax's face.

I thought it best to change the topic. "We have at least ten hours of flying."

"And only eight hours of darkness," Brax said. "The moment the sun comes up we'll be easily visible from the ground."

"We will have to risk it," I said. "If we wait a whole day, then that's the day the emperor might attack Avenus."

"I will speed our journey as I did before." Nameless raised his staff. "I'll summon up a powerful wind. This staff will add to its strength." He whispered some ancient word that made my bones vibrate and a glow appeared in his ash staff, and then a wind rushed up with such speed it pushed my hair forward.

Brax twisted to the left, the blast of air throwing him off course, then he twisted again, his wings flapping. "This is almost impossible to stay aloft in. It's too windy!"

"I am sorry!" Nameless shouted. "I am not gifted at windspeak and I can't correct it. This wind will follow us for the next few hours."

"Well, you had better hold tight, Carmen," Brax said. "Because I'll soon be going the same speed as a comet."

I lay myself flat against Brax's back because the wind was threatening to shove me right off of him. He wasn't kidding about the speed: with every sweep of his wings we rushed ahead, racing along the coast. Brax shook up and down, as if he were riding waves in the air. I figured it was best to shut my mouth and let him fly.

An hour later Brax raised one wing and lowered the other so we turned north, into the opening of the Ursa Sea, the body of water that led to Akkadium. After several wing flaps the wind let us alone and I could sit up straight.

"We have saved hours!" Brax shouted toward my brother. "You are relatively useful, Nameless."

"I am pleased to be of service," he answered.

We flew without a summoned windstorm because at that speed we would have overshot Akkadium by many leagues. Nameless chose a position several yards behind us, which meant the rich dead scent of his swan wasn't constantly in my nostrils.

We passed a fleet of Akkadian asitu warships in the water, their oil lanterns blazing brightly. They were moving quite fast, which suggested they were in the power of one of Sargon's spells. Immortals were massed on the decks, backs straight and facing forward. Would they stand at attention all the way to Avenus? Though my understanding of war tactics was limited, I knew that having all the ocean under Akkadian control meant they could just pile up the weapons, food, siege engines, giant barges and pack animals until the force was so overwhelming that Avenus would be crushed. Only the crossing of the strait had saved our allies so far.

"That is unwelcome news for our friends," Brax said after we had passed. "They cannot protect themselves from another fleet. The two fleets will become a pincer that squeezes the island."

I nodded. "All the more reason to move faster."

In time, the lights of Akkadium became visible. Though I had now seen the majesty of Dreki, the capital of the dragon land, it was still impressive to once again lay eyes on this walled city. It already felt as if years had passed since we had attempted to kill both Corwin and the emperor. My first paid assassin job, I recalled. Somewhere in my left boot I still had the coin that Naram-Sin, the executioner, had given me. I could not help but reflect for the hundredth time on the oddity of having Nameless, who was once Corwin, beside me.

"I am assuming we will land at the house of dung," Brax said. "I shall prepare my nostrils."

"It is close and should still be abandoned," I replied. "I doubt anyone with a sense of smell would hole up there."

We turned away from the city and in time found the familiar barn surrounded by hills of manure. Thord had once jokingly called this the "Offal" house. The name still fit. One swoop around showed the building to be empty—at least there wasn't a fire in the chimney. We landed and before I could dismount, Brax poked his head in the front door and let out a blast of flame.

"Was someone inside?" I asked.

"No," Brax said. "There were rats. Now there are no rats. I really don't like rats."

Nameless had touched down silently behind us. He slipped off Dust and led us all into the building. Little bits of straw were burning here and there, but Brax hadn't caught any of the walls on fire. Impressively, though, the old wood in the fireplace was lit. I pulled the door shut.

"It is an hour until sunrise," Nameless said. "May I suggest that we sleep? We won't accomplish anything in that time, and the rest will be good for our bodies."

"Yes," Brax said. "A wise idea. Can you ask your dead swan to sit as far away from me as possible? I find her stink is blocking the pleasant scent of dung."

Dust narrowed her strange gray eyes and, if I didn't know better, I'd believe the creature must have some sort of feelings. It showed that it understood Brax's every word. That said, I was in total agreement with him—the thing gave me the creepy crawlies all along my spine, and it stank more than manure.

Nameless whispered and the swan retreated to the far corner, near the fireplace.

"I am exhausted," I said. "Let us get our plans together after our nap. My mind will be less muddled then."

Nameless nodded and said nothing, but lay down beside Dust. The swan settled its long neck over his shoulder, and my brother promptly fell asleep. The swan just stared at us.

That thing disgusts me, Brax sent the thought to me.

You and me both. But I do need to sleep. You will watch over me.

Like a hound, he thought. *An angry, grumpy and handsome hound.*

I had enough strength to crack a smile, and then I closed my eyes. Just before falling into darkness, I felt one of his paws rest on my shoulder.

8

AN ICICLE IN MY HEART

I awoke to screaming.

I shot up, eyes open, and hands on the hilts of my daggers, but before I could draw them, Brax grabbed me and said, "Your brother is a fitful sleeper." He motioned with his nose.

The first sunlight, coming through cracks in the walls, was bright enough to show Nameless twitching and scratching at his chest as if he were bound. He let out another guttural scream that shook the rafters. Dust was awake—was always awake as far as I could tell—and looking down at him with what passed as concern. She let out a soft, caring hiss.

"I'd say our little wizard has some hidden demons," Brax said. "What say you?"

"I—I don't know," I lied. I knew that he was dreaming about Corwin. And there was a chance that Corwin would be the one who opened up that single eye and glared at us.

"I'm going to wake him," Brax said.

"That isn't wise." I sat up higher. "I've read about sleep-walkers and how they should—"

Brax shot out his tail and poked Nameless hard in the ribs and then whipped his tail back just as Dust bent her neck and stabbed at it. The bird got a beak full of the dirty floor and let out a bitter hiss.

"Well, that was satisfying on several levels." Brax kept curling and uncurling his tail like he might use it again.

"And it worked," I added. For Nameless opened his eye and wiped at his sweating forehead. He then shook his head and looked up at Dust, who was still hissing in our direction. Nameless glanced across at us.

"My apologies," he said. "Was I snoring?"

"Screaming violently is more like it." Brax slowly settled his tail. "You know, the scream that a torture victim would make as torturers peeled away his flesh."

Nameless frowned. "Screaming? That is very curious. I am usually a dreamless sleeper."

"Do you remember what it was about?" I asked. "Sometimes our dreams are closer to us when we first awake."

Nameless shook his head with so much force I thought he'd pass out. "I remember nothing," he said. "It was nothing. The mind is sometimes a monster all its own."

"Well, that's not a very comforting way of putting it," Brax said.

"Are you sure you remember nothing?" I asked.

Nameless stared directly at me and this time shook his head subtly, suggesting he wanted me to stop asking questions. There was a pinch of anger to his features.

"I just need breakfast," he said, and then he opened his saddlebag and distributed food to us. He handed a large hunk of dried meat to Brax. Within a brief time Nameless also had tea made using the fire. I knew Brax liked tea, but seeing him drink from such a small tin cup looked rather ridiculous.

Brax drained the cup and set it down. "Let me guess your plans." Brax tapped a talon on his jaw, doing his best impression of a teacher. "You two are going to trundle off to Akkadium in your best finery and I will have to hold down the 'offal' fort and enjoy the company of that winged dead thing."

"Dust is not dead." Nameless patted the swan's shoulder and what looked like actual dust came off. "She lives in a different state than you or I or Carmen."

"Well, it smells dead," Brax snarled. "Just make sure it knows to stay in its corner or it will be dead all over again."

"Dust will act properly," Nameless promised. Dust hissed directly at Brax but moved back against the wall. "And you are correct. We cannot fly into Akkadium on either winged creature because there will be too many wards and ballistae for that. Stealth is necessary."

"If you weren't so big and powerful, Brax," I said, "we'd be able to sneak you in."

"Now you are showering me with compliments just to soothe me." He gave that sharp-toothed dragon grin. "I accept your accolades with the grace and humility of someone as wonderful as me."

"We need your wonderful mind," I said. "For we have to put together a plan to enter the city, get past the walls of the palace and break into the White Tower. I have the palace memorized, so that's a start."

"It looked familiar to me from a distance," Nameless said. "It was as if I'd seen it from that angle before."

"That makes sense." I set down my teacup. "You—I mean Corwin—would have flown into the city on a swan many times."

"That must be where the familiarity comes from," he

said. "But I don't know that I have enough memories to be helpful."

"Can you picture the interior of the White Tower?" Brax asked. "I would guess that Corwin would have been inside it at some point."

"No," Nameless replied immediately. "I can't. But it may be as we near the tower it will become more familiar to me."

"Well, one thing I know," I said, as I took off my boots, "is that we cannot wear our assassin cloaks or regular clothes." We changed into the garments that the Avenians had given us. I looked like a simple peasant with a ragged brown cloak. I could secure the daggers hidden inside the trousers. There were pockets in the cloak for my potions and powders—the Avenians had thought this through.

"So let me get this straight," Brax said. "You are leaving without a plan."

"Perhaps the best way to look at it is that our minds are open to all possibilities," Nameless said.

Brax snorted. "That's just a fancy way of saying you have no plan."

"We have no plan," I admitted. "We also have no time. So we will have to go now."

I searched my memory for the spell the crone had taught me to disguise my dragon eye—no sense frightening people with the oddity of it all. I couldn't remember the word at first because it had been so long since I'd used it. Then it came to me: *"Oranu."*

Saying the word made Nameless glance up from tucking in his shirt.

"That's an impressive spell," he said. "And well spoken."

"Thank you."

"Where did you learn it?" He threw on his cloak.

"From an old woman in an Avenian market."

"Doubly impressive that it still works," he said, and then he motioned at me. "I am sorry the person I was caused that scar."

I shrugged. "That may be the first time you've apologized for it."

The patch over his eye wouldn't look out of place because many a peasant would have lost an eye in the fields, during military duty, or in a fight. And the patch made him less recognizable, though few in the city would have seen Corwin's face close up.

"Be careful," Brax said. "And please don't expect me to burst in there to bail you out when things go wrong. I'll be busy napping."

"Enjoy your sleep," Nameless replied.

We left the offal house, walked across the land of manure and headed toward the northern gates of the city.

I thought we would talk on the way there, but Nameless was brooding. When we got closer, we wandered onto one of the paved main roads that crisscrossed the empire, joining in with other peasants, traders and workers who would march into the city every day to sell their goods or their skills.

"I dislike this place," Nameless finally said. "They build it on blood."

When I thought of the history of the Akkad Empire, he was speaking the truth.

I patted his shoulder. "It is worse than that," I said. "It's built by grinding down other civilizations—blood, bones, spirit and all."

This idea was not new to either of us, but walking through those gates now, looking up at the guards, expecting them to shout or point or even send a bolt through our hearts at any second, it was easy to imagine how much destruction this empire had caused. Countless slaves had sacrificed their lives to make these walls and to construct every building inside them. I noted that none of the guards at the gate were Immortals and hoped that meant they were all away with Sargon. It wasn't like any of the defeated realms could mount a counterattack.

Nameless led us, and I wondered if he was remembering the streets. Corwin had been coming here with his maestru for years before he betrayed his fellow assassins. The streets had to be familiar to him.

"I truly hate this city," he said loud enough that I worried a passerby might hear.

"Hate? That's a strong word."

"No. It's the perfect word. Akkadium is too beautiful. These streets are a shrine to the ego of every emperor." He gestured to where the palace was coming into view, built above the rest of the city. "All designed to bring awe and display power."

"You really aren't Corwin," I said. "My guess is he loved walking these streets and loved being an important part of that power."

"Maybe that joy is what I am feeling," he said. "And it revolts me."

We walked a few more steps before I asked, "What did you dream of last night?"

"Cutting your eye," he whispered and I shuddered. "Over and over and over again. And the most horrible thing was that I felt no regret or sorrow. Perhaps there was even a gloating joy."

"I'm sorry I asked," I said.

"No. It was a reminder that I must be vigilant. Nothing

like that will ever happen to you again." He put his hand on my shoulder. "I promise."

He dropped his hand and kept walking. I followed, uncertain whether it set me at ease to hear his promise.

With each street we passed the homes grew richer—from mud brick one-room houses to four-room houses made of red stone followed by the richest homes, huge ones that were built from marble slabs and pillars. This progression only made sense—the higher on the hill, the wealthier you were, and the most powerful—the generals and ambassadors and merchants—would live nearest the palace.

We were the subject of a few looks by noblewomen with their hair high and layered on their heads, smelling of perfume. Even the servants, running errands for their masters, looked down their noses at our peasant garb.

So we sped up, since any attention, even snobbery, wasn't helping us stay unnoticed. We came to a long open space between the last house and the palace itself. It was a low garden with few trees, tall grasses and several benches. At first it surprised me that the emperors hadn't planted grand tall trees, but the strategic part of my mind recognized that if there ever was a siege, the soldiers in the palace would want a clear shot at their enemies from the heavily defended walls.

The emperor's palace was as impressive as it had been the last time I'd seen it. The royal palace in Drekia made this one look like a toy, but it had been carved by powerful dragons and constructed by great beasts that could haul half a mountain on their backs. This imperial palace had been built by much smaller beasts, oxen and mules and slaves—every inch moved into place by mortal men. And so in that way it was more impressive.

"The sight of it makes my heart grow cold," Nameless whispered.

At first I thought he meant the palace itself, but his one-eyed stare was locked on the White Tower. It rose higher than all the other buildings, like a smoothed tusk of straight ivory. This was a tower made to hold the mightiest of wizards. What spells were cast to imprison them inside? What sacrifices made to create such a powerful structure?

"It's like an icicle in my heart, too," I said.

"It's not the sight," Nameless said. "I knew seeing it would move me. But being this close, the tower is working at me. It is calling to the magic I have secreted in my heart, wanting to consume it. That tower is alive with ill will. With purpose. The emperor's purpose."

That explained the disturbing sense I felt that the dragon magic inside me was being drawn to that place, too. "You're right," I said. "I feel it, too. It's horrible."

He glanced at me, but said nothing.

We followed the paths, our heads down, stealing glances at the task before us. The main gates were open, but if we even attempted to go through there they'd behead us on the spot. We were peasants, after all. There were at least thirty Immortals guarding it—so Sargon hadn't taken every one of his elite soldiers with him.

"We won't be going in the front gate," Nameless said.

"There are side gates meant for the servants, but they are heavily guarded and locked up tight."

He pointed directly at the wall. "Then our only choice is to go over the top."

"Are you insane?" I hissed. "You expect us to climb that wall in the middle of the day with all those eyes watching every inch of this palace?"

"Yes," he said. "I am a little insane. You should know that

by now." He spoke with no hint he was joking. "But what I have in mind is an old trick—if they don't look, they don't see. And I can guarantee they won't be looking in our direction."

And then, without another word of explanation, he led me toward the wall.

9

THE DARK DISTRACTION

We followed the path that took us nearest to the wall. The guards marching in both directions on the wall walk were so high that they looked to be the size of little dolls. Nameless had timed our approach so their backs were to us, but that would change the moment they turned around. We crouched in a flowery bush of purple rhododendrons, hiding amongst all that color. Maestru Xerithus of the Red Adept gardens would be proud of me for remembering the names of the flowers. If he were alive today, that is.

It was better to focus on the living right now. And on ourselves living. "So what is the plan?" I asked. "I'd be honored to know it."

"This," he said. He clapped me on the back. "Do you mind staring at the wall ahead of us? It will make everything go smoother."

"Make what go smoother?"

"I'm changing the color of your clothes to match the gray wall. It's a relatively simple spell, but if you concentrate and picture the color, it will help. The brown cloaks we're wearing stand out too much."

I stared at the marble wall and thought about the color: gray, gray, gray. My back warmed, my arms tingled and the color of my trousers, tunic and cloak slowly changed to a whitish gray.

But so did my skin.

"What!" I spat out the word. "Look at my hands!"

"Oh, sorry." Nameless took his hand off my back. "I didn't mean for that to happen. I'm relatively certain it will fade."

"Relatively certain?" My skin was tingling. I examined the backs of my hands, frightened at how pale gray they were—as if I were dead. "It better fade!"

"We'll work it out," he said. "Are you well otherwise? I mean, it's not affecting your internal organs, is it?"

"Are you saying I might turn this color inside, too?"

His face was red. I'd never seen my brother blush before. "Let's not worry about that. As long as your lungs aren't failing and your heart keeps pumping, all is well."

"You mean this spell might stop my heart?"

He looked me up and down. "It shouldn't. And I'm encouraged by the fact you haven't collapsed—your insides must work properly. Again, my apologies."

He tapped his own shoulder and the color spread along his clothes. "Your skin hasn't gone grayish white," I noted.

"I pronounced the spell better this time."

"Well, we may be the same color as the wall, but it is far too smooth to climb." Even from here, I saw that the marble had been sanded to perfection. "Impossible to climb, in fact."

"Not impossible." Nameless bent and scratched at the ground with his staff. I peered over his shoulder as he drew a picture of a bird. It looked to be a raven.

"Is this art class?" I asked.

"It's our distraction," he said. And then he whispered "corvu" several times and followed that up with a little *caw caw* sound.

"The whole idea of a plan is that we discuss it," I said. "I'd like to know what this distraction is—just so I don't get distracted, too." A tingling fear was growing in the back of my thoughts. Corwin had always liked to keep things secret until the last moment. It gave him a sense of power. Was that why Nameless wasn't being all that forthcoming?

"There they are." He pointed at the sky. A dark storm cloud was coming across the city, but unlike a normal cloud, it moved low and with great speed. As it neared us, the *caw caw* of the cloud echoed off the walls.

"Are those bone ravens?!" I said.

"No, certainly not." He sounded affronted. "They are crows because they're easier to summon and friendlier. Ravens are too bitter." It grew dark as the cloud of crows blotted out the sun, flying just high enough to sweep over the palace walls. Their wings rustled because they were flapping so close to each other. The one good thing about them was they all looked alive—not a single one of them was showing any bones or rotted brains. They turned and followed the wall and then circled above the front gate. It was such a loud cacophony of *caw-caw-caws* that no one in the palace could ignore it. And I was certain it drew every eye on the walls and beyond.

"That is a brilliant distraction," I said. The Immortals at the gate were looking up and pointing, uncertain about what to do with this visitation. They ran along the wall walks toward the front gate, their crossbows raised. But the murder of crows had broken the soldiers' patrolling pattern, so no one was watching our section of the wall.

"Yes," he said. "It was a rather superb idea." He put up his hands, palm outward. "One last thing. Will you place your hands against mine?"

"Will I change color again?"

He shook his head. I swear his good eye sparkled with a bit of humor. "You'll be pleased with the effect."

I set my palms against his. His hands were warm, which had never been the case with Corwin. Could even his body be different now that it had this other person inside it? He whispered something in that ancient spell language and I felt a sharp pain. He had to struggle to pull his hand away. "What was that?"

"It is a gecko spell," he said as if that explained everything. "Just don't rub your hands together."

I looked at my palms. They seemed wet. I didn't even want to move a finger.

"And now all we have to do is climb the wall." There was a jaunty tone to his voice. "You'll find your hands are the best tools for that."

He ran the short distance to the wall and hopped high while raising his hands above his head. He stuck to the wall and then climbed, putting one hand above the other. It should have been impossible for him to grip that smooth surface, but it was happening right before my eyes.

I did not mimic his leap. Instead, I walked up and touched the wall and my hand stuck to it with such stickiness that I could pull myself up. Then I plopped my left hand in a higher position and discovered that if I pulled my right hand off palm first, it would break the hold. My feet gave me very little traction on the marble, but I had enough arm strength to climb toward the top, though the higher I went, the weaker my arms became.

I looked down. We were high enough that I could see

the tops of the houses and yards near the palace. Servants and rich Akkadians were in their gardens, staring up at the mass of crows. The birds continued to spin near the front gate which, judging by the sounds of clicking chains and shouts, the guards were closing.

I caught up to Nameless and then passed him. "You're getting slow in your old age, brother," I said.

He gave me a genuine smile and a chuckle. "I was holding back," he said. And then he added, "Sis."

We raced upwards, matching grins on our faces.

I was still in the lead when we were only a few yards from the top. Confident of winning, I swung my arm up and my hand failed to stick. I tried again, and it didn't work.

But Nameless hadn't seen my predicament and was pressing his advantage, climbing higher.

"Wait," I said. "There's something wrong!"

But he continued to grin. "Ah, you're trying to trick your sibling while you catch your breath," he said. And then his right hand failed to find purchase and he had already unstuck his left hand.

He slipped, then fell.

I reached out, stretching as far as I could, and grabbed at his flapping cloak, hoping to Belaz that his weight wouldn't jerk me off the wall. My fingers closed around the hem of his cloak and a jarring pain shot up my arm, but my left hand stayed tightly stuck to the wall.

Nameless swung below me.

"Oh dear," he said. "You weren't trying to trick me. I should have trusted you."

The fall from here was high enough that every bone in our bodies would break.

"Throw the spell again," I said, my breath puffed

between my teeth as the arm holding him began to weaken. "It must have... have... run out."

Nameless shook his head. "No," he said. "There's an invisible ward across the top of the wall. I'm surprised your one hand is still sticky."

The moment he said that, my hand slipped. Then the bond broke, and we fell.

I didn't even hesitate. Without a conscious thought, I grabbed one of my daggers and jabbed it into the wall and turned it so the blade was sideways.

We jerked to a stop.

"Well, that's a nice trick," Nameless said. "I've been meaning to ask you about those daggers."

"They're rather handy," I said, huffing. My arm had nearly been yanked out of its socket. Again. "Hold on to my belt. I will try to pull us up."

"You're strong, sister," he said. And there was something wonderful about the way he said *sister*. Corwin had always used it as an insult. "But not that strong."

"You don't know me all that well," I said. "Don't forget I'm part dragon."

Well, truth was it was only a small part of a dragon. But maybe that strength—that blood I got from Brax—would be enough. Nameless must have believed me, because he switched his grip to my belt and I drew the other dagger and stabbed into the wall and twisted. And just to prove him wrong, I pulled us up.

An inch.

Two inches.

Three.

It would take weeks. To his credit, Nameless said nothing.

I'd never get us to the top. Then I felt that sudden kick in my muscles, a flowing of strength being released in my blood, and I found I was stronger. I sped up, stabbing and twisting, rocks falling from the wall. We hit the warded area, and I worried it would stop my daggers, but the blades sunk in.

Despite that, my arms were at the end of their strength. I kept going, my brother hanging by my belt. It was a good thing I'd notched it tight.

What are you doing? Brax's voice appeared in my head.

I sent no reply to him. I was far too tired.

Come on. Tell me, he insisted. *I know you can hear me.*

I'm climbing the wall of the palace with my brother holding on to my belt. I stabbed the dagger in with my right hand, twisted and pulled up.

Oh. Well, you get yourself in the strangest predicaments. Guess you should have had a plan.

This is not a time to lecture! Why are you contacting me?

I'm bored. That dead swan is boring. This manure house is boring. Tell me a story.

What?

Tell me a story.

Are you insane! I both thought this and said it aloud.

You seem preoccupied.

I am. Will you please go away? Go away! I may have said this last bit aloud, too.

Fine. I was just curious if we could contact each other this far away.

We can. Now go!

Brax said nothing else. I had neared the top of the wall. With one last stab and heave I threw us over the edge and we landed on the wall walk.

An Immortal was looking down at us.

10

A PASSING SHADOW

The shock on the Immortal's face was briefly hilarious. Briefly, because his training kicked in a moment later and he smoothly drew his sword and swung it toward me. I raised a dagger to deflect the blow, bracing for the full-force impact of an enormous man swinging an enormous sword.

But the sword fell from the soldier's hands before he finished swinging the weapon.

Nameless, who had landed at the feet of the Immortal, was grabbing the soldier's bare ankle, just below his leg armor. The Immortal's eyes rolled back in his sockets and he collapsed onto Nameless, which was perfect because it prevented even the slightest clatter of metal.

Not so perfect for Nameless, who struggled to get out from under that weight. The Immortal's eyes were still turned back so all I could see were the whites. His mouth opened and closed like a landed fish gaping for water. Nameless gently shut his eyes and the man stopped moving and breathed normally. We dragged the Immortal into the nearest guard station and threw a few empty sacks over his unconscious body. A quick glance let me know that there were other Immortals further along the wall walk, but they were still gesticulating at the crows.

"Did you use a spell on him?" I whispered.

"No." Nameless was doing a weapons and supplies check, patting his pockets and sheaths to be sure every item had survived the climb. It was his assassin training kicking in without him knowing. I started doing the same. "You mustn't have studied as hard as I did. There's a freeze point below the ankle."

"There isn't!" I said. "*And* I studied twice as hard as you."

"Well, somehow I knew about it, so the only conclusion I can make is that I studied harder than you."

I rolled my eyes. "Let's change the topic. How long will he be out?"

"Hours," Nameless said. Then he pinched the side of the Immortal's neck and let go. "Now he won't wake up until tomorrow." I hadn't seen that move before either, but I bit my lip. Corwin must have learned these things from his secret lessons with Banderius. Nameless withdrew a small bottle from his cloak and splashed a bit on the Immortal. "It's actually a perfume, but it will smell like cherry wine."

"Good," I said. "Plus, when he wakes up he'll be in a cell, punished for falling asleep at his post. They'll be less likely to believe a story about two climbers coming over the wall."

"Correct," Nameless said. "Though I am uncertain whether they will execute him for being asleep at his post."

I thought about that for a second. "By the time we're done, one sleeping Immortal will be the least of their worries, I'm sure. Let's go."

We snuck down the nearest set of stone stairs and through a guard room that opened onto a garden. Nameless had taken the lead, but I pushed ahead once we were outside. After all, I had two eyes, and I knew how hard it was to judge distance and to peer around corners with only one. We met no enemies. After several quick steps, I put my hand on Nameless's chest to stop him from stepping onto one of the main paths. "We will do our best to act like servants, so we should take the back paths." I glanced at my hands and discovered they were still slightly gray. "I could just tell people I have the Gray Plague."

Nameless smiled. "Yes, that might work. Perhaps I should make my flesh gray."

"We don't have to be twins in everything," I replied.

There were fewer guards than I remembered from my last visit to the palace, but that had been in a full-fledged celebration of Emperor Sargon's ascension to the throne, so he had been trying to impress the rest of Ellos. We walked with confidence—well, as much confidence as servants would have—working our way through lush gardens and past the stables where I had once shoveled manure. The smell was the same.

One thing had changed: the sky was silent. From our vantage point, we could see part of the mass of birds circling the front gate.

"Your crows are quiet," I said.

"Yes, they now realize they were under a spell."

"You mean they're smart enough to know that?"

"Of course." He said this almost dismissively. "Let's just hope they don't figure out it was me who summoned them. They are legendary for holding a grudge." He eyed them warily. "Anyway, they did the job for us."

"Yes, they did. Do you—"

I stopped. An inky shadow passed over us and I had a fearful moment where I thought Brax had arrived, and soon every bow and ballistae bolt would crisscross through the air into him. It wasn't a dragon, though; it was a black swan with a familiar female rider on its back, heading toward the front gates.

"Who was that?" Nameless asked.

"It's Scyllia," I said. "She was once your closest friend. She's part snake and part poison."

"It sounds as if I didn't have the greatest taste in friends."

I bit my tongue and watched Scyllia fly into the murder of crows, and, well, murder them by drawing a sword and laying waste around her. The sky rained feathers and blood. Within several moments, the crows had scattered.

"She seems unfriendly," Nameless said. "I think it best we move on."

We turned down a stone path that led along the eastern wall of the palace and also took us closer to the White Tower. It loomed over the grounds, the wall, even the city.

"It is not good news that Scyllia is here," I said. "I would have expected her to be at the front, right beside Sargon."

"She may be the one who reins here in his stead. Even the greatest empire has its interior enemies."

"Well, it bodes ill for us," I said.

"She doesn't like crows." Nameless pulled at his hood to be sure it covered his face. "That's for certain."

Once we were under the shadow of the palace and out of sight of Scyllia, I felt safer. The nearer we got to the White Tower, the more any feeling of safety slipped away. I had not looked closely at it during my last trip to the palace; I had been concentrating on my task of killing both the emperor and my brother. Now that we neared the pale prison, it was becoming clear that the tower didn't fit with the rest of the surrounding buildings. Human hands had made all the other structures. But the tower was not composed of blocks of stone and didn't look like a single mortal hand had been used in its construction. It was like a giant ivory tusk planted in the ground, smooth beyond belief and reflecting the sun in such a way that it seemed the tower could vanish even as I stared at it.

"I am feeling ill." Nameless had his hand on his stomach. "This is not a natural place. It is a pit. A hole in the fabric of life made with a white blade."

"It makes me sick to my stomach, too." I breathed in, glad the air was pure. "Sick everywhere. Is it like the spell that Sargon cast on his troops?"

Nameless shook his head. "That is a trick. This is real. Death and consumption are woven into those walls. That any structure like this could be imagined and then created is horrid. What mind would dream of this?"

"I met the architect who designed it. He was a cold, hard man who was the executioner for several emperors."

"It sounds like he had the right mind to think of this." His shoulders were hunched and he appeared to want to fold into himself. "We will find a way into that nightmare, though I don't want to imagine how it will feel inside."

We walked the perimeter of the tower. No plants grew near it. Nothing of beauty. It was a stark symbol of the power of the emperor and his architect, to design a building that could reach into the very lifeblood of a wizard or witch and pluck the magic from them. A moat of what looked to be boiling blood surrounded it. The drawbridge was down and there was one door that led into the tower. It was closed.

An Immortal turned onto the path directly before us and we both cast our glances downward. I pulled my hands into my sleeves, hoping he wouldn't notice my gray skin. The Immortal passed within a hair's width of me, but said nothing.

We walked by the front gate of the tower for the third time. Surely an observant guard would notice we were going in circles, so I led Nameless over to a gazebo where we pretended to be clipping the flowers, doing our best impressions of gardeners.

"So how do we get inside?" I asked.

"I got us over the walls," he answered. "I leave this to you."

"What? I got us over the walls."

"Only the last bit, so it doesn't really count." He was grinning as he said this. It was good to see that his sense of humor was becoming stronger, or he was simply more comfortable with me. Maybe he'd joked with the wizard Goran all the time. "In truth," he added, "I am uncertain how to enter. It is not guarded by any soldiers, so other methods must protect it. Or the place is so horribly destructive that only an idiot would attempt to go inside."

"Or idiots," I said. "But let us run through our idiotic options. There is only one door. There are no windows. That makes me think the door is the only way in."

"Your years of training have paid off." Was that sarcasm? "But you're right—we will walk through the front door."

"Just like that?" I said. "There may be a million deadly traps." I tried to think of something deadly and came up with: "A hammer may fall and squash you flat."

"Yes, there is a chance of that," he said. "But we are here and despite my misgivings, we don't have another option. We could wait until nightfall, but it has been pure luck we weren't discovered yet."

"And," I continued for him, "every moment we wait means that the Emperor Sargon could be across the strait and marching on Avenus while we are standing here twiddling our thumbs."

"That settles it," Nameless said. "I'll walk in."

"You will?" I said. "And why you? Why not me?"

"Because I will detect any of the wards. Also, I can dodge falling hammers better than you. I studied harder." And without another word, he darted directly toward the White Tower.

11

STRONG BLOOD

Nameless strode forward, his back straight, and he was full of purpose and confidence. He looked tiny compared to the White Tower, like an ant approaching an iceberg. As he crossed the drawbridge, he fell to one knee. He caught himself before tumbling forward completely and stood up straight again. Nameless struggled forward as though he were fighting for every step, but he eventually reached the front door which was about twice his height and three times as wide. No hammers or other objects fell from the sky. Nor did flames suddenly burst all around him. In fact, he turned and waved to me, appearing a little cheerful as he pulled open the door and went inside.

I was about to follow him when a bird came out of nowhere and landed on my shoulder. I made a fist to whack it away, assuming it was a vengeful crow, but held back my blow when I saw the sparrow. "Are you Carmen Dore of the Red Assassins?" The spellbird had a feminine voice. "How are you feeling today?"

"W-what?" I asked.

"Oh, I'm just curious about both your emotions and your

physical state of health. I care deeply about you mortals."

"Did you bump your skull?" I blurted. I'd never met a spellbird that didn't have an attitude. "You care about us?"

"Yes." The bird nodded its tiny head several times with such speed its beak blurred. "I know that's not typical of my brethren, but I find the day-to-day travails of you mortals to be a significant concern for me. I want you to enjoy positive, fulfilled lives."

"Oh," I said. "Thanks. I am fine."

"That's splendid news and you are welcome," she said sweetly. "Now, I have to ask you the question again, it's all part of the command they gave me: are you Carmen Dore of the Red Assassins?"

"Yes, I am."

"Well, I have a message for you. Are you prepared to hear it?"

I glanced toward the White Tower. There was no further sign of Nameless. "Yes."

"Before you hear the message, would you like me to get you some tea? A biscuit? Or a soft chair?"

The wizards or witches had worked hard to make this spellbird friendly. "You can do that?"

"Yes," she said. "But the chair takes some time. I have to spit up the tea, but it still tastes good."

"Oh, forget the chair and the tea," I said, though my mouth was watering despite her description of how it was produced. "Please tell me the message."

"All right." She cleared her throat and then Thord's voice came out of her beak. "Carmen, it's Thord. I hope you have arrived at Akkadium and are safe as you hear this. And feeling good and strong and... anyway, it's on." The bird paused for a few moments. "By that I mean the invasion has begun. The emperor broke the blockade by launching hundreds of burning ships into the Avenian fleet, sending every trireme to the bottom of the strait. So all the emperor's forces have landed on the island of Avenus and are gathering on the beaches. We harassed them from the sky, but it was pointless. It is a massive army, and they will soon march on the city. If you have discovered any secret weapons, well, now is the time to use them." The bird paused again and glanced at me, and I swear it somehow wore a similar expression to Thord's. "I hope you are well, my friend. Keep safe. I'm sorry for what I said about you being different. I didn't mean it as an insult. In fact it was supposed to be a compliment. Goodbye."

I sucked in a breath. Well, at least he had apologized.

"Is there something I can do for you?" the spellbird asked. "Do you have a reply?"

"I —yes," I said. "Tell him—wait—I know how this works. I'll tell him. Are you ready?"

The bird blurred its beak with nodding again. "Hit me with it!"

"Thord, we are at Akkadium now, at the White Tower. We will gather what power we can and return as quickly as possible. And you—you don't have to apologize. I am different." And then I added, "Oh, and I wish you were here."

"Oh, that's a nice touch at the end," the spellbird said. "It was sweet. And I think he's sweet on you."

"What!" I spat.

The spellbird ruffled her wings. "I'm not trying to perturb you. It's just a guess by the way he says your name."

"The way he says my name?" I said this a little too loudly. The Immortals would be here in a second if I kept shouting.

"Oh, you look vexed. I'm sorry. I don't really understand you mortals, but I want you to have your best lives. Anyway, I'll take him your message."

"Yes. Good. Go then!"

She reached out a wing and patted my shoulder. "It will all work out," she said. I wasn't entirely certain what she was referring to. Then she flipped into the air and became a blur darting toward the heavens. Somewhere up there were the airstreams that would carry her to Thord in a few minutes.

I stopped staring at the sky and shook my head. I needed to keep my mind on the task at hand. There wasn't any sign of Nameless, and for all I knew he could have collapsed a few steps into the tower.

A quick glance let me know that no Immortals or guards were within sight, so I ran down the path toward the White Tower. As I neared, I saw that the moat was boiling and my nostrils were soon hit by an acidic stink. I was almost certain that if I stuck a finger in the blood-red circle of liquid, all I'd pull out were bones. My eyes watered, making the tower itself blur.

Nameless had left the door to the tower open, but I couldn't see him in the now revealed hallway. With each hurried step I went further under the shadow of the tower and into its influence. It had presence—that's what it was—and a malevolent, pitiless will. It was pulling at the parts of me that were magic—the dragon magic, at least. Walking became more difficult and only a scant distance from the door, my knees buckled and my legs nearly gave out. It wasn't just that it drained my muscles of strength; it was my faith in myself that was spiraling down a drain. I would fail. It was time to give up. This was a useless quest.

If Nameless hadn't gone before me, I might have convinced myself that entering the White Tower was impossible. A normal mortal would be prostrate before even reaching the drawbridge.

The feeling continued to press down, but I lifted myself,

took a deep breath and steeled my will. This was no worse than the worst lecture by Maestru Bolatrix, who spent hours talking about intestines. That thought made me chuckle. Maestru Alesius would be proud to know that I was using the hardship of an eye-watering, boring lecture for motivation. I could do this. I could.

Once I crossed the threshold of the door, my chuckle stifled in my throat. The sensation of the whole tower pressing down on me doubled and then tripled and became a physical thing that made it hard to open my mouth and suck in enough air to breathe.

I kept going because Nameless was in here. I couldn't abandon my brother.

The walls were a smooth, uncanny white that was hard to look at. The floor was white, too. The color made my head ache. I turned a corner, assuming the hallway would lead me into a larger room, but my path continued straight ahead and then curved, like I was walking a spiral. Nameless wasn't anywhere ahead of me. Perhaps he had gained some strength or he had vanished.

Then I saw the bottom of his boots far ahead. He was on the floor, the rest of his body hidden around a curve.

The sight gave me strength to push on, but I couldn't force myself to reach any speed. With each step, my legs were growing more tired. It took what felt like hours, but I reached Nameless without falling myself. He was prone, but not dead.

He was digging his fingers into the floor and pulling himself ahead. I tried to kneel beside him but fell forward. The shock of my knees slamming into the floor jarred me further awake. I put my hand on his shoulder.

"What is happening?" I slurred. The words didn't echo, as if this tower ate everything, even sound.

"A pattern," he whispered, lifting his head. "They lay the tower out in a very specific pattern. They designed it to consume magic." He rested his head and it looked like he was kissing the floor. "The further we go, the more the pattern leaves its mark on us."

"So that's what's happening," I said. "No need for guards. Anyone who entered here would only take a few steps and collapse."

"Yes," he said, speaking into the white stone floor. "And it works with great strength on those with magic inside them." He turned enough to look at me—his good eye was glassy with pain. "The charm hiding your eye is gone."

"It was probably the first thing to go," I said. "But why are you affected so much more than me?" I was, after all, not kissing the floor right now.

"I don't know. I stood in the timeless river and let the magic flow into my blood. It's all so new and strange, and right now its presence is weakening me." He swallowed. "I don't know if I can continue."

I could continue. I was certain. And so, with monumental effort, I rose to my feet. "We must keep going, Nameless. We don't have another choice."

"Maybe after I sleep for a while." His head was flush with the floor again.

"You can't sleep!" I shouted, but the tower immediately muffled my words.

"Sleep rests the mind. Sleep rests the muscles." It was a mantra we would repeat at assassin school.

"This is the wrong place to fall asleep. You will get up right now." I leaned down and grabbed his shoulder, bunching up his cloak. "Get up! We'll die if you stay here." I pulled. "You will not let your sister beat you! Get up, you weakling!"

My words must have awoken his competitive blood. He grunted a complaint but got to his knees, and I could now drag him further down the hallway.

"Not sister," he said, and the words made me feel cold.

"What are you saying?"

"Not because you're my sister," he explained. "That's not why you're winning." He was off his knees now and leaning on me. "Dragonstrong."

"Stop mumbling."

"You dragonnnnsstrong." He slurred his words. "Cheeeeter. You. Have. Dragonsssblood." That last bit sounded like he was swearing.

"I'm not cheating," I said. "I'm—" And then it became clear to me. It was the dragon blood that gave me enough strength to carry forward. Because there was old magic in their blood, older than the design of this tower and older than any mortal magic. The pattern I was walking on still ate at me, at my strength, but it could not break the dragon part of me.

And that realization made me feel even more confident and certain that each step meant something. That the pattern wasn't marking me or burning me. There was this blood inside me—Brax's blood—and in that blood was such endless strength.

"You're right," I said, patting Nameless. "Your sister is cheating. You'll just have to live with that. Come on, brother. I'll make sure this tower doesn't hurt us."

"Says you," he said. But he found enough strength to grit his teeth and stumble forward with my help. We eventually rounded the next corner.

A dead wizard hung on the wall.

12

THE WHITE TOWER

I sucked in a breath at the sight of the wizard. He was in a white wicker cage that dangled on what looked to be a thick ivory vine, as if the entire structure had grown out of the ceiling. I remembered wicker had a property that was important to wizards and witches.

"Wicker is for sacrifices," Nameless whispered. "If woven in the right pattern it can bind magic inside it."

I shuddered. They had sacrificed this wizard in a ceremony that I didn't want to imagine. All that remained were bones, though he had enough skin on his skull that his bright red beard, patchy in places, had been preserved.

"It's Redbeard," Nameless said. "My master taught me the names of my colleagues who were taken to the tower."

"That would be a long list." Redbeard looked as though he died a hundred years ago; the tower had robbed him of everything.

Well, not everything, I realized when I looked at his chest.

"The emperor tore out his heart," Nameless said.

"And ate it." I remembered the glee in Sargon's voice as

he told me how he'd attained his powers by eating the hearts of the wizards and witches. I associated that moment with a great deal of pain, because seconds before he revealed that little culinary tidbit he had broken my arm with a snap of his fingers. Now he was using those powers to break the land of Ellos.

"He will pay for that," Nameless promised.

Though the sight had made him go pale, there was something about it that also seemed to empower Nameless. He wasn't just an assassin; there was a comradeship between wizards and witches, and he shared in it. These were his people.

"He has a lot to pay for," I said. "We'll have to make a list." My attempt at humor fell flat, not even echoing off the walls.

Nameless limped forward with renewed vigor, and I had to struggle to keep up. When we turned the next corner, I nearly slipped because my body shook with surprise. The whole wall was a long line of wicker cages. Every single one contained a dead wizard or witch. Most of them were bones; others were so withered they looked like dolls, and each had a hole in his or her chest.

I stopped looking closely as we passed.

"Bori. Ange. Sarta. Earthbone." Nameless was muttering as he limped beside me, and I worried he'd gone mad, looking at so much death. "Hydrix. Shel. Browneye." He was saying the names of each magic mortal we passed, though I don't know exactly how he could identify them because they all looked the same to me—bones and withered skin and excavated chests.

"It's their spirit essence," he said, as if he'd read my mind. "I know them from it—even after death it drifts here—a hint of who they used to be. Goran taught me how important it was to remember the dead and give them honor."

No wonder the wizards hated us so much—we assassins had allowed this to happen. We took part. I almost wanted to forgive Blacktooth for trying to kill us. These were all the most wise and powerful wizards and witches in Ellos, sent here to be snuffed out one by one and have their knowledge stolen from them. No, worse than stolen: consumed. It was horrible.

We struggled around another bend in the hallway and discovered yet more wicker cages and death. I had stopped listening to Nameless recite their names, but saying each one continued to give him strength, as if he drew power from their essences. He didn't stumble. He moved a little more easily.

I concentrated on getting him to move forward faster—yes, it was good to remember them, but every single wizard or witch we passed was dead and beyond our aid. We were here to help the living.

The further we went along the spiraling hall, the worse the bodies looked. They were now mummified and some were turning to dust. The curious thing was the dead didn't smell. In fact, there was no smell, no scent that my well-trained nose could identify. Nothing at all. The walls of this place drew everything that remained of these wizards into its essence. One day not even the dust of their bodies would remain.

The floor slanted upward slightly, which made it harder to slog forward against the oppressive weight of the tower. The entire structure continued to press down on us, squeezing out who we were—everything we were—into a form that it could steal.

"I am uncertain how much further I can go," Nameless said. He had stopped whispering their names and was slowing down, and I'd been working harder to keep him moving. "I can't recognize them anymore—there just isn't enough of their essences left." There was a dark sadness to his tone. A despair. Corwin had never once felt despair. "Some are completely gone."

Soon there were no more wicker baskets. Just the long and bare curving wall of the tower. I had long lost any idea or sense of where we were inside, but we had to be near the center. Or maybe the inside was endless.

"We have to keep going," I said, though the words were hard to speak. The tower itself didn't want me or him to go any further. It was whispering *lie down now* into each of our ears, our muscles, our bones. *Go to sleep. Forget who you are.*

But I dragged Nameless forward, step by step, and he kept a tight grip on my shoulder. We passed through a doorway, and my skin suddenly turned to scales. The dragon magic had saved me from a dragon's flame, but could it shield me from the might of the White Tower?

"That's very interesting." Nameless was looking at the scales on my exposed wrist. He tapped on them. "So very interesting."

"Just walk. And stop staring at me."

The door led into yet another hallway, but now we were going down. Despite the angle it wasn't any easier to walk; in fact, each downward step felt like pushing through burning molasses.

"The weight of the White Tower," Nameless said. "The unbearable weight. Now I know, now I understand."

"I—I don't." The words were painful to spit out—it was difficult to move my tongue.

"It's not just a white tower; it's a wight tower."

He had gone demented. The tower had pressed out his brains. His reason.

"You're making no sense. Of course it's a white tower."

"W-i-g-h-t," he spelled. Then he coughed as if spelling out the word had given him a sickness.

I couldn't string the letters together to make it into a word. The scales were doubling on my flesh, across my face, my lips, even my eyelids. My skin was certainly dry enough to have scales.

"Wi—" I said.

"A barrow wight." Nameless had stopped coughing. "A veštĭ. I should have seen it. I know the dead. Goran taught me their names. Why didn't I see it?"

"Wight?" I repeated.

"Yes, it is a spirit. It's so plain to me now. A barrow wight is one of the undead who—who take the essence of the living. They sleep in barrows and wake to drag us all down to the underworld with them. This whole tower is alive. It is a presence. It is a wight. Made of some dead spirit."

"Whose spirit?" I asked.

He shook his head. "One of the long-deceased emperors, with bitter, consuming anger woven into every stone." Nameless was pulling on my arm, forcing me to go further along. He had the strength now. The understanding of where we were had given him power. "Or it could be several emperors—there are no mortals who hunger more than they do. This tower is alive, and its one purpose is to eat those who wield magic. No wonder none of the witches or wizards ever walked out of here."

"You're a wizard," I said. "You might not walk out of here."

He smiled, and it was a familiar flash of triumph. "I am only alive because I am an apprentice." He coughed out a chuckle. "I am not enough of a meal for it to bend its will to fully feed on me."

"And me?" I asked.

"You know the answer. Your magic is too old for this place."

I felt the wight, the tower itself, and knew he was correct about its past. It was alive. It was hungry. An everlasting hunger that would devour any magical mortal or creature sent into its circling hallways.

We both stood straighter, moved stronger with that knowledge. Until we turned a corner and went through a doorway to a room in the very center of the tower.

Because there we discovered another wizard in a wicker cage in the middle of a room.

This one wasn't dead.

13

THE ESSENCE

The wizard had his right hand clenched to one of the wicker strands of his cage and his head turned so he stared directly at us as we stepped in.

"It's the wizard Boqin," Nameless whispered. "He lives!"

But Boqin didn't blink, nor did he wave or make any motion to acknowledge our presence and as we moved into the room, instinctively pressing our backs against the wall, his eyes didn't follow us. Instead, they continued to watch the door.

I took a step directly toward the wizard and my foot did something odd—it turned in midair and made me step to the side. When I tried to go straight again with my other foot, the same thing happened.

Nameless pointed down. "There's a pattern on the floor." The smooth floor of the round chamber had a circular pattern of white and light gray imprinted on it. "If you don't follow the pattern, you won't be able to go to the center of the room. My guess is that it will drain us even deeper."

"Well, we can't turn around," I said.

"So we go forward," he finished for me. He took the lead

as we walked in a circle around the room. I watched each step, but also stole glances at our target. Boqin had gray hair, copper skin and was clean shaven, which made him seem younger than his years. He was clearly a powerful wizard—here at the center of this White Tower he could hold his shape and not surrender who he was and not be withered or broken by the power amassed against him.

A few steps later I learned that I was half right. Nameless and I shuddered in unison. For half of Boqin's body had withered into nothing more than skin and bones. One of his bone fingers still clung to the wicker bar.

He drew in a slow breath through one nostril and frost slowly emerged, making a cloud that soon vanished. His eyes—one withered, one perfect and clear—continued to stare ahead. His chest didn't have a hole in it which meant his heart was still there.

"Emperor Sargon couldn't break him," Nameless said. "Boqin has held his essence together for all these years. In the very center of this wight tower. It is beyond amazing."

We worked our way behind him, each step more of a struggle. What seemed weeks later we came around to his front again but weren't close enough to touch the cage. "His face is so familiar to me," Nameless said. "They replicated it in many of the spell books. For my master thought by drawing Boqin, they could summon him from this place. But this tower was too powerful. They failed."

We were now close enough I could reach out and touch his foot if I'd had the desire to do so. He still wore a leather shoe with a bronze buckle. His other foot was withered and shoeless.

We circled one more time. For all I knew the seasons had come and gone several times before we stood before Boqin again. We stopped.

"Boqin, master of the language of the dead," Nameless said. "Boqin, great scholar of the underworld, my master Goran sends his greetings."

At the mention of that name a whistling sound came out of those half-dead, half-alive lips. The painful breath turned into words. "Whoooo isss here?" Boqin said so slowly. "Whoooo bothhhhers meeeee?"

It was such a horrible sound. It must have hurt him to even speak. Every part of him must hurt. I hurt just standing in this oppressive prison. My joints ached and my bones trembled and my brain threatened to bleed. I couldn't imagine what it would be like to be here for years.

"I am Nameless," my brother said. "And this is my sister Carmen."

The good eye began to roll, and the head tilted and he looked down, down toward us. Only one eye could go the whole way. The other, too dry to move, continued to stare at the doorway.

"Namelessss?" He crackled the words out. "That ssssounds like a name Goran would choose for an apprentice." The wizened lips turned into a crooked half-smile. "He was always too clever with words."

"He would laugh to hear you say that," Nameless said. "We are here to learn from you."

"Learn?" Boqin looked slowly from Nameless to me and back again. "What can the almost dead teach you?"

"Everything," Nameless replied. And then he explained, without spare words or any flourish, our purpose. It took a minute or two, but Boqin was listening the whole time. He nodded once, which made his bones creak.

"I understand," he said.

"Can we take him with us?" I asked. "Imagine such a mighty spell wielder on our side."

Boqin laughed a crackly dry laugh. "Noooo. You cannot take me. No one can. I can only give myself to you."

"Give yourself to us," I said. "In what way?"

"I can give what remains of me." There was just an echo of his power in his voice. "I-I can invest myself in Nameless and his name will rise up. It is decided. I have decided. No more prevarication, since the sands of time are against us now." He slowly raised his withered hand, which only had a few fingers remaining intact. It creaked and the bones crackled. "One last breath," he said and then he inhaled, only one half of his chest rising. He exhaled out his last breath. "There."

He reached out his withered hand and Nameless leaned forward. A withered finger touched my brother's forehead.

It was over in a heartbeat. Boqin closed his eyes and one half of him fell to dust so he leaned, looking briefly alive, and then he collapsed in his cage.

"Too much," Nameless said. He put his hands to his head as if trying to squeeze out his brains. "It's too much!" He stepped away and danced left and right, slamming his fists into his skull and screaming. And then he let out one small cry and collapsed to the floor face first. He didn't even try to stop his fall. He lay still.

I knelt at his side. "Nameless," I whispered. "Nameless. Get up. Get up!"

But his eye was closed. At least he hadn't broken his nose. I checked the artery in his neck, happy to discover his heart thudded a slow beat. He was alive, but whatever had happened knocked him out. His flesh felt cold, but it was freezing inside this horrid tower. I pinched his hand and shook his shoulder and didn't receive a response. When I flicked back his eyelid, his eye was turned back in its socket.

Nameless would be my burden, that was obvious. I'd have to get him out of the White Tower.

Maestru Arvid had taught us assassins a special carry for the wounded, and so I grabbed Nameless by his right arm and moved him into position, so he was lying along my shoulders. He wasn't light, though he was thin. Perhaps whatever strength the dragon blood put inside me would be enough for me to bear him back through the spiral insides of this tower and into the fresh air. Into the world again.

I rose, my legs shaking, and took a step. Judging by how hard that was and how every part of me ached to drop him and collapse, it would be a lengthy journey. I took a second step.

A familiar and frightening noise echoed along the tower walls.

Laughter.

A shadow stood in the doorway. "You are about to die," a flat, gruff voice said. "And I am so happy I get to be the one to finally kill you."

14

THE GLOWING

I knew the voice and even as I lowered Nameless to the ground with my right arm, I was reaching for my dagger with my left hand.

A crossbow bolt struck my shoulder, forcing me to drop the dagger, and knocking me back into the wicker cage. I clung to it, gritting my teeth, and struggled to stay upright.

Scyllia strode into the circular room, cutting across the pattern like its power had no effect on her. She had a small, loaded crossbow in one hand and her leering smile was so wide it showed most of her teeth.

Here she was: my classmate. My brother's best friend and evil co-planner. Her gray armor caught very little of the light that glowed in the room.

"Maestru Alesius taught me well," she said, holding the crossbow up. "Ironic, isn't it? Your master gave me the skill that will kill you. I never, ever miss."

My shoulder was proof of that. The pain radiated out from where the bolt had thudded into my flesh. It was hard to feel my right arm or move my fingers. But I slowly let go of the cage and reached toward my other dagger.

"Nuh-uh," Scyllia said. "One more twitch and you'll get a matching crossbow bolt."

I held still. The only twitch I made was forcing myself to smile. "It's good to see you, Scyllia." I kept the pain from my voice. "I want my notes back from Poisons class."

She widened her eyes and then laughed hard enough that the bow no longer pointed at me.

"You've grown a spine," she said. "And perhaps you can throw a spell, or two. I'd love to know how you controlled the crows at the front gate. It was a summoning far beyond anything the healers or witchy-women could do. But the appearance of the crows made me think I should probably check this tower. And look what I find? Imagine my surprise to see you next to that idiot's cage. You! Brave enough to walk into the White Tower. You were always so meek and dim-witted."

"Dim-witted!" I spat. "I'm not dim-witted."

"Oh, you were a marvel in class. But I mean dim in the ways of dealing death. Dim, dumb and dreadful."

I had spent as little time as possible near Scyllia while in the Red Adept Assassin School. Corwin had always been mean, but at least his insults had intellect and finesse behind them. Scyllia used insults like she was swinging a hammer. Actually, she used most everything like she was swinging a hammer.

"You'll find I've learned a thousand ways to deal death now," I said.

"Oh, really?" She pointed the crossbow at my heart. "How many kills do you have? Not counting rabbits."

"I—I." I found it an opportune time to clear my throat. I hadn't yet killed any mortal. Which I didn't consider such a horrible thing.

"I'm at forty-nine kills," she said. "You'll be my fiftieth. I'm sure that deserves a cake. And poor little you—you've killed no one."

"Not true!" I moved slightly so my shoulders weren't square toward her—that way she'd have less of a target to shoot at. Not that she'd miss from this distance. "I killed a dragon."

"What? Don't be ridiculous."

"I did! I did." My voice squeaked a little. "It was a Hvitur dragon. It was big. Really big."

"Liar!" She shouted this word with great relish. "Oh, I can't believe it! Little Miss Prissy Trousers Carmen has become a liar. Or that so very brilliant brain of yours has cracked. Well, it's time to crack open the rest of your skull." She aimed right between my eyes.

"Why use a bow?" I asked.

"Huh?" I enjoyed the confusion on her face.

I spoke slowly, as if to an infant. "Well, you said it's time to crack open my skull. So why, my slow-witted friend, are you using a bow? Bolts only puncture, they don't crack."

"I know what bolts do, Carmen! Are you trying to teach me some kind of grammar lesson? I'll fill you full of holes for that."

"Nope." It took all my focus to not look at the crossbow; instead I stared her directly in the eyes. And then I winked, which surprised her. "It's a dare, is what it is, my sweet friend Scyllia." I spat to the side to look tougher. "I bet you can't crack my head open like an egg. You used to be the school champion at hand-to-hand fighting."

The whitening of her knuckles showed that her hand was tightening on the bow. "Are you daring me to smack that smile from your face? Including all your teeth?"

"I'm totally daring you to do it." I didn't have a hope of tangling with her hand-to-hand. No, wait, the *old* Carmen didn't have a chance. I was stronger and maybe faster than I'd been before. That would be a complete surprise to her.

I had momentarily forgotten I had a bolt in my shoulder and could barely move my right arm. This fight would be over in two eye blinks. But a bolt between the eyes was a sure thing.

"You dare to dare Scyllia the Great?" She spoke between gritted teeth.

"Scyllia the Great? By Belaz, did you just call yourself great? Like you're some kind of conqueror from the olden times. That's the stupidest thing I've ever heard."

"It's not stupid! I'll show you who's stupid." She raised the bow and lowered her head to aim.

Uh oh, I thought. *This will not end well.*

Any moment I expected her to loose a bolt, but she relented and motioned with the bow. "Throw your other dagger onto the floor."

I did so. Both daggers were out of reach now.

"Take off your cloak and turn around so I can see if you have any other weapons," she said.

I dropped my cloak and faced the wicker cage. Boqin continued to stare at me through his dead eye. Then I turned back. "I only have the daggers."

"Then hold very still." Scyllia came closer and I held as still as I could. I realized I was shaking. Not out of fear, but because the White Tower was still pulling at my essence and weakening me. I tightened my left fist but couldn't hold it long. Maybe I wouldn't fare so well.

Scyllia stopped and glanced quickly down at Nameless. He hadn't moved since he'd fallen. Or maybe he was playing possum. Any moment now he would reach up with a knife or special pressure point pinch and surprise her.

She kicked him in the stomach. Hard. His body moved, he *oofed,* but he didn't wake up or turn over.

"Your friend is rather useless," Scyllia said. If only she knew whom she had just kicked. She stepped over my brother and stopped an arm's length away and then narrowed her eyes. "What happened to your skin? Pimples?"

"What! I don't have pimples!" I put a hand to my face.

"Well, there's something on your skin."

She was staring at the scales. They hadn't lowered back into my skin. "It's nothing," I said. "Maybe I get hives when I'm around you."

"A shame you have such a blight. You always had such nice, smooth skin. I often dreamed of peeling it off of you and using it for paper. Today that dream will come true."

"I'll keep my skin, thanks," I said.

"It won't be up to you." She stuck out her tongue and I was reminded how childlike she could be. A horrible, dangerous, murdering child. "Anyway, let's make this a little more even." With a quick motion, she yanked the bolt out of my shoulder. I let out a squeak of pain but didn't fall to my knees. "You'll be happy to know I didn't use my flesh-tearing boltheads. These are for hunting game. You don't want big holes in your steaks." She inspected my arm. "Ah, it's perfect! A clean wound with very little bruising. If you were a deer, you'd already be on my table. You're lucky you interrupted my game hunt."

"Oh," I said, resisting the urge to put my other arm up to staunch the bleeding. Maybe whatever healing powers I'd received from Brax would close the wound. "I do feel very blessed and lucky to see you again."

"There will be no more sarcasm when you're dead." She set her bow down and put up her fists. "Before we start this little lesson in face pummelling, I want you to promise not to use any weapons other than your fists. Just in case you have some magic powder hidden in a pocket."

"You want me to promise it will be a fair fight?" I said. My words were slightly slurred. The wound was hurting me more than I'd first thought.

"Oh, it's not a fair fight. It's very one-sided." Then she shook both her fists. "Well, two-sided. But I don't want any surprises and I know you always keep your word."

I glanced at my daggers on the floor. "I swear it," I said.

"Good! I will turn your teeth into a necklace."

I slowly raised one fist, but didn't even try to move my wounded arm. "You seem to have planned out what to do with every part of my body."

"I'm clever that way," she said. "Never waste, never want."

Her skin glowed slightly, which I at first assumed was just her being excited about getting to pummel me, but then I realized I was noticing the glowing through my dragon eye. An actual light radiated from her.

"Why are you glow—" I started.

And then her right fist hit me full in the face.

15

INVESTED

She was an expert puncher—the best of our graduating class. Yes, Gregum had such enormous hands and size on his side. And Corwin was someone who never wanted to get his knuckles bruised because he preferred using sharp things. Scyllia, though, always hit with the force of a smithy's hammer. I don't know how she perfected it, but she once even knocked out Maestru Dornar during a demonstration. He didn't wake up for three days.

I was not an expert, and I was far too awake as I fell backward. The pain in my lower jaw radiated through my head and made me forget to put out my hands. I skidded across the pattern on the floor. Once you'd walked the pattern, you could cross it—this punch had proven that.

I shook my skull. She had knocked my thoughts out of the room, maybe even back to Avenus, and just as my wits, or what remained of them, returned I looked up to see Scyllia standing over me.

"You can take a punch," she said. There was grudging respect in her words. "That will make this so much more fun." And then she grabbed my leg, spun me around, and threw me into the white wall. My wounded shoulder struck first, which didn't much help the wound. I let out a strangled cry.

That was a horrible mistake. Scyllia liked hearing others in pain. "Ah, the sweetest note of music," she said. "Let me play you like a violin."

Despite the hurt, I got to my feet. "Did you practice that saying in front of a mirror?" She didn't like my reply—she answered with another blow that I barely dodged. Her fist struck the wall and she knocked out a chunk of stone.

A chunk of stone!

Something wasn't right. Either the wall was weak—unlikely, since magic reinforced it—or she was incredibly strong. She didn't grimace in pain from hitting something so hard, nor did her knuckles bleed. I thought back to the warning that assassin had given us just before he died. It had been about Scyllia, but I couldn't remember exactly what he'd said.

"Yes," Scyllia spoke flatly, not even winded in the slightest. "I see the realization in your weird, weird eyes. I am invested!"

“You're what?”

“The great and powerful Emperor Sargon has invested me with the strength of a thousand warriors."

"I'm sure he didn't mean that literally," I said.

She swung again and I ducked. Then she followed up with a short left-handed jab and a quick roundhouse which caught my wounded shoulder and drove me backwards. This time I didn't let out a peep of pain—even though I really, really wanted to. She was targeting the shoulder on purpose, which only made sense: they had trained us to exploit weaknesses.

I stumbled to the middle of the room and her next blow

missed my head by a hair's width, but she knocked the wicker basket from its mooring and it flew all the way across the chamber and shattered, spilling out what remained of Boqin. Maybe the emperor *had* literally invested the strength of a thousand warriors into Scyllia. How was my head even on my shoulders?

But her confidence meant that she had lowered her right hand enough that I saw an opening for a quick jab. I caught her below the left eye, fully expecting her head to snap back because I had hit her with all my dragon strength behind the blow.

She didn't even blink.

Not once. Nor did her head snap back. In fact, it felt very much like I'd smacked a statue. My wrist may have fractured, and my knuckles immediately bled.

"Did I forget to mention my skin?" she asked. I had jumped back, shaking my hand to get the pain out of it. Scyllia did a mocking pirouette. "It's made of stone. Well, it's still soft and attractive, but it's impervious. That means nothing will puncture it."

"I know what impervious means." In this brief lull, I had brought my knuckles to my mouth and tasted blood. Winning this battle would be impossible. My daggers might puncture her skin since they were elder magic, but I had sworn not to use them. Plus, they were halfway across the room.

Stupid, stupid oath. She wouldn't keep her oath for a moment. And then when I thought back, I realized she hadn't sworn an oath to only use her fists. My stupidity was legendary!

"Well, as lovely as it is to see you again, Carmen, I am growing a little bored by this. I wonder what prize Sargon will give me for your head?"

"It's not worth much," I said, dodging because she'd jumped at me. She was faster than she had been in our school days. My guess was she'd been invested with speed, too. But I didn't dodge quick enough because her punch landed directly on my shoulder again, and it was as if another bolt had gone right through me. I staggered back, trying to keep on my feet.

"Oh, that one stung." She kissed her fist. Again, I pictured her practicing all this in front of a mirror. "I don't feel pain anymore, just to let you know. But I remember it, and it's so good to see you cringe."

"It didn't hurt," I whispered. "It didn't." That whole side of my body was aching.

"Now, don't go out with a whimper, Carmen," Scyllia said. "Let me send you to the shadow realms. Say hello to the shades of our maestrus."

"No, I'll send you," I said and grabbed her hands. A now familiar roaring came into my ears, the rushing of dragon blood in my veins, bringing with it a surge of strength. Dragon blood was stronger than the magic that built this tower. Stronger and older than Scyllia and the magic within her, and I pushed her back a step and another, and her eyes widened and then she bore down to shove me, but I kept forcing her to make another backward step and another until she was against the wall, pressed there. Words were echoing in my head, *power dragon blood ancient strength,* each of them strengthening me. Scyllia was driven to her knees.

A smile twisted my lips. It was hard to smile with such exertion, but I was beating her. I was winning against the great, cold, angry Scyllia who had always hated me because of my connection to my brother—I was driving her down. Her eyes showed the slightest bit of panic and I admit I enjoyed it. She and my brother and Gregum had laid waste to my school. I was getting the revenge for all of my maestrus, all of my fellow students. All assassins.

Then I pushed her hands against the wall, forcing her even further down, and when my knuckles scraped that icy wall I shuddered. The tower responded to that physical touch and drew at my strength.

And invested its own strength into Scyllia. It was a wight. And it had a mind of its own. She rose, pushing back, so I had to retreat. Then she broke my grip and shoved me so hard that I flew into the center of the room.

And that was when I learned she had been holding back. She moved faster and faster, jumping from one side to the other as I reacted just a moment too late. Her blows rained down on me like hail, then came up like hammers, hitting me in the head, the chest, the shoulder—all before I could react. The room spun. Her lips were moving now, but her caustic words were drowned out by a ringing in my ears. It was the sound of death coming. I landed one blow that only hurt my hand. Then she connected an uppercut to my chin, and I flew upwards. For a moment I thought I'd hit the roof, but skidded to a stop on my back. I couldn't move or even raise an arm to defend myself.

Scyllia landed with her feet on either side of me. Her lips were moving as she leaned forward to grab my collar, and at that moment my hearing returned.

"You will be dead and gone forever," she was saying. "Forgotten. Bones. Nothing. That dragon will be torn to shreds and no one will miss either of you at all."

My lips wouldn't move. I could only stare upward as her fist came down like a stone from the heavens.

"Don't kill her," a familiar voice said. It was Nameless. He was awake. But the timbre of his voice had changed and even with the ringing in my ears, I could tell he was not himself.

Scyllia stopped her fist an inch from my nose and looked to her right.

"I get to kill her," Corwin said. "After all, she is my sister."

16

A MEMORY

Scyllia lowered me gently to the floor and, more importantly, lowered her hand. My brother sat up and rubbed his head. He gave that brief head shake he'd perfected, designed to make his hair land in a fetching style on his forehead.

"Hello, Scyllia," he said. "It may surprise you to see me."

"Corwin!" She was up on her feet in an instant, yanking her dagger from its sheath. "How in the seven hells of Hades are you here?"

"That, my dear and loyal friend, is a very long and entertaining story." He offered his hand. "Help me up."

The only movement Scyllia made was to point her dagger at him. The blade was curved to cause maximum damage. "How do I know you're not a—a mirage? A dream?" Her face had turned pale as alabaster. "Or maybe you're some stupid spell left by that dead wizard? How can I believe it's you?"

"Simple." He laughed, and it was fully Corwin's demeaning chuckle. Even in my dulled state a chill prickled my skin. It felt like my scales were rising again to protect me from that laugh. "I'll tell you something only I know: I was the first person you ever kissed."

Her eyes widened and I sucked in a breath despite my injured ribs. My brother grinned. He'd always had perfect teeth.

"Only you would know that." Scyllia had brought her left hand to her lips as if she'd just been kissed. "I told no one."

"Well, my sweet little sister knows now." He pointed his index finger at me like he was pointing at a pile of dung. "But she'll be dead, so the secret will be safe between us. Not that you should be ashamed of kissing me. You should be proud."

"Yes. Yes." Scyllia lowered her dagger. I wondered if she'd rush right over, and what? Kiss him? Ugh! "But... but how did you get here? You've been gone for such a long time. We assumed you were dead."

Another typical Corwin chuckle followed. "I don't die." He breathed in through his nose as if enjoying the cold, stale air of the White Tower. "Oh, let me give you the short version: she and that dragon and her two friends cut out my eye, strapped me to a swan and sent me west. I was deposited in the land of wizards and witches and was trained as a wizard apprentice." He jabbed a thumb toward the broken wicker cage. "I tricked Carmen into bringing me here and now, after sucking up Boqin's magic, I am the most powerful and handsome being in all of Ellos."

It was definitely Corwin.

"You are?" she whispered. Scyllia explored her lips with her fingers. "You are. You must be."

He raised his hand, but this time it was glowing red. "I have the power of life and death," he said. "At the touch of a hand. And I have the power of sight." He tapped his eye patch and it fell away. There was a glowing orb inside his socket. "I have Boqin's eye. His wizardry is in my blood and bones and brains now. And I also have my brilliant, brilliant wit. I am so powerful even the emperor's army will kneel before me when I snap my fingers."

"You are all powerful," she said. "I can sense it. It... it—"

"Emanates from me?" He nodded several times. "Yes, you are right. And do you remember how after that kiss, you promised to serve me forever and ever?"

"Yes." She raised her fist and spoke with such fervor she spat a little. "Yes! And I meant every word. I am yours, Corwin. Forever!"

"And I am honored to have you," he said. "I have two tasks for you, Scyllia. The first is to help me to stand."

She slid her dagger into its sheath, walked over to him and grabbed his hand and easily pulled Corwin to his feet. She was still a good two inches taller than him. His grimace was the only good sign I saw in that entire display. He wasn't at full strength, yet. Or the White Tower still acted on him.

Alas, I couldn't move a muscle and foggy pain surrounded me.

Corwin touched Scyllia's face. "He has made you even more beautiful and more powerful."

If I wasn't already in such pain, I would have retched.

"Oh, thank you, Corwin, thank you." She put her hand over his.

I would have shut my eyes, but I needed to watch for some weakness I could exploit. *Wake up, brain! Wake up!*

Corwin pulled back his hand. It trembled ever so slightly.

"Well, I have my second request." He turned to glare down at me. "I've failed to do it properly the last couple of times, so I want you to butcher my sister."

"Really?" she said. "You'd gift this honor to me?"

Corwin patted her on the shoulder. "You deserve the glory of sending her from this world."

Scyllia didn't say a word. She turned and walked toward me with her dagger out and a giant, fervent grin on her face.

17

THE DECISION

Scyllia had likely dreamed of this moment from the first time she entered the Red Assassin School and saw me standing next to Corwin. I was his sister, so he had some affection for me. She had always wanted all of his attention. At least this was what my addled brain was putting together at a very slow speed. She glanced at her dagger and then slid it back into its sheath and approached with her bare hands.

She would make my death very, very personal.

I had been playing possum. It was an old trick and would probably fail, but some strength was returning to my muscles. When she leaned down, I swung my fist toward her head, putting all of my strength into one blow that would knock her sideways.

My fist landed right on her temple, but she didn't even blink. She really was invulnerable. Even that punch meant nothing.

Her hands found my throat and her face was now right in front of mine. Her mad grin was the last ugly sight I'd ever see. "This is for getting better grades than me," she said, tightening her grip around my neck and closing my windpipe. "And for always looking down at me."

I tried to answer these charges, but couldn't get a word out or a breath in.

"And it's also for being born."

She really, really hated me.

The blood, my dragon blood, was in my veins but being cut off from reaching my head. The hope that I could find strength to fight back ebbed away, and the next time she started speaking I no longer could hear anything. At least I wouldn't be haunted by whatever uncouth insults she was spitting at me.

Then I remembered that I had a dragon hanging on my chest. *Brenna,* I sent my thoughts toward her. *Brenna sister of Brax, help me.*

There was a sensation like she was turning over in her sleep. Almost awake and aware. The soulstone grew warmer.

Brenna!

But then she turned again and the stone cooled. There was no reply. Darkness came over my vision and I felt myself slipping away from where I was. From life. Then a momentary brightness flashed and I saw that Scyllia was still there, gritting her teeth and grinning harshly. Darkness fell again and I drifted away. But the light returned when my heart beat one more time—it refused to stop. My vision was gray. My lungs empty. There was a shadowy movement behind Scyllia that I couldn't make sense of—something reached out and wrapped around her neck.

Darkness again. Then blurred light. But the pressure on my throat was gone.

And so was Scyllia.

I took a deep, hard breath and some color returned to

my vision. Another breath brought back my wits and some of my strength. I could turn to one side.

A shudder shook me. I was face-to-face with Scyllia. Her eyes were closed and there were dark shadows around her neck—no, not shadows, but arms cutting off her air. They released her and she lay still.

"That was more work than I hoped it would be," the man behind her said.

I blinked. It was Corwin or Nameless, I could not tell which.

"You—you put her in a sleeping hold," I said.

"Yes," Corwin or Nameless said. "It made the most sense for the situation. She is rather invulnerable." His tone was steady and not sarcastic, but I was still confused.

"Are you Nameless or—or Corwin?"

"Nameless," Nameless said. "I'm certain of that." He pointed at his temple. "But he was here."

"Corwin was here?"

"Yes. But I overcame him, and then I overcame her." He shook his head. "These details can be explained later. We do now have to exit this tower with great speed."

"Yes. Yes." By this point I'd taken several more breaths and some strength trickled into my muscles. It felt like I was climbing a mountain, but I slowly sat up. Nameless stood unsteadily. He wavered back and forth. "And are you all-powerful like you said?"

He shook his head. "I am sorry but that was a lie."

"You made your hand glow!"

"Starlight paste," he said. "It was in my pocket. Something happened when Boqin touched me and he—he gave me himself—his power, but the gift is too big for me to understand at this moment. Or perhaps ever. I mean, I do have a new eye—a wizard's eye." He blinked his glowing eye and it grew a little less bright and obvious. "I can see through it. So that's something."

"Believe me, I know how weird it is to get a new eye." Scyllia continued to breathe in and out like a sleeping fawn. Well, an invulnerable killer fawn with a bow and fists of stone. I stumbled across the floor to pick up my daggers and then returned. "What do we do with her?"

"If we were both true assassins," he said, "we would slay her here and now and let her blood stain the White Tower."

"Why do you think I wouldn't do that?" I said. The words were more defensive than I'd intended.

"Because you didn't kill me when I was tied up and unconscious."

"That's true," I said. "But we blinded you and sent you away."

He nodded. "Yes. I have the actual memory of that event now. If you hadn't chosen that path, I wouldn't be here. It was a gift to me. You gave me life."

I patted his shoulder. "I guess you owe me, brother. If only I had chores I could get you to do." I gave Scyllia another glance. "Well, we can't blind her in one eye and strap her to a swan."

"That is true," he said.

"And it'll take all of our strength to get out of this place, so we won't be taking her with us."

He nodded. "Yes, that is also true."

"And if we leave her here, she'll awake and come after us."

"An enemy left alive today is an enemy who fights again tomorrow." It was something Maestru Alesius had said many times.

"Well..." I drew in a breath and shrugged. "You're right. I can't kill her. She's defenseless."

"Then I am at a bit of a loss as to what to do," he said. "You don't have any corporthium pills?"

"Used my last one on you," I said.

"I thought as much. Well, we won't have to deal with the moral quandary of taking away someone's personality and everything they are." He said this without bitterness, but I still felt a pang of guilt. "I believe I have hit upon an answer. Will you give me your dagger?"

"What! No."

"I know your daggers are special to you," he said. "In fact, they are one with you." What did that mean? He put out his hand. "But the dagger will solve the problem we find before us. You can trust me, Carmen. I'm not Corwin or you would be dead."

I slowly unsheathed one of my Uriken blades and handed it to him, hilt forward. He took it, knelt beside Scyllia and turned her so that the back of her neck was exposed.

"What are you doing?" I asked as he stabbed the blade toward her.

"Don't worry, Carmen." He paused a finger width from her spine and began cutting upwards, but not into her—the blade was a short distance from her skin. "She has an invulnerability layer and it is an actual physical thing—a living spell. These wonderful magical blades can cut it, though. I'm just opening it up a bit." He used another hand to peel back something invisible. "The shell of this protected her from the White Tower. But by puncturing it the tower itself will act on the armor."

"Eventually draining it," I said.

"Yes. And her. Not to her death, but it will bring any powers Sargon invested in her to nothing." He gently set Scyllia on her back and even folded her arms over her chest so she looked comfortable. "She will be purely mortal when she wakes up."

"How long do you think that will take?"

He shrugged. "Several hours unless someone discovers her. But I bet only Sargon goes this far into the tower, and he's a little occupied right now. We have taken her off the board."

He stood and handed back my dagger. I sheathed it. "Let's not tell the others we left her alive," I said. "They're still kind of mad I insisted on not killing you."

He laughed lightly. "I won't bring it up. But if they ask—I'm not good at lying. Now, can you give me a hand? I need your help to get out of this horrible building."

I slipped my arm under his shoulder and we limped toward the door, leaving Scyllia sleeping on the cold, hard stone.

18

FINDING A PLAN

A decade passed before we reached the front door of the White Tower. The sun had gone down and it was dark. By the time fresh air was on my face and moonlight on my skin, my strength had returned. I looked left and right, but the courtyard was empty. There would be guards in the towers above the palace, but we only had to get to the grove to be hidden from their sight.

It still took too long to cross that short distance—we were that exhausted. After a few steps Nameless moved away, saying, "It'll look too suspicious if you're helping me."

He walked on his own like a two-hundred-year-old man, each step a struggle. And I wasn't doing much better, maybe fifty years younger. The oppressive weight of the White Tower pressing down was lifting from my back as we crossed the path and lurched onto the next one. I still felt the tower reaching toward me, but it was nothing like being in its belly. If I'd been stuck there it would have consumed all my magic.

I expected a crossbow bolt to rip through my back at any moment, but we eventually stumbled into the foliage and out of sight of any watchful eyes. We collapsed onto a stone bench in the shape of a lion and leaned against each other. Like a brother and sister. I wanted to stretch out and sleep forever. Instead, I inspected the wound on my shoulder. Scyllia had been right—the bolt had left a small hole but there was no extra tearing. The bleeding had stopped, but the pain continued to radiate outwards.

"You should still be bleeding," Nameless said. He was even more observant with two eyes. And frightening, truth be told, since his wizard eye glowed. Was that what people saw when they looked at my dragon eye? "That was a deep wound."

"I heal quickly," I said. "It's a blessing and a... well, it's just a blessing."

"A good trait to have." He pointed at his eye. "I guess we aren't exact twins anymore—different eyes. Although, we have one thing in common. We didn't make an escape plan."

I nodded and then took a deep breath that made me grimace: it felt as if Scyllia had cracked every rib. "I was hoping your beautiful and brilliant brain would think our way out. I can't do all the work."

"I will take that as a compliment, even though our brains are exactly the same size." He coughed lightly, but it was clear he was holding back a bigger cough. He didn't want to alert any Immortals. "Neither of us is strong enough to climb the wall again."

"I couldn't even climb down off this bench."

"Do you think a week has passed?" he asked.

"A week?" I snapped. "Are you kidding?"

"No. I do not kid. Time was shifted inside there. Like it wasn't moving inside the tower, but continued to flow outside those white walls."

"If a week has gone by, then Avenus has fallen and this

has all been for nothing." I failed at keeping the fear from my voice.

He looked up at the moon. "Oh, wait—it's only been a few hours judging by the quarter moon. Sorry to alarm you, sister."

It was still odd to hear him say "sister" without regret or anger or sarcasm.

"Do you... do you have any of Boqin's powers?" I asked.

"I have something," he said.

"Can you be more specific?"

"Boqin touched my forehead and created a wellspring inside me. But we are too close to the White Tower to look down into that well. The tower interferes with my awareness of what gifted me."

"Oh," I said. The tower was sending waves of exhaustion over me. They would be even harder on him. "And what about... about Corwin?"

"That too is strange. I have all his memories now, but they aren't my memories. They are his. And... I hesitate to give further details on him."

"Give them." I put my hand on the lion's head beside me, bracing myself for bad news.

"Well, it's more than his memories. It's him. He's inside me now. When I was talking to Scyllia it was actually him. He seized control."

"Seized control of you?"

Nameless scratched at the back of his skull. "Yes. He wrestled me aside and became me. But I was able to fight him off and push him down."

"Do you think it's possible that he might come back?"

Nameless shrugged. "Anything is possible."

"That's not comforting!"

He lifted a hand and looked at it for several seconds. It

was like he was seeing his hand for the first time. "It's not my intention to be comforting," he said dreamily. "Right now Corwin is far away from me. Sleeping."

"Just don't let him wake up!"

"I will do my very best to prevent that." Nameless wasn't good at pretending he had control over the situation. He didn't even try. "But our more important problem is figuring out how we will leave this palace. We can't climb the walls. We aren't rested enough."

There was a crack several feet away, as if a twig had snapped. I sat up, staring through the underbrush. Was someone sneaking up on us? But there wasn't another noise and I couldn't see any sign of movement.

"Whisper," I said. "Just in case there's someone listening. How do we get out of here? Its not like we can ride: Brax can't come to us."

"That is correct." Nameless was turning his staff in his hand. "The wards around the city would slow the dragon enough so he would easily be pierced by a ballistae bolt. He was able to fly in last time because of the distraction of the fireworks."

"You remember that?" I said.

"Yes. It was an incredible sight." Again, he spoke without emotions. "The dragon coming in toward the emperor—spells, bolts and arrows bouncing off him. I saw it—I was below the balcony on the grass. I mean, Corwin saw it."

"So flying out on Brax won't work. And getting through the gates means battling a horde of Immortals."

"Yes. That way is closed to us, too." He put up his index finger. "I just searched through all of Corwin's memories that concern the palace. There are secret tunnels, but they were never shown to him. It's almost as if Sargon didn't completely trust your brother."

"Well, the emperor isn't stupid," I said. "Corwin was an assassin. So if we could find the tunnels we might get out. I have the plans memorized, but there was no obvious place for them to be."

"We could search for hours or days. Assuming we got inside the palace without being killed."

"Yes, they—"

There was a movement to our left in the leaves. I reached for my daggers. Nameless pointed his staff toward our visitor.

A dark, large eye stared at us. Something tall and huge stood in the trees; perhaps a magical guardian had sniffed us out. I drew back my arm, intending to stab that eye out.

Nameless put his hand on my wrist and gave a soft shake of his head.

"Hello, friend," he said. "Don't bite me."

Then he reached into the leaves.

19

GET BEHIND ME

What he brought out was a black swan's head. Well, it was attached to the rest of the swan's body, but the head was all we could see at that point. "Carmen," Nameless said, though the timbre of his voice changed enough that he sounded like Corwin. "You remember Snake-Eyes, Scyllia's brave and resourceful mount."

"Yes, I do," I whispered.

The swan hissed at me. "Ah, and he remembers you. 'Like master like swan,' as Maestru Arvid used to say. Well, you may recall that I spent many hours with Snake-Eyes, and we have bonded. I'm rather a natural with swans." He cleared his throat. "By that I mean Corwin was a natural with swans."

"That's what I assumed you meant." I had moved, so he was between us and the swan. He kept petting the beast's head and Snake-Eyes eyed me with a malevolent, murderous gaze.

"Well, as I'm sure you've surmised, Scyllia left her swan outside the tower and like a good swan, trained by assassins, he found a place to hide. It really is fortuitous that we sat here."

"Are you about to suggest we'll ride Scyllia's swan out of the palace?" I said. The thing took that moment to snap at me, catching my shoulder. "Ouch! By Belaz that hurt!"

Nameless shook a finger at Snake-Eyes and the swan retreated. I was very proud that I resisted the urge to stab it with my dagger.

"You have guessed my plan," Nameless said.

"I'm not getting on that that thing." I pointed at the swan. "It's Scyllia, but with feathers. He'll dump me off the first chance he gets."

"He might," Nameless admitted. "But consider this: the wards guarding the sky will not be set off by Snake-Eyes and he is a recognizable form to the soldiers and Immortals, therefore a flight on his back won't arouse any suspicions. I expect there is only a fifty percent chance that they'll kill us with crossbow bolts."

"Those are horrible odds."

He waved a finger at me, taking on a lecturing tone. "Well, we have a hundred percent chance of being caught if we remain."

"You were always far too good at simple math."

"I recall—that is, I have discovered in Corwin's memories—that you consistently had a higher mark. He found that rather aggravating."

"He would," I said, then I blinked and my left eye felt a sharp pain—an old pain—and I asked, "Did he stab out my eye on purpose?"

"It wasn't a stabbing motion," Nameless said as if he were talking about a cloth pattern. "It was a downward slice."

"Oh, don't get caught up in specifics." That came out more bitter than I'd intended—but I was bitter, and I had every right to be. Why did the gods give me a brother like Corwin? "Did he do it on purpose?" I held my breath.

Nameless was quiet for a moment. I had no idea how he worked his way through the memories inside his head, but he eventually cringed, perhaps reliving my blinding. "Corwin didn't know whether it was on purpose," Nameless said finally.

"He didn't know? He had to know. He did it!"

"That's right. But sometimes we do things without understanding why. It suggests to me he didn't plan to do it beforehand, and it may have happened in the moment."

Well, that would have to be enough of an explanation. "I'll get on that evil bird," I said.

Snake-Eyes squawked, loud enough that it might alert a guard. He also took another snap at my head, but Nameless deflected that and patted the bird again. He gently turned it away from me.

"I suggest you stand behind me," Nameless said. He slowly rose to his feet and looked more steady than I felt. He pulled on the reins and the bird forced its way through the bush, snapping a few branches. It was a beast of a swan, not just in personality, but in size, too. Maestru Arvid had found the perfect mount for Scyllia.

Just thinking of Maestru Arvid reminded me of the day I handed the swan egg off to him. It had been such a wonderful moment with a wonderful man. Now that man was dead and the egg may well have been destroyed. There would be a future time to list all the names of the dead and light candles to their shades. Today, we just had to fly out of an enemy's palace on a beast that hated me.

"I said stand behind me," Nameless repeated. I'd not moved, and Snake-Eyes had turned to glare. Maybe he saw me as a big mouse he'd like to eat. I stood, discovering I was shaky on my feet. The pummelling I'd taken was enough to tenderize every muscle in my body. Nameless motioned, and the swan turned his head in the other direction. "Now, here's the tricky part. We have to mount him at exactly the same time, so he doesn't know we're both on his back. And then you hide behind me because you know how well swans can see from either side of their heads."

"He'll know by the weight that I'm there."

Nameless slid the staff back into his belt. "He's used to carrying Scyllia in her armor, so we won't be too heavy. When I count down from three we both jump on."

"Fine," I said. My aching body didn't want to jump or even hop, but I would not give it a choice.

"Three-two-one-go," he said and my legs managed to get me up into the air and, as if we were twins—which we were—we both landed on the swan's back at the same moment. I let out an *oof* of pain. "Now grab tight and stay behind me." Since Nameless had the reins, and I had nowhere else to hold, I put my arms around his stomach and locked my fingers. He whistled, and we took three gigantic steps, burst through the last few branches, and ran along the garden path. Snake-Eyes kept racing faster and faster like a flightless bird.

"This isn't working," I whispered. "We're too heavy."

"Shhhh," he said, then he whistled another order and Snake-Eyes spread his wings, wide enough to fill the whole pathway and we were slowly, slowly leaving the ground and entering the air. I hoped we would gain enough height to clear the wall. We flapped toward one of the guard towers. "I'll try to disguise the fact there are two of us on the swan." Nameless pulled back on the reins so that Snake-Eyes flew just over the tower and the soldiers ducked as we went over them. One of them shook a fist, but it was dark enough they couldn't see me. At least he wasn't pointing a crossbow at us.

This might work, I thought. I patted Nameless on the shoulder, then returned to hanging on tight. He turned his head and gave me a grin and a sense of warmth and comfort came over me even though I was high in the air on an angry swan. I was with family. Family. This was what it felt like.

Then I felt something else. Pain. And Snake-Eyes let out a horrible hissing shriek. It took all my will not to do the same.

A ballista bolt had gone right through the bird and directly into my leg.

20

A BEAUTIFUL BEAST

The sky became dazzling with brightness as a magic ward went off. And then another and another, lighting us up and making it very obvious there were two riders, and neither of us was Scyllia. The wards *boomed* as we flew through them and the swan continued to scream. Some sharp-eyed guard had seen us, or Scyllia had awakened and alerted the Immortals.

I moved my leg to discover that the tip of the gigantic bolt had poked into the top of my thigh. It was not a deep wound, but it hurt horribly.

"Oh dear," Nameless said. "I'm so sorry this happened." I thought he was addressing me, but he stroked the bird's head. "Keep flying, keep flying, dear creature." Snake-Eyes was jerking up and down, losing altitude with each dip, and we were only halfway across the city. It wouldn't do to crash into any of those stone-roofed buildings. Nameless shifted so he could glance at me. "Are you all right?" he asked.

"It's just a poke. No major arteries hit. It'll heal." I spoke through gritted teeth.

"Well, we have a bit of a wild ride ahead, so hold on even tighter."

He pulled on the reins and Snake-Eyes climbed despite the pain. The arrows that were zipping our way were now coming for us from the outer walls of the city. Another giant ballista bolt whizzed next to my head. Any closer and it would have decapitated me. "Higher," I said, even though he didn't need my suggestions. I just had to do something.

Do something! That was it.

Brax! I shouted this thought inside my mind. *Brax! I need you.*

There was no answer. My brain was a void, and I felt a coldness in the part of my thoughts where he usually rested. Was he dead?

Brax!

Nothing. Then: *Who dares to wake Brax the magnificent?*

Brax. Get up. We need you. Get to the walls of the city. Now!

I haven't had breakfast.

We swerved suddenly, forcing me to shift back, and the protruding bolt stabbed me again.

Get here now. We're on the back of a swan. Being shot at by ballistae bolts and arrows.

Sounds like you have it under control.

Get here now! I shouted inside my head.

There was no further answer.

Brax?

Then Snake-Eyes dove and I checked to see if a bolt had gone through its head. "Are we going to crash?"

"I believe we're harder to hit if we use the buildings to protect us," Nameless said.

He was correct. We zoomed past taller houses and a massive temple for the great man-bear god Ak, out of sight of the soldiers. The bird—what a tough, lovely bird it was even if it hated my guts—kept pumping its wings and following his commands. We flapped down an alley and an Akkadian citizen, holding three loaves of bread, gawked up at us, his face wild with shock. He dropped the bread and ran. The entire scene would be funny if my life wasn't hanging by a thread.

Or a few feathers.

We went left and right, and only the occasional arrow came in our direction. "The ballistae aren't designed to point this low," I said. "Excellent idea."

"Pure luck," Nameless replied. More proof he wasn't Corwin. My old brother would have accepted the glory, even if it wasn't his. "I'm aiming for the southeast wall. I just don't know if we have adequate speed to ascend high enough to clear it."

Then we turned and flew directly at the wall. There were Immortals and other bowmen on the battlements, loosing their arrows as we aimed right at them. We ducked against the swan to make ourselves smaller targets, but there was no way to make Snake-Eyes smaller and arrows hit him in the chest, and still the bird—the brave giant bird—flew forward. I didn't know what kept him in the air, but he arced upwards under Nameless's command.

"I just want to let you know," Nameless said. "It will be really, really close."

In the end, it was too close. We smashed into the battlements, knocking Immortals and sending them flying. Snake-Eyes crashed through them, rolled and we were thrown from his back and flying through the air over the wall. I was spinning so quickly I couldn't make sense of what was sky and what was earth below us. If we hit the ground at this speed, we'd be dead.

It would be the perfect time for Brax to swoop out of the

sky and rescue us.

But he didn't.

21

THREE IS A CROWD

We hit the surface hard.

And it broke below us.

For, whether Nameless had been intentionally planning this or not, we had smashed over the wall, missed the docks and crashed into the Ursa Sea, splashing down a few feet from a massive barge.

The impact ripped my grip from Nameless and down, down I plunged into those depths. It took some time to remember to kick and kick and kick, my lungs begging for air because I hadn't taken a deep breath. Finally, I broke the surface and sucked in air and then went down again in case bolts or arrows were being loosed at me. The next time I surfaced, I saw Nameless swimming several feet to my left. Down I went again and kicked toward him. We came up at the same time. No arrows were hitting the water, but I wouldn't take a chance, so I grabbed him by the cloak and pulled him farther along.

"Water!" I said to him once we'd stopped. "What luck. We hit water."

"That's why I chose the port wall. I thought it was

obvious since we could not fly very far. We would be dead if we hit the ground."

"Oh," I said. "It was obvious. And it was still good thinking!"

Several feathers floated up, but Snake-Eyes did not surface. "He was a magnificent mount," Nameless said. "May he take flight with his brothers and sisters in the nether realm."

"Yes," I said. "He was a good swan. Now we had better get out of here. They'll soon be on search boats with lamps and—"

Without a noise a great black shape hit us, and a tearing pain burst in my shoulder. The impact shoved me under the surface, and I sucked in a mouthful of water.

Then, before I could try to swim away, I was pulled out of the sea and lifted skyward. Nameless flew beside me in what I first thought was a spell he had cast. Then I saw the talons wrapped around his shoulder and mine.

"You two splash like wounded sheep in a lake," Brax said. "Not that I've seen that."

I coughed, spat out a gallon of water and tried to say something, but only gargled up more liquid.

"Thank you, dragon, for saving us," Nameless said.

"I didn't save you," Brax said. "I accidentally picked you up because you were right beside her."

"Dragons do nothing accidentally," Nameless said.

"Oh, now you know everything about dragons. Great!"

I opened my mouth again to get my own thanks out, but resumed coughing and spitting. My throat, my nostrils and my eyes burned with salt.

"How eloquent," Brax said. "Now both of you shut up while I do all the hard work of carrying you to safety. I don't want to inadvertently feed you to the sharks."

He swished his wings and sped up, his grip strong around my shoulders. Dust flew behind us, watching Nameless carefully. The dead beast of a bird looked like she might attack Brax if she saw a hair missing from Nameless's head.

Thank you, I thought.

Never disturb my naps, he answered.

I managed a chuckle that made my ribs hurt. He carried us across the water for hours, searching out the opposite shore of the Ursa Sea. I yawned and stretched, his talons holding me tight. Nameless had his eyes closed and was even snoring slightly. Wizards must naturally have the ability to sleep anywhere. I closed my eyes and let slumber overtake me.

I awoke with a thud—Brax had lowered us onto a patch of grass, letting us fall the last few feet. I groaned because Scyllia had rearranged every bone in my body with her fists, but Brax, who had landed beside us, just gave me a shrug. "You'll heal," he said. "And I couldn't carry you two clods any further."

I sat up and patted my cloak and clothes. I had dried off but was shivering—had perhaps been shivering the last few hours. Nameless put his arm over my shoulder and pulled me close. I held still. Was this a gesture of caring and warmth? It was so far beyond anything my brother had ever done. I was growing slightly warmed, though. I imagined a lifetime of having a shoulder to lean on.

"I suppose you want a fire," Brax said.

"Yes." I stretched out my legs and rubbed them with my left hand. "I can't feel my toes. Once we're dry, we can speed back to the fight."

"Well, I don't gather wood," Brax added.

"I'll get it." Nameless took his arm from my shoulders, made a motion with his hands so they looked like two wings, and then let out a strange squeaking. He followed that show by standing up and limping away. Dust walked after him.

"What on earth was that?" Brax asked.

"I don't know. You didn't hit his head on a boat in the harbor, did you?"

"Not intentionally." Brax turned his head so he could see me with his good eye. "Maybe he was talking to his bird in swan-talk." Brax then yawned, the moonlight catching his teeth. A second later, he spit on me.

"What was that for?" I said.

"Oh, how quickly you forget the healing power of dragon spittle."

I looked down at where the gob had landed—directly on my wound. Already, I felt that area warm and the pain recede.

"Oh," I said. "Yeah, thanks."

"Yes, yes, whatever." Brax waved a talon as if waving away my words. "Nameless has an eye now. Did you notice that?"

"It's the wizard Boqin's eye."

"Oh, great, so now the eye of a powerful wizard is staring through your brother's skull." Brax made his eye roll. "That is a level of creepiness that I'm not comfortable with." He raised a talon. "There is one interesting fact—it makes you two look even more alike."

"We are twins in our strangeness."

"That's one way of putting it," Brax said. "So you two appear to have bonded. Is that wise?"

"Wise? He has a good heart."

"Or is it you wish his heart was good?" Brax shook his head. "He is a blank space left when you erased his mind. Yes, a personality grew like a weed in there, but who knows what else will grow up?"

"You're always so suspicious, Brax."

"Suspicion is a lifesaving habit. Especially when it comes to mortals." He snorted out flames from his nostrils. "Did he find his memories?"

"Yes," I said, and I shivered, thinking of how he had sounded when he spoke with Corwin's voice.

"And?"

"He remembers everything—that is, he says he can just look at Corwin's memories." I left out the part where Nameless had mentioned that Corwin might step into his body.

"And what of the wizard? Did you pluck out his eye? I hope you got permission first and, oh, maybe tell me why you are bruised to pieces."

I told him what had happened as quickly as I could, ending with: "Scyllia thought he was Corwin and so he surprised her with a sleeper hold."

At that moment Nameless came into the circle, his arms full of saplings and branches. He placed them on the ground and, before he could properly back away, Brax lit it with a blast of flame.

"Oh, sorry," Brax said. "I was a little quick there. I hope you didn't get singed."

"No, no," Nameless said. "All is well. I appreciate the extra warmth." Perhaps a sense of humor was growing in his heart.

I shot Brax a glare and he shrugged. Then I sat closer to the fire.

"So are you an all-powerful wizard now, crusher of emperors and so on?" Brax said. "I'm really hoping the answer is yes."

Nameless shook his head. "I don't know what I learned."

Brax narrowed his eye. "Is this some wizard philosophy?

'I know nothing but know everything' stuff? Or did you actually learn nothing?"

"The lessons are not easily digested," Nameless said. "They swirl around inside me. But I know they are there and that Boqin is whispering to me. In fact, right now he says to do this." He reached toward me and I pulled back a bit, but he drew out the soulstone so it was lit by the firelight. He held it in his hand, but the chain was tight around my neck. He examined it with his wizard eye. "Was she always this angry?" he asked.

"Who?" Brax said. "Carmen? Yep, she's a horrible grump. You should know that since you have her brother's memories."

"No." Nameless turned the stone around in his palm. "Your sister, Brenna. You may not want her to walk the earth again."

"She had a temper," Brax said. "But why wouldn't I wish her to walk the earth again?"

"Because she says she'll tear out your eyes and your liver. She's not sure which one first."

"That sounds like Brenna," he said. "I guess she's mad about that whole killing her groom thing. Are you truly communicating with her?"

"No. Not communicating. She is... she is talking. In her own head."

"You mean she casually mentions tearing my liver out, all the time?"

"No. She reacts to those surrounding her. And to the situation."

"She knows where she is?" I asked.

He was now turning the stone slowly in his hand. "In her own way. That's why she spoke aloud at the wizard council. She likes you." He said this last bit to me.

"She does?" I blushed a little, though I wasn't certain why. They trained assassins not to blush.

"My sister liking a mortal?" Brax spat the words and a few flames out. "You are lying."

"She has been in this form for a long time," Nameless said. "And the longer I hold it, the more Boqin sees of her through my eyes." He let the soulstone go and I tucked it back into my shirt, hiding Brenna from the world.

"Do you mean that wizard is still alive inside you?" I asked.

"No. Not like that. He is... he is a wise ghost."

"Or you're going mad," Brax said. "But let us humor you in this whole 'I have a dead wizard inside me' thing. It must be crowded in your skull. Anyway, what does he say about my sister?"

"I can bring her back to this world," Nameless said. "It is possible. I know the method now. The books you brought will be helpful because they contain the spell words I need."

"What about the sacrifice?" I asked. "Doesn't someone have to die to bring her back? Last time Brax wanted me to plunge a dagger through his heart. There had to be a sacrifice." I was a little bitter when I thought of how Brax had made me stab him.

"No one living has to die," Nameless said. His wizard eye glowed slightly.

"You are telling the truth about all of this?" Brax whispered those words. "You aren't just playing some semantic game, or trying to get on my good side so I don't eat you just to see what a wizard assassin tastes like? Brenna can walk this earth again? Whole and perfect."

"Yes," Nameless said. "As I said, I now see how it is to be done."

"And no one has to die?" I repeated.

"That's correct," Nameless said. "No one has to die."

"That's not exactly what you said earlier." I pointed at him. "You said 'no one living has to die.'"

"No one has to die," Nameless repeated. "No one."

"That sounds like you're just playing with words," I said. "Sorry to insult you."

Nameless was momentarily quiet, as if he was thinking. Or he was consulting all the people squeezed into his skull. "No insult taken. It's Boqin's wording. They were not my own words and I don't know exactly what he means."

"You sound like you aren't all there," Brax said.

"Oh, I'm here," Nameless replied. "The problem is that Boqin is here, too, and Corwin's memories and the lessons of my master. It's cozy inside my head. Crowded, in fact."

Brax itched at the side of his face. "Well, just hearing you talk about your stuffed brain makes my scales prickle. I'm speaking to a crowd when I speak to you."

"Yes. That's an excellent way to think of it."

"Well, Crowd," Brax said. "What are we going to do about the emperor bearing down on Avenus? We need to kill him so I can see my sister again."

Nameless was quiet for a minute. Then another. He closed his eyes.

"Has your crowded mind gone silent?" Brax asked.

I shushed him.

But Nameless had fallen into a trance. He breathed in and out so slowly it didn't seem like breathing at all. And then he raised a hand, and it glowed red. For real. His lips began moving, but no sound came out.

"His hand looks to be heating up," Brax said. "Should we put a teakettle on it?"

"Just wait. I'm sure he's looking for the answer to your question."

Nameless then snapped open his eyes and lowered his hand. "We know exactly what to do now."

I felt a sense of relief. There was such confidence in his voice and his words held power, so that I was drawn to him. Dust moved closer, too, and lowered herself. Nameless easily climbed into the saddle. "We must take to the air," he said from his perch. "I know the right windspeak words now."

"Oh, but what exactly is the plan?" I said. Dust was already in the air and Nameless was too far away to hear.

Brax cleared his throat and I did a weapons check, happy to find my clothing dry. I climbed up onto his back. "He called himself *we*," Brax said. "I hope he isn't completely crackerbrained."

And then we followed my brother.

22

UTMOST SPEED

We flew in a direct line toward Avenus because it no longer mattered if the emperor's forces spotted us —speed was of the utmost necessity now. Nameless easily summoned up a wind, and this time it wasn't a gale that blew us off course. Brax spread his wings, and they puffed out like sails as we raced through the heavens. It was the smoothest and fastest ride I'd ever had on his back, but even at this speed we were too many hours from our destination.

A black streak zipped by me on the left side. "Someone shot something at us," I said. I looked up and all around, but the sky and land below were empty.

"There is no one near us for as far as I can see," Brax said. "Though we are moving with great speed, so it is harder to spot objects before we pass them. Maybe it was just a stone falling from the heavens. They do that sometimes."

"That doesn't make me feel any better," I said.

"The sky falling isn't comforting?" Brax snorted. "You mortals worry about the smallest things."

Then the blur whizzed past again, this time on my right

side, and I heard a warbling. It was either spinning in such a way that it made that sound or...

"Slow up," I said.

"What?" Brax shouted.

"Slow up," I shouted back. "We're going too fast."

"I don't follow your every command, mortal," he said. "Unless you say please."

"Please!"

He straightened his wings, so they didn't catch as much wind, and we slowed to an almost normal velocity. Nameless, seeing us fall behind, had Dust straighten her wings until she was near us.

"Why are you slowing down?" he asked.

"Because," I said. This time I heard the warbling before I saw the object shooting toward me. And it was not a stone. I pointed. "We are going too fast for our little feathery friend."

Shortly before the tiny brown blur reached me it opened up its wings, stuck out two clawed feet, and then landed on my shoulder.

"Well, you were setting the sky on fire with your amazing speed!" the spellbird said. It was the same female I'd spoken to before. "You are the swiftest creatures I've ever seen. Well, except for spellbirds like me. Congrats!"

"Hang on," I said. "Let's get back up to speed."

Brax began to work his wings, and Dust, too, so we were soon catapulting through the sky. Nameless stayed above us and to our right, close enough to hear the spellbird.

"Are you Carmen of the Red Assassins?" she asked.

"You know I am," I said.

"Yes, but I have to ask and you have to answer. It's how the message spell works."

I sighed. "I am Carmen of the Red Assassins and you may tell me your news in front of everyone."

"Oh, you beat me to my next question. Good work!" The wind was fluffing her feathers, but her voice was clear and strong. "I'm afraid it's bad news. I know I'm not supposed to give away any of the content of my messages, but I wanted to prepare you for the painful, emotional blow. So take a deep breath and—"

"Just get on with it," I barked, and the hurt look in her eyes made me instantly regret my outburst. "Please," I added. "Please, sorry. We are prepared for bad news."

The spellbird nodded. "Hello, Carmen," it said in Megan's voice. "Things are not well." Was Thord dead? I wondered. "The emperor has burned his way to Avenus in a few short hours. They surround the city at this very moment. The Avenians are good fighters, but they are facing the full might of an empire. I guess I'm saying all is lost. And many have died." It was horrible news. *But what about Thord?* I wanted to shout at the bird. "The walls will soon be breached and, well, we'll all be dead in a matter of hours. They have cut off any chance of fleeing to the ocean with a second fleet of Immortals—another fleet!"

The bird began coughing. "That smoke is getting to me," she said in Megan's voice. "Anyway, Thord is on the west wall helping to keep it from being overrun. Last I saw him he was alive. Just race here with any help you've mustered. And if you get this message a few hours after sundown, I suggest not coming at all. It will be a bloodbath. No sense in you three dying, too. There, that's it. Someone get me another bow."

The spellbird stopped. "And that's the end of the message. I hope my previous warning softened the blow of bad news. Is there something I can do for you? Do you have a reply?"

"How long ago did you receive this message?" I asked.

"About two thousand wingbeats ago," she said.

"What?" I wanted to grab the friendly bird around the neck. "What does that mean in mortal terms? In hours and minutes!"

"Two hours and five minutes," the bird, unperturbed, answered.

"And how far are we from Avenus?" I asked.

"I'm so sorry, but I can't calculate that," she said.

We were now over the ocean, and so had left the mainland. But that didn't help me at guessing the time it would take to get there. Nameless put his hand up like it was a compass and made a measurement. "My guess is we are about four hours away," he said.

"We must go faster!" I exclaimed.

"We can't go faster without my wings falling off," Brax shouted.

"I have an idea," Nameless replied. "Well, I have an idea that Boqin passed to me through his memories. It'll take me a second to prepare a spell. I'm mostly certain it'll work."

"Mostly certain?" Brax said. "Mostly certain isn't good enough for me when it comes to magic."

Nameless had retrieved his staff from his belt and was waving it around. "Boqin would use this spell when he traveled, but he was used to going to death and back. He had done so many times and had traveled to many other realms. At least I believe it's the right spell."

"What does traveling to death and back have to do with getting to Avenus?" I asked.

"This all bodes ill," Brax said. "And it bodes stupid, too!"

"Just let him work," I said. I turned to the spellbird. "Thank you, my friend. Please go ahead of us and tell Megan of the Red Assassins this message: we are coming. It's a promise."

"Done!" the bird said. "Good luck! It was so great talking to you again. Do have fun traveling to death and back!" Then she flapped her wings and arrowed straight into the heavens.

"I prefer the smart alec spellbirds," Brax said. "Her cheeriness is nauseating."

I was going to leap to her defense, but I couldn't find the will. The bird was gone anyway.

"I am ready," Nameless said after several minutes. He pointed his ash staff at an invisible point in the distance. The tip was glowing red. "A rip will appear in the sky ahead of us. Please fly directly into it."

"A rip?" Brax said. "You're ripping open the sky and you want me to then fly into whatever is there?"

"It will be a void," he said, as if he'd made everything clear. "And yes, please do fly into the opening. I am now very confident that we will survive."

With that he spoke a word and the red glow on the staff shot forward and exploded a short distance in front of us. A darkness ripped a hole in the sky. It looked like a giant demon was opening its mouth. "Just to be clear," I shouted. "We are flying into that?"

"Yes," Nameless said. "I'm uncertain why you two keep asking that. I was very clear with my instructions. Also, I want to tell you to not stop for anything. No matter what you see."

"Well, you can't say being with me is boring," I said to Brax as we approached the opening. "Here's hoping we make it to the other side."

"I'll blame you if I'm torn into a thousand pieces," Brax

said. "Every one of those pieces will send guilt your way, I promise. The only consolation is you won't be able to ride on me again."

And then we flew into the demon mouth void.

23

INSIDE THE VOID

There was darkness. And screaming. Like a choir of a thousand tortured prisoners all around us, their voices so high-pitched and piercing I was certain my eardrums would burst and blood spurt out my ears. Colossal figures made of crimson light appeared in the distance and reached long burning arms in our direction.

"Faster!" I shouted, but my voice didn't even carry beyond my lips.

Faster, I sent to Brax.

You don't have to tell me that!

The giants stretched, reaching closer and closer, their red-nailed hands cutting through these skies like fireworks, mouths opening and closing. The nearest one had at least a hundred eyes and a hundred mouths on a massive, jagged head. Were they gods? What sort of horrible beings existed in this place, just beyond our reality?

The screaming hit an even higher pitch, so I had to cover one ear with my hand, hold tight to Brax with the other, and hope my right ear didn't go deaf. Brax could do nothing but fly.

The fingernails on these giants were so sharp they left ribbons as they cut through the air and would soon slice through us. A hundred eyes glared down at me, and those mouths moved with such hunger. We would be little more than one bite.

Then Nameless gestured with his staff and another rip appeared only twenty yards away. He flapped through first. The hands raced toward us and, at the last moment, I ducked, feeling a blast of air as one finger passed only inches above my head.

We rushed through the rip and it snapped closed behind us.

We were over the ocean and moving at such an incredible speed that my hair was now straight behind me.

"Well, that was horrible," Brax said.

"Are we back?" I asked. "Is this our world?" It was hard to speak with the wind rushing down my throat and drying out my eyes. I blinked several times. The ocean looked familiar. The sun was the same shape as the one I remembered from Ellos, but it was the wrong color.

"This place looks darker!" I shouted. "The sun is too red! It's not right."

Nameless was several yards ahead of us, his cloak flapping like mad. "That's just your vision." His words blew back to me. "It will correct itself. We have jumped ahead many leagues, but not far enough. Let us go through another rip—that one wasn't so bad."

"Wasn't so bad?" I said. "What do you mean by that?"

"We all have our heads," Nameless said. He didn't appear to be joking.

"I'm not doing that again!" Brax said. "My ears ring like a thousand bells are playing in a madhouse."

"Your friends wait at the other side," Nameless said in

that aggravatingly steady voice. "They face certain death. You will not forsake them." He made another motion with his staff and a maw of darkness cut across the sky. There was a red world waiting on the other side. "Do not pause for a moment in this realm," he warned.

"Why do I feel like we're flying into the open mouth of a sky demon?" Brax said.

"Because that's exactly what it looks like," I replied.

But Nameless was correct. There was no way we would forsake our friends. So we followed him inside.

This time there was only a redness. No giant shapes or screaming or silence: this unknown place was endless and filled with hopelessness. It truly was only a red void.

The hopelessness pressed against me.

Do you feel that? I asked Brax.

I feel nothing, he answered. *Nothing at all. We should go back.*

But the weight was pressing on us from all sides. Brax swept his wings and yet we didn't go forward or move in any discernible direction. There was nothing to measure against.

It's pointless, he said. *We are stuck here.*

I was in total agreement with him. It was all pointless. Nameless had pulled ahead; the image of him on Dust's back—getting smaller and smaller—was the only sign of movement. He did not look back.

He's abandoning us, Brax said.

Yes, I answered. *Yes, of course, he is.*

Some brother. Everyone betrays you in the end.

Brax had slowed the flapping of his wings to once every ten or twelve heartbeats. *We're lost, aren't we? And we've been here for hours.*

Days, I thought. *Time here is different... it's, it's dripping.*

We should stop. Stop. I need to rest.

Brax slowed his wings and stretched them out in the open redness. There was no noticeable change. The red world would never change. It didn't matter if we moved ahead or backwards or up or down, because none of those directions existed. There was nowhere to go.

Maybe if we sleep, I said. *We'll find strength to move on and find a way out.*

He's a traitor, Brax continued. *No matter what name he takes, Corwin is a traitor. He planned this all along.*

Yes, he must have. It's in his nature. But sleep, Brax. That is our best option now. A rich lethargy permeated each bone in my body, each muscle, and surrounded every thought in my head. A suffocating sense that I must slumber. How much time had passed? Was there ever anything before this red void?

I lay down my head, loosening my grip on Brax but staying on his back.

Yes, sleep. Sleep, he thought. *Sleeeeeep.* It looked as if the redness was on the tip of his wings, moving inwards. But maybe my eyes weren't working properly.

Your wing is red, I sent to him.

Brax didn't answer and that was the right choice. Answers were pointless. In the back of my head I remembered there was something we were supposed to do. We had a task. What was it? And a warning had been given to us, but I couldn't find any concern in my heart. I'd remember the warning tomorrow. If there were tomorrows in this place.

I closed my eyes tight and slept, and when I dreamed all I saw was red.

Time passed. Then:

A smack hit my head and a lightning bolt of pain—something real in this world—went down my spine.

"Wake up!" a voice said. "Carmen, wake up!"

The urgency was not appreciated and it was unnecessary—there was nothing to be urgent about. Nothing in all of history. But I was smacked across the top of my head again, and it took all my will to open one eye.

Nameless was above me, looking down, his ash staff in his hand, and he hit me with it again.

"Hey." My voice was muffled.

"I said don't stop," he shouted.

Then he cracked Brax twice very hard on the top of his skull. The dragon opened his one eye. "What? Who?"

"You are Brax Andorium, Prince of Drachia and"—he hit me again—"Carmen of the Red Assassins, and you are both harebrained idiots."

I found enough concern and strength to rub my head.

"You are weak and foolish and oath breakers," Nameless shouted with such force he launched spittle toward us. "You are nothing and no one fears you." He smacked me again in the temple, and this time it was a sharp whip-like pain. Then he surged ahead and hit Brax on the end of the snout, which, I remembered, was a particularly sensitive spot on a dragon. "You are useless twits."

"Hey," Brax said. "Hey. Don't say that. Not twits."

"Your sister is a putrefying mess of nothingness," Nameless shouted. "Brenna is a bag of bones and a shrill mindless shrew of a dragon."

"Hey!" Brax said. "She's not a shrew!" He was flapping his wings now.

"And I took out your eye on purpose," Nameless said to me. "My useless, ugly sister. You should have died at birth—the world would be a better place for it. All of Ellos would rejoice. And Thord is an idiot. You might as well be enamoured of a stone."

"What!" I said. "You'll pay for that!"

Then Nameless took off on Dust. Brax let out a burst of flame, too late, but he was still angry enough to push his wings until we reached full speed. He aimed right at Nameless. My anger had driven away any sense of lethargy. "Get him! Get him!" I shouted, banging on Brax's back, and kicking his sides like he was a horse. Something else red was filling this world: anger. I focused only on Corwin. Or whatever his name was.

We got closer and closer, cutting through the redness. I was gripping one of my daggers before I knew it and ready to slice him into tiny little ribbons of Corwin. I would pay him back for all he did to me: taking my eye. Killing my friends. Brax roared when we neared our enemy, shooting flame that reached for his cloak.

Nameless aimed at a dark opening in the redness and dashed through.

"You won't escape us!" I shouted. I threw the dagger and it flew through the rip.

And then we hit the opening and emerged in a land of smoke, fire and screaming.

24

THE CARTHENON

The rip in the sky that we had just raced through snapped closed with a crackling bang.

The city of Avenus was spread out below us. To call it a city at this point was being kind, for it was mostly a fire pit, buildings burning, broken wagons scattered across the streets, and the bodies of horses beside them. Citizens were fleeing down the street and hoplites carrying long spears marched in formation to meet the enemy. Several hundred columns of smoke filled the sky, which was crisscrossed by burning arrows and catapulted balls of fire that smashed into buildings.

Nameless circled back toward us, holding up my dagger. He had caught it in midair, which was a rather impressive feat.

"Are you coming to the same conclusion as me?" Brax asked.

"Yes," I said, blinking several times. The "red" vision had slipped from my eyes along with an overwhelming anger. "Nameless saved us."

"That was brilliant," Brax said. "He came up with some

extremely motivating insults. I still want to burn him from the sky, though. Can I fry him a little?"

Nameless approached and Dust did us the courtesy of screeching at us like we were idiots. The bird was unruffled, as if it hadn't traveled through several hells to get here. It was as ugly as death and unflappable. Nameless patted the bird's head; it quietened and then he flipped the dagger through the air. I caught it by the handle and sheathed it.

"Welcome to the real world," he said.

Those words made my heart break a little. Because somewhere in my head I was hoping we had mistakenly flown to a different Avenus and that the one we left behind was still untouched. "I apologize for my cutting words," Nameless continued. "I had to draw some of them from Corwin's memory. I couldn't come up with that kind of vitriol on my own."

"They were really well chosen," I said. "Thanks. I think."

"You're welcome." He took a moment to survey the city. There were bodies on the street and soldiers fighting hand to hand. "They have breached the eastern gates." He motioned toward the main gates of Avenus. I'd walked through them on foot several times and now they were broken and lying to the side. A battering ram shaped like a bear's head sat abandoned on the street, burning from the oils that had been poured on it. The enemy flowed into the city through the twisted front gates, like a dam had been broke. They were led by squadrons of Immortals in their shining armor. "We have arrived either at the perfect time to help our friends or in time to see the city fall."

"Thord was guarding those gates," I said.

"Well, he may guard them with his bones," Brax said, then he glanced back and saw the look on my face. "Sorry.

He may also have escaped that horrible destruction and is right now fixing his hair."

"We should check the gates," I whispered.

"No," Nameless said. "That would be death. Look at the archers and the catapults." The rows and rows of archers outside the walls were sending a rain of arrows ahead of the advancing Immortals. On the fields beyond the city walls, the emperor's catapults continued to launch stones and burning spheres of fire. The army stretched as far as I could see outside the city.

"It would be death," I admitted. At least Thord had his swan. He could have fallen back like much of the Avenian army was doing.

"Somewhere outside the city is Emperor Sargon," Nameless said. "Despite all his power, he doesn't lead his army into battle. He never liked to get his hands dirty. Bloody, yes. But never dirty."

"He doesn't have to lift a sword if he can strike from there," Brax said. And then he snapped his wings close to his body so we dropped ten feet in a heartbeat. A burning ball of flame went through the space we'd just occupied. "I'm going to pretend that wasn't aimed at us."

"The Carthenon still stands," Nameless said once he'd rejoined us. He pointed toward Avenus's impressive government building that had been built at the top of the highest hill. The Avenian senators and other leading citizens would have a heartbreaking view of the battle now.

Red and green columns surrounded the outer building. The columns were pretty, but offered no protection. The Carthenon itself was three stories high and made of thick white stone. This was the home of their democratic discussions, and it was a temple, too—the place where the Avenians worshiped their many gods and goddesses. The

Carthenon had escaped most of the attack, though there were flames where catapulted firestones had hit it. Their assembly, the Ecclesia, was inside the building. It was funny the things that came to mind from our many political classes at Red Assassin School. I was certain no one had ever sacked the Carthenon before.

"We had better find the archon," I said. "Or whoever is still in charge."

We flew across the city. We were relatively safe to do so because the Avenian ballistae had been knocked out, so they wouldn't be able to target us by mistake. As we got closer, I saw that the large wide steps that led up to the Carthenon were flooded with citizens and soldiers alike fleeing toward safety. We passed over a dead black swan draped across a broken statue, and I couldn't tell whether the bird belonged to Thord or Megan. At least I didn't see a dead cloaked rider next to it.

The roof of the Carthenon opened into a square garden. There were fig trees, olive trees and benches and several painted statues of Avenian deities. From above, it was a perfect, untouched place of serenity. Except for the far corner where a stone had smashed through one side of the wall, broken several benches, and knocked over trees and toppled a statue of Dion, their portly wine god. He still looked happy, despite his broken arm. The statue of their warrior mother goddess, Exthena, stood unmoved in the middle of it all.

We landed next to Exthena and several Elites rushed out of the shadows, their bows at the ready. "Halt!" one yelled. His red armor was dented and bloody, and a few other Elites were bleeding from head wounds. I remembered from my studies that the Elites wore red armor so even if they were wounded it wouldn't show. These warrior men and women were legendary for being incredibly well-trained and fearless. They clearly weren't showing any trepidation at the sight of Brax. He moved his tail, like he was thinking of striking them.

"Bows down!" a powerful female voice commanded. "These are the ones the spellbird told us to expect. I'd prefer they don't get a single arrow in them."

"I'd prefer that, too," Brax said.

The Elites lowered their bows and Thena, the archon of Avenus, strode out, clad in gold. It was not a gold dress. It was golden body armor that was scuffed and dented and seemed to have a black substance—blood—spattered here and there. She held a long spear with a leaf-shaped blade at one end and a spike at the other. It was as if the goddess Exthena herself had come to life, and the sight of this archon left me a little breathless. "Welcome to the endgames," she said. She stopped before us and leaned on her spear. "I would offer you wine and a fine meal but as you can see..." She gestured to a collection of broken wine jugs, the wine itself looking like blood. "They broke all of my wine. The barbarians!" She then laughed a little madly. There were several worried-looking men and women in togas behind her, and behind them stood an assassin.

I rushed to Maestru Beatrix, and she opened her arms. "You are alive," I said as we gave each other a quick hug.

"Yes, and I've gone back to wearing my assassin garb." She gestured at her clothing. "Mostly because these pimplewarts won't take orders from someone in a librarian's toga."

Then a familiar figure limped toward me. Megan had her left arm in a sling and her face was bruised. "It took you long enough to get back." She patted my shoulder, grimacing at the movement.

"It did," I replied. "Longer than I could ever imagine. Was that Naga in the courtyard?"

She nodded. "A lucky bolt struck her while we were carrying messages back and forth. She stayed alive long enough to get me to the ground."

"She was a good swan," I said.

"Her death is the least of our worries." Her words were cold, but her eyes had watered slightly. The bonding between a swan and an assassin was never easily broken.

"We do have many worries," I agreed. "What about—"

"There isn't time for a proper reunion," Archon Thena said. "My city is burning and the enemy surrounds us on all sides. Now tell me you have brought some powerful spell or an army of dragons." She glanced at Brax and Nameless, who both looked tired and ragged. Almost like we'd flown through the mouth of Hades. "I could really use some good news."

"Well, I have only a modicum of good news," Nameless said. "We found Boqin in the White Tower and he was still alive."

"Where is he then?" she snapped.

"Well, he died. But that is not bad news. He was able to—"

At that moment, the sky darkened with wings and a shadow fell across us.

"Another interruption!" Archon Thena lifted her spear. "What is it this time?"

25

THE HEAD OF A SERPENT

The black shape fell from the sky and a moment later its wings opened, revealing it to be a swan. It landed in the middle of the courtyard, only a few yards from us, and Thord slid off the saddle and stood unsteadily. His hair was slick with sweat and his armor slick with blood. He bowed toward the archon. "The eastern gate has fallen."

"Thank you for helping to hold it as long as possible," she said. "We gained valuable time and many of our citizens are safe in the Carthenon because of that." She gestured toward us. "You will be pleased to see that your friends have returned."

"Welcome back," he said. He looked directly at me. "Things have been rather boring without you."

"I'll bet," I said. A cut above his eye bled freely and before I could reach out a hand to quell the bleeding, Megan had already slapped a wad of healing gum on it.

"You were getting all blinky," she explained. "It's a bad look for you."

He wiped away the excess blood. "You always have my best interests at heart."

"Well, now that the touching reunion is finished," Brax said, "Nameless was about to inform the archon about some great magical feat that would save us all from the maws of utter destruction."

But Nameless didn't speak at first. Instead, he gave a measuring glance around the room, pausing to look at Brax, then Megan, me, Thord, his swan and at the Elites and hoplites. This was all done with speed, but I could tell his brain was calculating our battle readiness and where he could fit us into any plan that was unfolding in his head. Corwin had always had a very tactical mind. I was certain Nameless accessed that part of him.

"Well..." Archon Thena said. "I am a patient person, but this silence is allowing me the time to hear the screams of the dying and the crackling of my burning city and, frankly, I've had enough of that. We must strike back at this emperor. What happened after this wizard died?"

"My apologies, Archon Thena." Nameless bowed slightly.

"If you bow to me again," Thena said, "I will stab you. I'm an archon, not royalty. Now spit your plan out."

"Boqin ascended to another plane," Nameless said, slightly faster than his usual talking speed. "But we have returned from the White Tower with his eye and heart."

"I noticed your new eye." She pointed at him. "And I assume congratulations are in order for having his heart, though I don't want to know how you got it. What does it mean for us? Be quick in the telling."

Nameless nodded. His wizard eye was glowing as he spoke. "There has not been enough time to fully unlock all that the wizard Boqin has gifted me. I have much of his knowledge and some of his powers so with what I now know, a plan has formed that could end this war: all we have to do is cut off the head of the snake."

"I assume Emperor Sargon is the snake," she said.

"That is correct."

"You had me at beheading," Brax said. "I'm enjoying this plan so far."

"Yes, I like the goal of the plan." Archon Thena absently tapped the spike on the end of her spear into the floor, scratching the marble tile. "Now tell us how this feat will be accomplished. There is a massive army between us and him. Not to mention he has the power of a multitude of wizards. We have seen what that means firsthand."

Nameless looked at a point in the sky, then back again. "I have taken his army and his powers into my calculations." He said this as if they were nothing. "I need nine of your Elites. I assume they are trained as *hippeis* and so know the ways of the wings."

"Yes, each of them has flown in glider attacks," she said.

"Then I want those nine." He pointed at a group of Elites, six men and three women who stood behind the archon with narrowed eyes. They didn't seem surprised to be picked. "Send for their gliders at once."

Thena made a simple nod and a hoplite ran from the room.

"The rest of the plan involves me, Thord, and Carmen on our mounts." Brax cleared his throat, but before he could complain, Nameless spoke again. "I did not mean to suggest you are just a mount. You are a powerful entity and the most important piece on the game board."

"I'm gradually learning to like your new brother." Brax patted my shoulder. "He has a nice way of putting things."

"What we will do." Nameless's voice was growing louder and more confident with each word and filled me with certainty in his plan. Was this a spell? "Is we will launch ourselves from the top of the Carthenon and fly directly toward the enemy."

"I take that back about the wisdom," Brax said. "He's gone insane."

"I assume there's something I'm missing in your plan," Archon Thena said. "Because the only ending to a full-on frontal attack will be death."

"There is one more thing." Nameless gestured at the group. "I intend to turn all of us invisible."

He had made himself invisible once right before our eyes, but he'd admitted it was a trick. This sounded like it needed more than sleight of hand.

"Invisible?" Archon Thena said. "So you have learned some powerful magic from Boqin. How effective is this spell?"

"It is complicated and it could easily fade or fall apart. But..." He motioned. "With this experienced group of fighters we could—"

"You're not leaving me behind!" Megan had stepped up, so she was face-to-face with Nameless.

Nameless didn't even blink. "You have no mount and a fractured arm, therefore it isn't practical or beneficial to take you."

"You will find a role here, Megan," I said.

She gestured at Brax with her good hand. "Can't two of us ride on your dragon?"

Brax shook his head. "I'm not a flying cart. Plus, two of you would weigh me down."

"Adjust to your fate, Megan," Nameless said. "Accept it. You are wounded and would hamper our ability to strike hard and fast. If it's any consolation, you'll likely be fighting the enemy soon enough."

Her eyes were angry slits and her nose flared like she was about to draw a blade and start fighting for a place on the team. Thord reached out and patted her shoulder. To my surprise, she didn't punch him in the head. "The fates have been unkind." His voice was soothing. "You deserve this stab at glory, but take a measure of yourself. The great god Belaz has made this decision for you."

Megan glared for several moments, her good hand on her small crossbow. She wasn't one to be fond of the god of assassins—she didn't enjoy bending her knee to anyone. But mentioning our god was also a way of saying this was out of her control. Megan nodded. "You're right," she said.

She patted Thord's hand, then left her hand over his. I gritted my teeth and looked away, concentrating on my brother's next words.

"The spell will hide us from their eyes," Nameless continued, "but not their armaments—so we are at risk of being struck by arrows or catapult stones. We will have to fly straight and with great speed. Our goal will be to land behind the lines of the enemy right where Sargon stands directing his armies. We will kill him and his generals and the army will, without commanders, soon stop fighting and scatter."

"That plan might work," Archon Thena said.

"Yes." Nameless put up a finger as if he were giving a lecture. "There is one major problematic factor. I can only turn myself and others invisible by holding on to them. So if I were to lay hands on Carmen she would become invisible and if she were to touch Thord, he would turn invisible and so on."

"Oh," the archon said. "How is it possible to stay connected while you're flying?"

"Brax will be above us and I will hold his talon."

"Hold my talon?" Brax shook one of his talons at Nameless. "I don't let mortals hold my talon!"

"Let me rephrase that," Nameless said. "Brax will clutch my weak mortal hand with his powerful talon and he will turn invisible. Then Thord will hold Dust's talon."

Thord looked a little green at the prospect of that, but said nothing.

"And below them, grasping either talon of Bolt will be two lines of your Elites with their glider wings stretched wide and their hands on the ankles of the comrade in front of them."

"Like a double trail on a kite," I said.

"Exactly, sister!" Nameless said. "Because we cannot maneuver easily, we will have to aim ourselves directly at the enemy."

"So one lucky catapult stone could smack all of you out of the air," Archon Thena said.

Nameless nodded. "Yes. That would be the result."

"Well, these do not sound like great odds," Archon Thena said. "But let's not bring math into this madness. This will be a feat that minstrels will sing about for a thousand years."

Brax flexed his wings. "If you're taking notes for those minstrels then let them know this: I am not excited about playing a part in this fodder for bards. I'm certain the story will end with a handsome dragon full of arrows."

"It's the best plan we have," I said.

"It's the only one," he replied. "And, as always, the dragon has to do the heavy lifting. Ah, I've spoken my piece. Let us get on with it."

26

THROUGH THE SKIES

We assembled at the broken section of the wall. Nameless ordered several hoplites to shine their shields and then block the hole. He didn't explain his reasons for that.

The Elites assembled their glider wings with such speed and efficiency it was almost mesmerizing. The devices were black triangles of bone-thin metal stretched with sewn-together bat wings. Once finished that the Elites donned their red helmets, partially hiding their grim-set faces behind their eye-slits, and then stood in two perfect lines—looking for all the world like red metal bats. They each held a long doru spear.

I did a quick equipment check: the most important part was being certain my daggers were properly tight on my belt. The poison pockets in my cloak were mostly empty, though I had glow dust. What felt like many years ago, I'd used that same type of dust to brighten the cave and to get my first glimpse of Brax. The dust would be useless in a battle in the middle of the day. I tied my hair back so tightly my eyes watered—I wanted nothing to block my line of vision.

I left my backpack against the wall, knowing that the books we'd been loaned by Goran were still safe inside. They had survived our trip across the ocean, but I doubted they'd last through a battle.

There was still enough of a crack in the wall to give a view of the outside world. Even more of the great city was burning now as the Immortals and the regular Akkadian soldiers worked their way through the streets, putting everything to the torch. The wind shifted the smoke into different horrifying images—floating beasts, dead bodies, giant gaping mouths—it was some frightening spell Sargon had cast. As if watching their city burn from inside it wouldn't be terrifying enough for the Avenians. The Green Dome, a massive coliseum with a green dome for a roof, was belching smoke from its center. There may never be chariot races in that building again.

As the Akkadians marched nearer, it became clear that Brax would be visible to them if they had a spyglass or were using birds as their eyes. "I wonder if you should crouch down a bit," I said.

"I don't crouch," Brax replied.

"Few spotted us when we arrived," Nameless said. "And right now they can't see our huge winged friend, or any of the swans." Nameless motioned at the wall of perfectly shined shields held by the hoplites. "Those shields are looking glasses now, reflecting the sunlight toward our enemies. It will be enough to distract their eyes—another sleight-of-hand trick I learned from Goran. They won't guess our purpose. That said, we shouldn't dillydally."

"Dillydally?" Brax said. "What kind of word is that? It's bad luck to say silly words while girding for battle."

"As if girding is any better," I said.

One of the Elites glanced over at us and I was certain she thought we were insane.

"My apologies," Nameless replied. "You are correct about the importance of words. How about this? Let us not pause in our preparations: we will face the fury of our enemy with fortitude and fiery bravery."

"Now you have it." Brax patted Nameless hard enough on the back to make him stumble a step forward. "I'm inspired."

"Not everyone likes your sense of humor," I said.

"That's for certain," Thord added.

Brax shot him a wicked one-eyed glare. Before this could get any messier, I climbed on my dear dragon's back and with a nod from Nameless, we flew up several feet in the air. We were higher than the shields now and I wondered, as we sat out here in the open, how long those shields would distract the enemy from a dragon floating above the Carthenon.

I glanced down to see Nameless had climbed onto Dust and was now waving his white staff in a circle. Nothing happened the first two passes, then the swan hissed and they vanished. Archon Thena looked a little surprised, and even the Elites took a small step back in unison. The first part of the turning invisible plan had worked.

And then I felt a buzzing sensation go up my body, starting at my feet and zipping right to my skull. My hands and arms and the rest of me had vanished, along with Brax. It was almost enough to make me fall off, except I could feel Brax below me. I tapped on his neck to be certain.

"Yes, you're invisible," Nameless said. "The other tricky part I neglected to mention is that we can't see each other. Now please ascend another yard or two and we'll get Thord to join the line."

We did so. I watched Thord move into place below us and vanish, and then the Elites lay down on the rough floor in two lines and grabbed the legs of the man or woman in front of them. The lead Elites reached for the invisible talons of Bolt, and all the Elites blinked out.

"Fly, Brax," Nameless said. "Fly steady and slow."

And with that command Brax began pushing his wings forward and, at the same time, the hoplites moved their shield wall and stepped aside. Soon we were clear of the Carthenon and, since I couldn't see any of our companions, I assumed everyone was with us.

"A little faster, Brax," Nameless said. "Please."

Brax began flapping a bit harder. We aimed directly toward the eastern gates and the emperor who waited on the plains beyond them. A few moments later we were passing through such thick smoke that it briefly took the shapes of our bodies, revealing us, and then we went through that column of grayness. I held my teeth tight, preventing a cough.

Below us, citizens were running through the lanes, some bloodied, others limping. I spotted a mother screaming and carrying her child, and that scene made the bile come up in my throat. I wanted to land and defend her. But there was no point to that. As we flew further along, we came across Avenian troops who had formed into square phalanxes with their long spears—dorus—held out before them to prevent the enemy from charging down the alleys and streets. It was clear from our vantage point that long columns of spotless and fresh Immortals were converging on the defenders, and soon the hoplites would be overwhelmed and surrounded. There were just too many streets to defend.

They are brave men and women, Brax thought to me.

Yes, I wish we could aid them.

We are, he answered.

An arrow passed near us. Then a catapulted stone, flying at such speed that it made a hissing sound, went over my head.

We are one lucky shot away from being turned into mincemeat, Brax thought.

Then I will keep crossing my fingers and repeating: don't be mincemeat. Don't be mincemeat.

That at least got a chuckle out of him. *It's as good a saying as any for a mortal,* he sent.

It was so odd to see through him to the horrors below. And I was growing used to the sense that I was flying on my own through the sky according to my human sight. But my dragon eye, if I squeezed the other one shut, would give me the slightest outline of his form and our trailing companions.

We flew over a swirling mass of anger and shouts—the Akkadian soldiers were caught up in their bloodlust. Behind them a squadron of bowmen sent a swarm of arrows our way, not knowing we were there. It was impossible to avoid the wooden missiles, so Brax spread his wings even wider to protect our companions. The arrows stuck into him, some bounced off and if anyone had been looking at that spot, they would wonder why so many had broken in midair.

It almost worked perfectly. But the last grouping of arrows were at an angle that made them miss Brax and thud down, striking the tail end of our line. An Elite—a male—suddenly appeared in the sky, holding his shoulder where an arrow had pierced his arm, forcing him to let go of his companion. He twirled downwards into the side of a brick building and then smashed into the ground. A moment later we were too far to see what became of him.

I wasn't certain whether his sudden appearance would be enough to warn Emperor Sargon.

We crossed the center of the city and at one point I recognized the Library of Avenus, its roof crumpled in and smoke belching out. There were librarians, despite the enemy coming toward them, rushing with pails of water to douse the flames.

There is none braver than the protectors of knowledge, Brax thought. *We fight for them, too*, he added because he knew, possibly from me clutching tightly to his back, that I wanted to jump down there and guard the librarians.

We went on with our invisible flight at a speed that felt too slow. The battle would be over before we reached our targets. And now that we were fully over the enemy forces, it was disheartening to see exactly how vast their numbers were. Immortals in their glistening golden armor, their long spears pointed forward, led lengthy lines of troops. Calvary raced through the other streets, hunting down Avenian citizens and soldiers alike. The only good thing was that the arrows and catapults' stones were now zipping high over our heads because the Akkadians were aiming so far ahead of their own troops.

It felt like we were flying over burning buildings and enemy troops for hours. Emperor Sargon had brought the four other realms to their knees with this army. Avenus had never had an actual chance. And it was feeling like our little group didn't have a chance either.

We crossed over the broken gate and onto the flat land surrounding the city. A land still massed with troops.

"Go a little to the north." Nameless's voice sounded distant.

Brax turned ever so slightly and I saw what Nameless had spotted.

There was a long line of great catapults being loaded by crews of workers. They rolled stones into each bucket, drenched them with oil and then set them afire and loosed the burning mass toward the city.

And right next to the catapults were a dozen huge, white war chariots, a bear flag flapping from each.

The largest wagon belonged to the Emperor Sargon.

27

SILVER BIRDS

There were eight muscular horses per chariot. The wheeled craft were large enough to hold at least twelve Immortals each. These were the absolute best of the best of his fighters—Sargon's personal guard. The brightness of their armor dazzled me but, despite the near blindness, I counted at least one hundred and forty of them, including the ones arrayed in front of the wagons. My assassin-trained brain couldn't help doing the math—that was twelve Immortals each in hand-to-hand combat. No, even more since we'd lost one of our Elites. It was impossible odds!

Well, maybe not impossible. At least we had a dragon on our side. And a wizard inside a wizard apprentice who happened to also be an assassin.

Emperor Sargon's chariot had a small tower in the center that elevated him above the rest of the army so he could see where his blows were landing. He stood on that tower, generals on either side. A golden crown glittered from the top of his head. His arms were crossed and he was beaming with a beatific smile, as if the sight of the fallen walls and the burning city and dying citizens was the most beautiful vision he'd ever seen. And perhaps it was: this was the culmination of his years of planning.

I drew in a breath, trying to calm my racing heart. So odd to have something invisible beat so hard. We were getting nearer and nearer and the land grew quiet around us. The only shouted orders were coming from the catapults, followed by the clacking of their gears and that tremendous rush of sound as a burning rock flew in the city's direction.

A troop of Immortals were in a crescent before the emperor's chariot, waiting silently for a command—perhaps they had been standing that way for hours. Each of them was holding a loaded crossbow.

I squinted my dragon eye, getting a close view of Sargon's face. It was clean-shaven, his hair had been well-oiled and styled and he wore a crown of golden leaves. He looked so perfect it was as if he were standing in the center of a painting. It surprised me he didn't have a painter capturing his pose at this very moment. And a minstrel writing his song of conquering.

Behind his wagon, laid out on the ground, was a carpet of white furs. Was this carpet there for his dainty feet to walk upon once he'd achieved victory? Maybe he'd have it unfurled all the way to the city's gates.

Occasionally Sargon would move a hand, and a glowing falcon would appear and race to the city. Other falcons were zipping over to the white-robed engineers commanding the catapults. Those birds were his eyes and ears and his mouth—helping the catapults to aim and letting him know how the battle for Avenus was unfolding.

Those birds were also our undoing.

For Emperor Sargon, oblivious to us closing in on him,

continued to grin like mad, salivating as he watched his victory. I was sure Brax would take that smiling head from his shoulders, just for the wounds the emperor had given him. This man had killed the wizards and witches, eaten their hearts and had crushed the Five Realms. He had also helped my brother destroy all the assassins. And the image of the Library of Avenus burning came to mind.

We had plenty of motivation.

He would deserve every cutting blow of our revenge. I used my anger to stamp out any last vestiges of fear that remained in my head.

Sargon opened both hands at once, and two bright silver falcons appeared and shot straight up into the air and directly toward the city. The first one flew forty yards, hit Brax right in the chest and bounced off, then fell dead to the ground. That wasn't too bad, because no one seemed to notice it fall.

The second falcon was rotten luck on wings. It struck one of the Elites directly in the face. When I looked down, I saw that a lead Elite had lifted his hand to his eye, breaking his hold with Thord and bumping the Elite next to him. Now all eight of the Avenian soldiers appeared out of thin air, at least forty yards from Sargon.

There was a gasp from below, proving even the Immortals could be surprised. The Elites spread out, aiming downwards—directly at the royal chariot. They gained speed and passed us. It looked like they would reach our target without being wounded.

But a general on one chariot barked out a command and the Immortals on the ground brought up their crossbows and bolts flew into the air, hitting many of their targets.

Three Elites spiraled down, either dead or soon to be dead because half the Immortals were drawing their swords and preparing to fight. The remaining Elites, whether or not they were wounded, aimed true, their long spears held out before them.

Emperor Sargon was standing still as a statue. His smile was gone, and a look of confusion had replaced it. This interruption had not been anticipated. Good! The longer he stood shocked, the better our chances of killing him!

But he hadn't survived palace intrigue for so many years by being slow-witted. He quickly moved his hands in a circular pattern, and I knew it would mean something horrible coming for us.

"Unleash the fire of Hades," Nameless shouted.

"Consider it done," Brax shouted back.

Nameless let go of Brax's talon, and in an eye blink two swans and a dragon and their riders appeared in the air before the emperor. It was enough to make him stop his motions and open his mouth in a gaping, comical fashion.

We had definitely surprised him.

28

GETTING THE PICTURE

Brax dived toward the royal chariot, the wind from his wings flattening the Immortals on the ground, the horses yanking at their reins at the sight of him. He let out a blast of flames, parting the remaining Immortals who stood between us and the emperor.

We reached the chariot and Brax, on purpose, smashed into the tower nose first, knocking it down. The emperor flew backwards, arms waving madly, and landed on the pile of white furs behind him.

I leapt from Brax's back, booting an Immortal general over the side of the chariot before he could even draw his sword. Thord had landed next to me while Bolt dug his talons into another Immortal general, lifting him skyward and then throwing him to the ground. And next to Thord, landing with quiet skill, was Nameless clutching his staff. He blasted a hole right through two Immortals who fell over without a sound.

No one stood between us and the emperor. He was on a patch of grass between the white furs, trying to get to his feet. His crown had fallen off and blood dripped down the side of his skull.

Before any of us could move, a female Elite came running across that flat ground at full speed, shouting, "This is for Avenus!" Her battle spear was held straight out, and she performed a flying leap that proved these soldiers were agile and well-trained. Sargon continued to look confused. His brain hadn't accepted what was happening yet, and that hesitation would be his death. He didn't even bring up his hands to protect himself.

The spear caught Sargon in the side of his chest and went right through him. The Elite landed on the ground, a cry of victory on her lips, and she kept pushing the long spear further and further along its bloody path.

It had been a blow that would be spoken about for ages.

But it wasn't enough. Because Sargon hadn't even grimaced. Instead, he stood in place despite being pierced right through and when the Elite was near enough, he touched her with his bare hand and her victorious cry suddenly halted. She turned bright red, as though a molten fire were lit inside her, and then she fell to smoking pieces.

Emperor Sargon rubbed his hands together and then pulled the spear the rest of the way through him and tossed it, unerringly and easily, through another Elite. Again, he didn't make the slightest grimace. There also was no blood nor sign of a wound.

"This is all delightfully surprising," he said. "I do not understand how my right-hand blade, long thought dead, is now standing before me, right next to his sister. I will get the answer to that no matter how many entrails I have to twist. Or hearts rip out. I would mention plucking eyeballs, too, but I'm sure you get the picture."

Having seen the Elite's flaming death and the spearing

that followed, we had all paused. Nameless whispered and at first I thought it was an order or suggestion, but the air between us glowed and a moment later Sargon pointed his right hand, and the red line of fire that came from him was deflected into the sky.

"I will hold him at bay," Nameless said. "The two of you attack from either side."

Thord leapt one way off the chariot and I the other and we circled around, trusting that the invisible shield Nameless had summoned would continue to protect us.

I spared a glance to see that Brax had used his flames to drive the Immortals back from the main chariot, giving us space to fight. There were still three of the Elites left, battling their way toward us.

Sargon shot a flaming ball and I put up my hands but was shielded by Nameless. The heat still reached me and the scales rose on my skin. I wasn't confident they would be strong enough to stop his magic.

"Oh, I see your plan," Emperor Sargon said. "Single me out like a helpless lamb, then devour me. But I am not alone." He clapped his hands and the white fur blankets that were all around him rose—and stood. Because they had been so immobile I'd mistaken them for rugs—white bear rugs. But these were not rugs, they were the actual beasts getting to their feet. They had slept through the battle, but not his hand clap. Each of them was several heads higher than the emperor. "I'm never alone when I'm with my pets," he added. "Perhaps you'd like to meet one." He reached behind him, grabbed a bear by the scruff of the neck and threw it at me as if it were no heavier than a pillow. It came through the air, its jaws open, its arms out, claws catching the light. Its black eyes were focused directly at me.

I froze. Assassin school hadn't trained me to defend

myself from flying bears. The snarling creature broke through Nameless's shield and smacked into my chest, throwing me backward with such force and speed that I rolled across the ground. It was on me before I could get to my feet, slashing its claws across my shoulder and then biting into the other shoulder. I grabbed at its neck to pull it away, reaching with my free hand for my dagger, but it pinned my arm to the ground with a massive paw. The weight of the thing was like having a castle plunked right on top of me. A castle with claws.

Then a fist hit it in the head and grabbed its snout to pull back its jaw. Thord was lifting, using his legs as if trying to lift the world, straining and yanking the bear's toothy, tearing grip from my shoulder.

Which was very kind of him. But the bear turned its attention to Thord and, using me as traction, pushed into him, throwing him down and going straight for his neck.

I pulled back to throw a dagger.

But a shadow came out of the sky between us. Brax lowered himself down, grabbed the bear by the scruff and tried to take off. He pulled it away from Thord, but he couldn't get any higher. "This thing must have eaten an army!" he said, straining.

And as if in answer to his cry, another shadow descended. Dust grabbed the tail end of the bear, and between the dragon and the swan they got the thing off the ground. They swept their wings in unison, the swan hissing as it worked, Brax grunting until they were up into the sky.

One bear gone. Five more to go.

I rushed over to Thord but he stood before I got there. "I'm fine," he said, waving me away and picking up his sword. "We need to help Nameless."

I turned to see that Nameless was floating above the

ground near the chariot. The glowing shield he'd placed around himself was being bashed and pushed by three bears; the rest were dead. His face was locked in concentration, and his wizard eye glowed.

Nameless struggled to point his staff and fight back. He slowly brought it around so it was directed at the emperor. I hoped fiery destruction would come out of the end of that hunk of wood.

But all Sargon did was point at him like an admonishing teacher, and then he snapped his fingers.

The white ash staff, a focus of Nameless's power, cracked in half.

29

A NEW SUN

The first thing to happen was Nameless screamed as if breaking the staff had broken a part of him. A green blast of fire burst from the staff, bashed the white bears away and struck Emperor Sargon, knocking him back a step or two. Nameless fell to the earth and lay still.

Emperor Sargon ran a hand through his hair, drew in a deep breath and stalked ahead, gesturing so the bears—which had found their feet again—backed away. He stopped beside my brother and looked down. "What is it about you that changed?" Sargon asked. "What brought you to this place?" The emperor reached down and placed a palm on Nameless's forehead as if feeling for a temperature. My brother shuddered and shook, letting out another brief cry of pain. "Oh, I see. I see," Sargon said. "Well, well, isn't that interesting? You aren't really you. You're someone else."

Thord and I were dashing toward him from two different angles, hoping Sargon wouldn't look up. The remaining Elites had fallen, leaving the battle in our hands alone.

Thord got there first and leapt. It was a good jump and he braced his sword with both hands, preparing for impact.

Emperor Sargon didn't even look away from Nameless, but pointed his hand and blasted Thord with a ball of fire that smashed him to the ground. Thord screamed, wiping at the fire burning along his armor.

I had a moment for that image of Thord all aflame to register and then I leapt, both daggers out, hoping that whatever magic was in those ancient blades would defend me from what Sargon threw my way. I flew straight as a bolt at him.

He snapped his fingers, and it felt like a giant hand had grabbed me, crushing the air from my lungs and smashing me into the ground. Again and again and again. Then the hand let go and I struggled to raise my head.

Sargon was stroking his chin, as though deep in thought, and then he raised his finger as an idea struck him. "So many quandaries to figure out," he said. "It's a challenge." Then he glanced over at me and winked. The remaining bears were pawing the ground near him. "Oh my dear bears, have a meal," Emperor Sargon said. The massive creatures came straight toward me, and stopped. One sniffed my hair, but I couldn't even raise a hand to swat at it. It opened its mouth, releasing a blast of eye-watering breath that stunk of decay.

"No, not that one," Sargon commanded. "The Woden boy first. Then her."

The bears sniffed once and then rumbled past me. Out of the corner of my eye I saw Thord rise, shakily, his sword in hand. They were so much bigger than him. At least the fire no longer burned on his armor.

"So you did this to your brother," Emperor Sargon said to me. "Look at me when I'm talking to you." His words, a spell, made me snap my head to glare at him. "I spent all that time cultivating Corwin, and you had the audacity to taint him with... with goodness. What a waste of potential." Nameless continued to open his mouth in a silent scream. It wasn't clear what was causing the pain, for all I could see was that the emperor had his hand on his forehead. "How to fix a broken assassin? Now there's a question I've never asked."

"He doesn't need fixing." I pushed myself into a crouch. His magic held me down, but my dragon blood, given enough time, could fight against it. And through it all, my dragon eye was seeing him clearer and clearer. He glowed with all the magic he had consumed.

"You really don't die easily," he said. "One has to respect that. And speaking of respect: learn to kneel before your superiors."

He gestured with his free hand, and I slammed to my knees. The pain went up my legs. Thord had wandered far enough to enter my line of vision. He was already bloodied and clearly exhausted, but he had killed one bear. He stabbed another, but the one behind him clawed him across the head, ripping the hood of his cloak and his skull. He stumbled and the bears fell upon him.

"Thord!" I shouted.

"I commanded you to look at me!" My head snapped toward the emperor again and my gaze locked with his. "Now, say this: 'You are the god emperor and I worship you and the ground you walk on.'"

I opened my mouth to spit in his direction, but my traitorous tongue formed these words: "You are the god emperor and I worship you and the ground you walk on."

I couldn't stop my mouth from moving, my lungs from pushing out air so that the words were louder, echoing across that part of the battlefield. I wanted to cut my tongue out. But my body betrayed me, by forcing me to sheath my daggers.

"That wasn't so hard," Emperor Sargon said. "Every single mortal in Ellos will bow to me and speak those words as I ride my chariot through their cities—*my cities*—and I will glory in their praises. They will look upon my face and be blinded by the beauty of it."

He did something so his face began glowing. He was so perfect that looking at him made my eyes hurt. I felt I didn't deserve to view such perfection. It was some powerful spell, but knowing that did not stop my mind and spirit from wanting to worship him.

"You're mad." I took all my will to spit those words out. "Total damn madness."

"No." He waved a finger at me. "I am the only one who is sane. You are the mad one for opposing me and you don't get to live in this wonderful, new world I am creating."

I had dug my feet in behind me, raising myself slightly while hoping my cloak hid my movements.

"You will not see the glory of one banner, one land," he continued. He sounded sorry for me. "All of Ellos combined under a beautiful empire that stretches from ocean to ocean."

"You won't see it either," I said.

That statement had enough confidence in it that it made the slightest look of consternation cross his face—a frown in all that glowing perfection. And in that moment I pushed, willed my legs to work, willed all that was in me—dragon blood and pure determination—to give me strength. The bear had wounded my left arm, so I drew one dagger and held out the blade with both hands. I pointed it directly at his heart.

He was bringing up his hand, the one that had been upon Nameless's forehead, but it was too late. For I had crossed that space between us in a heartbeat, and my arm was steady. My maestrus had trained me well.

My dagger found him. I found him. I drove that magical, warded blade right into his heart, so we were looking face-to-face. He was knocked back a few steps, but I stuck with him. The shock on his face made me smile. "I was paid a copper coin to assassinate you," I said. "That's all your death is worth."

He let out a gasp, a rasp of breath and a groan all wrapped into one death rattle. My first kill of a mortal was here. Right before me. It was justice, and it would save so many lives.

He continued to make that horrible noise; it grew louder, his face contorted. The spell that gave him god-like beauty was gone.

I tried to pull my dagger out and push him away, but the blade was stuck as if his heart were a hard thing.

And the thudding in my ears had grown quieter, so I now recognized the guttural sound he was making.

Laughter. He was laughing directly in my face.

"I didn't dine on the hearts of so many wizards to be killed by a blade. Even one forged in magic as old as this." He grabbed me by the throat and lifted me up, so I was without breath, without hope. He squeezed.

With his other hand he withdrew the dagger and dropped it to the ground. "I will discover who paid you that coin. There will be blood for the audacity of that purchase. I am worth so much more."

He continued to squeeze and I struggled, banging my fists against him, pushing at his arm, gasping for air. Nameless was below me and several feet away. He looked to be moving slightly.

I tried to shout at him. But no words came out.

"No," Emperor Sargon said. "You don't get to speak. Not in my presence. Never again." He touched my head with his free hand. "Ah, so it was the Executioner who paid you. He will have his head removed by his own axe—ending his ancient life. And now I end yours."

I kicked. I fought. But my vision grew darker and darker so that only his glowing face floated in front of me, his smile a collection of perfectly straight teeth. That grin would be the last thing I'd ever see.

I hope your scales still work, Brax said in my head.

And before I could respond there was the sound of wings swooping and the world grew bright, despite all the smoke of war blocking the sun, for there was suddenly a new sun forming above us.

A sun full of heat and power. An ancient flame. The most powerful flame produced by a Scythian dragon.

Brax was burning the emperor and me, hitting us hard with his dragon fire. The scales grew immediately over my skin and the power behind those flames split us apart, so Emperor Sargon dropped me and put up his hands and tried to block the flame. I fell to the ground, but saw the flames hit him; Brax drove Sargon to his knees with such intense heat it melted his face. In time, the emperor became one lump of blackened flesh.

And then he fell over, smoking and dead.

30

AN OPEN DOOR

Brax set down beside me, the wind from his wings sending the ashes of all the burnt grass drifting away. It cooled my face.

"So that's what a fried emperor looks like," he said. "I've always wondered."

I had found the strength to get to my knees and Brax was kind enough to extend a talon and pull me to my feet. I leaned on him and looked down at the still-smoking body before us. Sargon was unrecognizable—his face a black, burnt mask. His long, well-oiled hair had been scorched to ashes. All around him was the devastation wreaked by dragon fire. The ground was still hot to the touch.

My cloak had withstood the flame and protected enough of my clothes that I wasn't standing here naked. Nameless lay just outside the radius of the fire, but the blast had singed his hair. He groaned, then put his hand to his head and sat up painfully slow.

But where was Thord? Whatever bears that were still alive had fled. Two dead bears had fallen on Thord, one with his sword right through it. Thord wasn't moving, but I couldn't tell from here whether he was still breathing. Once I had my strength back I would go to him and check on his wounds.

"More proof that you should always bring a dragon to a wizard fight." Brax continued to support me—I needed to lean on him now to keep my feet.

"If you were limber enough, you could pat yourself on your back," I said, my voice ragged.

"I will accept that snark as thanks for saving your mortal life," he answered. "Again. In fact, it looks like all of Ellos owes me their lives. I assume they'll build statues of me to worship."

The Immortals who remained had backed away from us, but I didn't know how long their hesitation would last. Seeing their god-like emperor brought low had taken away some of their bravery and most of their purpose.

"We may have to kill a few more of them," Brax said. He spread his wings threateningly and several of them stumbled backwards to get away. He laughed. "That'll help keep them in line."

"Let's hope it doesn't come to that," I answered.

The ground shook below us and made an indistinct rumbling sound, as if the earth itself were complaining about having to hold the body of the emperor. "What was that?" I asked. At first I thought it might be a catapult throwing a stone, but they were all still. The land rumbled again with such force that I lost my balance and had to lean hard into Brax. He put an arm over my shoulder.

"I don't like this," he said. "We had better take to the air."

Nameless limped toward us, clutching a broken section of his staff. "Get gone!" he shouted. "Both of you get gone!" The ground shook a third time with such force it threw Brax to one side.

"Dust, to me!" Nameless shouted. He shoved the broken staff into his belt and put up his hands as if in supplication to the sun. "Dust! I call thee!"

The ground—the very earth itself—split open below Sargon's body, the foot-wide cracks spreading like lightning between my feet and widening with each passing second. Sargon glowed as if an unquenchable heat were rising inside him. His burnt body was now so bright I had to shield my eyes.

The emperor, as if nothing had happened at all in the last few minutes, got to his feet and faced us.

"Not by blade, not by fire, nothing shall rend me," he said. "For I am the god emperor of Ellos and all shall kneel before me."

Bright as a thousand suns he strode toward us and I expected him to unleash his power, but he stopped and felt his head. "You burned off my hair!" He patted his bald, glowing scalp. "Ah, it will grow back. Until then I shall have yours as a wig."

Thord rose up from the corpses of the bears and drew his blade from the beast next to him, and then took a limping step toward the emperor and another. *The blade won't harm him*, I wanted to shout, but before I got a word out Sargon waved a hand and Thord fell to his knees. "You are the god emperor," Thord said, though it pained his bloodied face. "You are the sun in the sky and you hold all of Ellos in your palms."

"Yes, sing it. Sing it!" Emperor Sargon said. "All of you will sing it." He pointed toward Thord. "Now battle for your life as you praise me." Thord turned. One of the bears, clearly dead, had risen up and began to roar a horrible garbled roar and approach Thord.

"You are the stars in the heaven!" Thord said, and he

swung at the bear. "You are the moon in the sky, great emperor!"

The bear knocked him down, but Thord got up again, still yelling praises as he fought.

"This is a worrying development," Brax said.

Dust dropped from the sky, hitting the earth hard, but her legs held steady. She hissed at us, and then hissed at Sargon. Nameless struggled to climb onto her, and ended up throwing himself over the saddle. The great black swan gave a cry then swept its wings once, twice and lifted off the ground.

"Get on my back," Brax said. "Get on now!"

Before I could move Sargon pointed, and a beam of light came out of the sky and struck Dust. The swan gave out a horrible screech and then its head was severed and tumbled toward the earth, still screeching. Its body kept flapping its wings, carrying Nameless away, and I thought he might escape on a headless swan, but the remains of Dust suddenly twisted in the air and plummeted to the ground. My brother thudded to earth only a short distance from us.

Then the crossbow bolts of the Immortals flew, and Brax stuck up a wing, blocking them from me. I could hear the *thud thud thud* as they struck his flesh. Many of them bounced off, but, judging by his wincing, others hit home.

And then Emperor Sargon gestured and an invisible fist struck Brax and me, knocking me onto my back and smashing Brax away from me.

Sargon strode toward us, signaling his Immortals to stop their rain of bolts. He walked with such confidence, each step certain even though he was stepping on bodies and dead bears. I noted he actually floated a foot or two off the ground.

Then a screech came from behind him as Thord's bird

dropped out of the air, too, landing to grab Thord. My friend, my dear friend had fallen and the bird was squawking at him, nudging his side and turning to hiss at the bear. Sargon looked in their direction and said, "What a noble beast." He snapped his fingers and Bolt's neck broke; the bird fell over and the bear leaped on it.

I tried to get up. A shadow fell over me and I turned my head to see what fresh horror was about to take place. Brax was coming down, bolts stuck into his side. He grabbed me in his talons, stumbled another step and grabbed something else and then he was flying up, up into the heavens. I got a glimpse of Emperor Sargon sending more flames toward us, but they missed.

I couldn't see what had happened to Thord.

Brax flew left and right, dodging the magic fireballs that Sargon sent our way. I looked over to see that Nameless, eyes closed, was clutched in his other set of talons.

"Go back!" I shouted. "Thord needs our help! Go back!"

"No," Brax said. "There is no returning. It is done."

"But you left Thord!" I banged against his talon.

"I can only carry two of you, and just barely. I chose the strongest of the two." He was grunting with each movement of his wings. We were now flying over the walls of Avenus and Sargon's forces looked up, but were too slow to strike us other than loosing the occasional arrow in our direction. "And I would not leave you, Carmen. I would never leave you," Brax added.

"I command you to go back," I said.

"You cannot command me," he shouted. "I am your friend and I have made the hard choice. Now, save your breath."

I wanted to scream and pry myself out of his talons, drop to the ground and run back, slaying Immortals and soldiers as I went. But squirm as I might, I couldn't get out of his grip.

We crossed the rest of the city and reached the Carthenon, which was now surrounded by Immortals and the regular Akkadian soldiers. They were bringing battering rams up the long steps leading to the building.

Brax drifted down into the rooftop courtyard. He deposited us on the marble floor and before I could stand, Archon Thena said, "I imagine this means we failed."

"Well," Brax said. "Emperor Sargon was speared in the side and he lived, a magic dagger was shoved through his heart and he plucked it out, and then I burned him to a crisp and yet he stood up and walked. So we gave it our very, very best." The walls of the Carthenon shook when another catapulted stone struck it. "And, as you have surely noted, he is getting closer by the moment. We may have made him a little angry and even more unforgiving."

"Then it is done and undone," Archon Thena said. "All of Avenus thanks you for your efforts." I got to my feet, this time without Brax's help. Nameless was unmoving on the floor, though he still drew breath.

Archon Thena turned slightly so the senators and remaining Elites and soldiers would hear her words. "We have fought the very best fight, and we will have to hope the tale of our struggle inspires those who come after us."

"I'd rather be alive," Brax said, though I wasn't sure the archon heard him. "That's my favorite kind of story."

"Where is Thord?" Megan had come up beside me, holding a blade as if she might run me through if I gave the wrong answer.

"Brax left him behind," I said.

"Get over it!" Brax snapped. "I wasn't going to grow another arm. And this is not the time to mourn. Thord knew his chances, and last I saw him he was alive." Brax drew in a wheezing breath. "He would have made the same choice."

I opened my mouth to spit out a retort, but Brax was right. And I was not thinking logically.

"I didn't hate him as much as I pretended to," Brax said with a quieter tone.

"Then he was alive," Megan said. "He has a chance, then."

I thought of what Sargon might do to him. "A chance," I whispered.

"Well, I'm sure he'll bumble his way out of destruction," she said with forced lightness. "He always does."

Before I could reply, Archon Thena spoke in a commanding voice. "We will continue to barricade the walls. Have the citizens gather in the center of the Carthenon, out of harm's way. And perhaps he will let them live."

"I don't think this will be that kind of day," Brax said. "When Sargon has smashed down the doors of this building, he will not leave a single mortal alive."

"Then we will fight to the last living Avenian." Archon Thena held her spear in the air as she gave her next command: "Arm everyone."

"No." The voice was ragged and, at first, I didn't know where it came from. It was almost as if someone had thrown it from another realm. Then I looked down to see that my brother had sat up and was rubbing his head. "There is another way," Nameless rasped. "There is one more thing we can do. The head must live."

Were his wounds affecting his brain? "What can we do?" I asked.

"Yes, tell us," Archon Thena said. "We are all ears."

I helped Nameless to his feet. He lifted the remaining piece of his staff. It looked like all the magic had drained out of it, but when he whispered an ancient word, it crackled with crimson energy.

A stone struck the wall behind us, making it collapse. Smoke and sunlight came in.

"Sargon is here." Maestru Beatrix was looking out the fresh hole down at the steps. "He has brought his chariot to the foot of the Carthenon stairs. We have only a few moments."

"We can save everyone in this room," Nameless said. "It is just a matter of opening the right door."

Another flaming stone smashed into the wall.

"See to the citizens!" Archon Thena said. And three of her hoplites and the Elites ran down and left the room. That meant only a few male and female senators, Archon Thena, and my companions remained.

"Speak in terms that make sense," said Archon Thena.

"The head must live," Nameless said, but he wasn't looking at her. He spoke to me. "The head must be taken to Drachia. There you can fall on your knees before Brax's brother and ask for protection. It is the only place that is safe."

"Drachia?" Archon Thena said. "Nameless, you've gone mad. How can we get to the land of dragons?"

"I will open the door to an in-between place," he said. "It will be safe. You know what to do." Again he spoke this last line directly to me.

"Megan, Maestru Beatrix—to me," I said.

And with that Nameless began whispering words of power, words I was sure he had learned from Boqin. He held up his staff and pointed and, with little fuss at all, an opening was ripped in the air in front of us. All I could see through it was darkness, so there was no way to know what lay on the other side.

"What in the seven hells is that?" Megan asked.

"My question exactly," Archon Thena said. "Though we Avenians don't believe in hells. Until today, that is."

"You know what to do," Nameless said to me. His arm was shaking as he pointed his broken staff, struggling to keep the doorway open. "I will follow."

And before anyone could react, I grabbed Archon Thena by the arm and pulled her toward the opening. She was taller than me, but not stronger.

"I'm not going in there," she said. "I intend to stay with my people."

"Megan," I shouted and, without another word, she grabbed the archon's other arm. She was a powerful and strong woman, but the two of us had just enough strength to pull her.

"You had better be right," Megan said. "I don't like the looks of that opening."

"It will be safe on the other side," I said. "He promised. We can trust his promises now."

And then Brax spread his wings, roared behind us and swept those remaining in the room before him. A male senator, squeaking with fear, jumped into the opening and we all followed.

All of us, except one.

31

TAKING STOCK

It was not like the other opening we had flown through. There was a sensation of coolness and of being carried forward and of the world behind us folding away—we were bodies and spirits floating through a formless space, and then I struck something hard and rolled across a floor. That first senator was already standing, checking his toga. I got up to see Archon Thena and Megan on either side, also getting up. And behind us came Brax, Maestru Beatrix and the three remaining senators.

Nameless had promised to send us somewhere safe. There were no torches burning in the room, but light came through the slit windows and the far end of the room was open to the air—it had a large, familiar balcony. I knew where I was the moment I got to my feet. This was the safest place Nameless could imagine.

We were in the Grand Hall of the Red Fortress. My school. My—

"Home," Megan said. "We're home."

It was such a strange way for her to put it because she had grown up in Allesaria. But it was the truth. This was our home. The place we had trained and learned how the world really worked.

"How is this even possible?" the archon asked. She was leaning on her spear. "Avenus is nowhere near the Red Adept Fortress."

I turned, for there was one person who was not here and the opening—the space between worlds—whatever we had passed through had closed up like an eye and vanished.

"Nameless didn't come through," I said. "My brother isn't here!"

"He didn't have enough strength left." Brax spoke quietly and perhaps with a bit of compassion. "He couldn't hold it open and walk through."

I stared at the blank wall. Nameless would be dead in minutes. How could he defend himself against Sargon?

"My people are dying as I sit here," Archon Thena said. She grabbed the spear with both hands, and I wondered if she were thinking of skewering me. "Why did you pull me through?"

"The head must live," I said. "Nameless meant that you must survive. The only way to fight back is to use your knowledge, your command and whatever influence you'll have over the factions that remain to fight the emperor. Nameless suggested going to Drachia and that there might be safety there."

"I'd say chances are half and half." Brax had moved closer to me, knocking over a chair with his wings. I guess he wanted to be near in case Thena tried to strike a blow. "My brother doesn't like mortals. Well, most dragons don't because you have a tendency to poke us with sharp things."

"But how do we even get there?" the archon asked. "The distance is so great. And, excuse me for being blunt, your dragon doesn't look to be in flying shape."

"I'm not *her* dragon." Brax rustled his wings. They were torn, and bleeding in several places. "I am my own dragon, but I appreciate the bluntness. Only Carmen can travel on my back."

The place smelled of old smoke and dust. It felt as if years had passed since I was last here. Lifetimes certainly had. And yet, in some secret part of my heart, I wanted to run up those stairs at the end of the room and into Alesius's study and demand that he save us. But there would only be dust, dried blood and bad memories there. Same as right here.

"First a fire," Megan said. She was already at the hearth, placing logs in the fireplace. "And then we will do a weapons and items check." It was the assassin's way to do things. Plus, it calmed the mind.

"I'll help you," Maestru Beatrix said. She found kindling and, after a few sparks from a spark rock, a warming flame came out of the fireplace. The heat immediately made me feel better, and I sat at one of the wooden chairs the Immortals hadn't broken. There wasn't a part of my body that didn't hurt. Archon Thena, who had been silent the whole time, sat near me.

"I will check a few things out," Megan said. She left the room, taking the stairs that led to the elevators. Maestru Beatrix had also slipped out of the room without me noticing, which was a dangerous sign; my senses had been so battered I was losing track of people. The senators had all gathered on chairs near the fire, though one was lying on the floor and shaking. Or maybe he was weeping. No one comforted him. They likely hadn't ever fought a day in their lives.

"And I have a sheep in my future," Brax said. "By that I

mean a sheep in my gut soon." He went to the balcony and spread his wings and was gone.

And that left only Archon Thena and me.

"You did the right thing," Archon Thena intoned as if each word burned. "By bringing me here, that is. Though I would prefer to die a thousand times with my people. Stories of fighting to the last woman or man make for delightful firelight tales." She gestured at the fire. "But it is better to use my skills as a negotiator and as a commander —revenge and regrowth is more likely. All of those things could pave the way to a brighter future."

"Thank you," I said. "Though it was my brother who thought of it, despite his wounds. His words drove me to action."

"Then I owe him, too," she said. "He has given a lot to aid in our cause."

"Yes, he has."

"And I am sorrowed, too, that Thord has fallen on the battlefield."

I only nodded. She was saying they were both dead now. She was a woman who was used to speaking hard truths.

"I have found a feast," Maestru Beatrix said. She walked into the room with a large tray of preserved dried meats, cheeses that had been in the cool box, jars of jellies and hard crackers. She placed the bounty on the foot table before us, brought water in a jug and settled down on a bench.

"I whittled a lot of the mold away to find edible cheese," she admitted. "But it won't kill us."

Archon Thena reached out and chose a dried fig and some cheese. The senators joined us, even the one from the floor who now had a splotched, red face. The food was beyond delicious. It didn't matter how hard the crackers were, they tasted heavenly spread with bilberry jam or tomato paste. I drank several mouthfuls of fresh water, too.

When half the plate was gone Megan entered the room. "Oh, food, yum!" she said. "I've never salivated for Maestru Orgrix's cooking more so than now."

She stuffed a dried beef strip in her mouth and chewed somewhat loudly. "I have delightful news. I discovered a way to Drachia."

"How is this possible?" Archon Thena said.

"I heard a sound." She paused for dramatic effect. "It was a familiar sound, and I thought I should investigate."

"You went off to investigate a mysterious sound on your own?" I said. "Why in the Five Realms would you do that?" Even as I said it, I realized that saying no longer applied to our world. It was one empire now.

"Because I'm a big girl," Megan said. "And you weren't in any shape to back me up."

"And what did you find?" Maestru Beatrix asked.

"I went to the swannery, and it's the most wonderful thing." She wasn't the type to talk this way. She moved her arm in its sling and grimaced slightly. "There were four swans nesting there. They must have fled during the battle for the Red Fortress and then returned and made the swannery their home. We have a way to travel to Drachia. To go anywhere."

"It is weeks of travel to get there," Archon Thena said. "According to the stories."

"No." Megan pointed up. "There are paths high in the air that the spellbirds use. The mage dragon Vecterix showed us the paths and, with the proper spell, a way to breathe that high up. So it is possible to travel to Drachia in hours. Thord and I did it." She faltered after saying his name. "I can lead us. I remember the spell."

"I hate to say it." Archon Thena looked at each of us. "But I am feeling a tendril of hope grow in my heart. Only a few hours of traveling and we will speak with a dragon who could become a powerful ally."

"Yes," Megan said. "Though it may take several hours to tame the swans. But even in my brief time up there I could hand-feed them oats. And I only got one nip." She rubbed her side.

"I am afraid you don't have hours," a male voice said from the main doorway. "You don't even have minutes."

32

BLAZING BRIGHT

The voice had startled me, and we all turned to look. Standing in the doorway, his broken staff clutched in one hand, was Nameless. He was grinning. He had somehow crossed the distance from Avenus and sneaked into the room with none of us knowing.

His grin was off, though. It wasn't happy; it was more of a leering smile, and it sent a chill through my heart.

"Yes, sister, you will not be training swans to flee from the glorious power of the emperor; you will shudder out your last breaths on the same floor your fellow students died on. All of you."

"Corwin," I said. "How—"

"I traveled here the same way as you did. And the answer to what is surely your second question is this: Emperor Sargon brought me back. He—he took that other putrid creature who has been in my head and strangled him. Nameless is no more. I am the one and the only Corwin. Your dearest brother."

There was a click, and a crossbow bolt flew across the room. It turned to ash before it made it halfway there. He jerked the staff to one side, and the crossbow flew out of Megan's hand and shattered on the wall. "Don't interrupt me," he said. "Never ever interrupt me again."

He took several steps into the room, the light of the fire making it clear that all traces of Nameless—the gentleness, the understanding I'd seen there—were gone. He looked hardened and angered.

We rose slowly from our seats. Archon Thena had taken up her spear. I had my remaining dagger. And Maestru Beatrix clutched her throwing stars.

"There are four of us," I said. "You will not find it easy."

"Well, sis," he said. "It seems I have a wizard inside me. How glorious is that? Just when I thought I couldn't get any better, I now can pull spells out of his dead mind. So you four are nothing but rats to me." He sniffed and shook his head sadly. "But I am not the one to kill you, for you have angered my dearest friend. My comrade. The emperor wants to take his own revenge."

The Emperor Sargon took a step out of the doorway and into the open. He hadn't a scratch from our previous battle. His outfit was no longer torn or burnt and there was no sign of the wounds I and the Elites had given him. His face had been fried off and still it had returned. He had even taken the time, or whispered a spell, so that his hair had grown back.

There was an overwhelming wave of power coming from him. It was that familiar spell that forced us to feel as if he were more powerful than us—a god. A feeling of insignificance came over me, and it was hard to look at him. There were stories of how when the gods showed their true selves, mortals would go blind. I understood that now.

"Thank you, Corwin, for being my herald and my harbinger," he said. His voice was smooth, even pleasant.

"There is something symbolic of the choice of this place to meet. A place that was so useful to me, until it wasn't. How the assassins swaggered through all of Ellos, and I brought them down in one night of crimson perfection."

I glanced at Corwin to see if he would try to share that glory, since he had been the one who had planned so much of that operation, but he continued to smile. He had once explained to me he saw the emperor as a pawn. Would he turn on the emperor one day? Or would the emperor turn on him?

"Avenus has fallen," Sargon said. "And my intention is to march the remaining population—the women, men, children, hoplites, grocers and poets—all the way through the four old realms—provinces, that is; to Akkadium. A glorious conquering display for every part of the empire to see. Those Avenians who survive will become slaves or bones for imperial hounds. The great march will be a lesson for all the ages to remember the power of the Akkad Empire. And what happens when you don't bend the knee to me."

"You are beyond evil," Archon Thena said.

"No. I am a brilliant student, that's what I am—I like reading. That march will be a symbol. You Avenians so like your symbols and your stories. Well, this will be one of them. Added to the memory of Ellos forever. And you'll get to see it firsthand."

Archon Thena shook her head. "No."

Sargon gave a sad, sarcastic sigh. "Yes, my dear archon. I will take you back to lead the march in chains. I will provide you a cart. I don't want you to die of exhaustion on the first day. The citizens of the Akkad Empire will line up to throw their filth at you. Another glorious symbol. I learned so much from your books before I burned them."

"And what about us?" Megan said.

"The dead don't have to march," he answered. "See, I can be kind. Though your heads will be there on pikes, with your cloaks still tied around your necks. Another clever symbol. I've really thought this through."

"And you will stand by this, Corwin?" I asked. For there was no doubt in my mind that Nameless was now gone.

"Yes, sister," he answered. "You have been a thorn in my side since birth. You tainted the air with your breath and stole accolades from me, so I will bless the day that you leave this world. You have dared to scar my perfect face."

"I was the one who scarred you," Brax said. He had landed silently on the balcony behind us. His lips were still dripping blood from his feed. "I should have ignored your soft-hearted sister and taken off your entire head."

"That would have been the wisest course," Corwin agreed. He showed no sign of fear at seeing Brax. "You cut me. For that I will cut you, scale by scale, into itty bitty bits."

"I shall eat the dragon," the emperor said. "It may take time to consume every portion of you. But I will leave your heart for last."

"A mortal eating a dragon." Brax rolled his eye. "Yet another fairy tale I don't want to hear. And, to be clear, that little scenario will not come true." He stalked further into the Grand Hall, his talons scraping along the stone floor. He was gathering his breath. I knew he needed to do that to get the fire inside him burning hot.

"For the third time the dragon has dared to come into my presence," Emperor Sargon said. "He slithers in with all the arrogance of the dragons. Well, your arrogance has ended, snake, for you will bow before me."

"You are dreaming, child emperor," Brax said. "You will no longer dream when my talons slice you into ribbons.

And I will be the one who eats you. Heart, head and all. I'm certain emperors taste salty. I may have to add pepper."

"No." Sargon shook a finger at Brax. *"You. Will. Bow."* The words boomed through the chamber. The force, the will behind those words, came over us in waves and as the emperor walked toward us, displaying no fear, that will grew stronger and stronger. The sense that I was in the presence of a god crushed me. I was an insect next to him. My one and only reason for breathing, for my heart beating, was to worship him.

The senators fell to the floor. I collapsed to my knees along with Megan, followed only a moment later by Maestru Beatrix. Archon Thena used her spear to hold herself high for a moment, then she let out a cry and fell to the ground. My head bowed of its own accord, no matter how hard I fought against my neck muscles. And when Sargon got within stabbing distance, I threw myself prostate to the floor. The emperor walked by, his sandaled feet only inches from me. If I had any strength or will I could have killed him. But he was a god and I was so insignificant that there was nothing I could do but worship him.

My position had pressed the soulstone into my chest and that globe was burning now as if Brenna, somewhere in there, were filling it with anger.

"What trick is this?" Brax said. I could raise my head enough to see him. He let out a tiny puff of fire, but didn't draw in his breath. The emperor continued to walk toward Brax and the dragon, my dear, brave friend, grew paler. "My body betrays me," he hissed as he lowered himself so he was now bowing his head toward Sargon. And I kept expecting Brax to rise up and bite off a hand or the head of this vain emperor, but my friend went lower and lower until he too was flat against the ground in the emperor's presence.

"And now you see," Sargon said. "Who I really am. I am your god. Emperor of all creatures, mortal or dragon, who come into the realm of Ellos. Every single living being with a mind and soul will bow before me. The Akkadian Empire will blaze with my glory."

The emperor stroked the top of Brax's head, touched the spikes along his back. "Your teeth will make a fine necklace," he said. "And your eye a pretty bauble. And your heart a perfect meal." He gave Brax's head one last pat, and then faced us.

"You may begin with your sister," he said to Corwin.

Since my head was turned I only heard the approach of Corwin's soft footsteps. He grabbed my shoulder and lifted my dead weight, so I was on my feet and now we stood face-to-face, dragon eye staring into blazing wizard eye.

"Use whatever method you want," the emperor said. "But do it now, my bright assassin."

Corwin pulled back his staff.

33

TO THE LAST BREATH

I didn't know what he could do with a broken magical staff, and so I didn't feel as much fear as I should have.

Corwin stabbed it into my chest and tiny bolts of lightning sparked, making me shudder and cry out. He held me in place so we continued to be face-to-face. The soulstone grew even warmer and I wondered if it were somehow reacting to what he was doing. If it could save me.

"That's for beating me in mathematics," he said. Then he struck me again and, despite gritting my teeth, I still let out a cry of pain. The shocks went up and down my body, making every muscle spasm, but there was nothing I could do to fight back.

"Stop," a voice said. "Stop!" At first I thought it was mine, but then it became clear it came from below me. "Choose me, Corwin," Megan said.

"Your death will come soon enough," Corwin answered. "This is a family matter."

And this third time he plunged the staff against my chest and held it there so that the power went through me over and over. His face in front of me became all that I could experience. That anger and hatred. A brother's absolute derision. Corwin kept pressing harder and harder, looking me directly in the eye. "I will take our parents away from you."

I didn't know what he meant, for they were long dead, but then an image of a mother holding me and Corwin clutched to her chest, and a father with his arms around us all, rose into my thoughts. This was a memory from my infant mind. A recollection of safety and of love. This was a moment that had formed me and made me believe that love was natural. It was real. And bit by bit my parents faded.

"No," I whispered. "No." But they were gone and I soon couldn't recall what I was mourning.

"There," he said. "That felt good. Now, this is for everything you did to me."

I kept my eyes open and looked directly back into his. The dragon blood, the power inside me, gave me some strength, but I knew I would fail. I was too weak to fight such wizardry. My resilience quickly faded. And it was clear my mind was fading, too, because I saw us as children again, growing up here in this very fortress. The two of us. A twin to my core, no matter what he did.

"We have always been together," I whispered.

"Yes," he hissed. "And that is why you have to leave me alone. This is my world now."

"We have always been one." Each word burned as it came out. My tongue was crackling with the energy he forced through my body. "We are one."

"Don't say that," he barked. "It's not true!"

"And I have always loved you, brother, always." Those words burned the most, but I saw they were a deeper truth. Even now, as through all his life, I was ready to forgive him.

To believe that he would change. That the best of Corwin would shine through as it had with Nameless.

He pulled back the broken staff, and the pain stopped. "You lie. You lie!"

"No," I said. "It is not a lie. I see it all." My voice was so hoarse I didn't know if he could hear me, but I kept speaking. "It is the truth. The heart truth. The one truth even I didn't believe. I see it. Nameless is you and you are Nameless and you are Corwin, each just another side of you. Another way you could have grown."

"He's dead," Corwin said. "Gone. Sargon killed him."

"No. He is you. He was always there waiting somewhere below. Bring him back. Bring yourself back."

"No," Corwin said. "No!"

"In my first breath I loved you as my brother, and in my last breath I will still love you. You cannot change that fact. It is immutable."

"Kill her, Corwin," the emperor said. His voice was closer, perhaps just behind me. "I grow bored with this familial display."

"Yes, my emperor," Corwin said. But he had something strange and terrifying in his eyes.

Tears. There were tears.

He pulled back the staff and plunged it directly at my heart. And in that moment I knew, somehow could sense, he was putting every destructive thing he had learned as a wizard into it. Whatever spell he was whispering would turn me to ashes and wipe me from this world forever.

And at the last moment, he pushed my shoulder so the staff missed me and plunged directly into the emperor's chest.

Sargon blinked. He looked down at the staff, then up at

Corwin. His smile faltered. "This is disappointing," he said. "I guess my right hand assassin will have to die."

The staff crackled and popped, but nothing happened to the emperor.

Emperor Sargon lifted his hand, making a sign that would be a spell, but before he could complete the motion Corwin shouted three words. They were ancient words he had plucked from the dead sorcerer inside his head. The sparking of the wand stopped, and next came a *crack-crack-cracking*. Emperor Sargon took a step back, clutching at the spot where the staff had hit him.

There was a hole burnt in the side of his chest and from that point, spreading outward, the cracking continued. He was turning to stone.

"You will pay," he said. He moved his hands, but the action failed to stop the spell. "This cannot happen to a god. I will rise from this and you will—" But his lips froze and his eyes, showing fear, turned to stone so he now was a statue in front of us. A hunk of rock. But I could look directly at him now—the god-like brightness was gone.

"Be quick," Corwin said. "He will soon defeat the spell. He cannot die this way. We have to break him."

Archon Thena stepped in and struck him with her spear, stabbing the emperor over and over, failing to chip even the slightest pebble from that stone. Megan had found a sword, and she joined in, but the blade bent. Brax pushed both of them aside and slashed at the emperor with talons that were tough enough to cut stone, but Sargon didn't even fall over. Even my dagger bounced off.

"Nothing can break that stone," Megan said.

Sargon began glowing and his feet looked like they were taking the color of flesh again.

"We have to flee," Maestru Beatrix shouted. She pulled

back the archon. "To the swannery. We'll take our chances with the swans and get out of here."

I didn't move, though. Because the stone on my chest was burning. A stone carved from rock as ancient as anything on this world.

Child, a woman's voice said inside my head. It was Brenna. *You know what to do.*

But I didn't know. I didn't. Sargon's body was glowing; in moments he would be whole again and we would all be prostrate on the floor and, seconds after that, dead.

And then it became clear. I snatched the burning stone from my neck, letting the necklace dangle, and gripped the soulstone tight.

I struck the stone emperor again and again and again.

He began to crack. The glowing of his body grew less bright. A chunk of his ear flew off. Then next, a piece of his nose. And that encouraged me so that I was swinging as hard as I could. The stone I was holding was formed by an ancient magic summoned by Vecterix, the mage dragon. So the stone was truly solid. And it was a soul, too. It had purpose and will. Brenna added her strength to mine.

Harder. Harder. Strike harder. She put these thoughts into my head. And, somehow, her intensity came into me, too.

I swung so hard that a crack formed from Sargon's skull to his chest. I could hear a noise like he was yelling, but then he shattered into hundreds of pieces before us and all that lay at my feet was a broken emperor.

34

TO KILL OR NOT TO KILL

There wasn't any cheering. Only a sense of satisfaction. We gathered around the collection of stones that had once ruled this entire land.

"Tell me he won't be coming back from that," I said.

"He won't," my brother answered.

"Well, just to be certain, I'll do this." Archon Thena picked up a chunk of stone that looked to be part of the emperor's head and tossed it over the balcony. It was a superb throw. She came back toward us, brushing off her hands.

I turned to my brother, who was looking down at the remaining stone. His expression was hard to read. He had always been hard to read. "And tell me who you are," I asked him.

He shook his head and wiped at his eyes. "I honestly don't know. You have worked your own magic in me. For the first time I don't know who I am."

"Maybe we should just kill him then." Brax had moved closer to me, in a protective position, and he lifted a paw. I stabbed him with my stare. "I'm just being logical. He tends to cause us trouble."

"He's my brother," I said. "And you would do anything for your sister."

"Fine, I won't kill him." Brax lowered his paw and shook his head. "Don't expect me to hold back from saying 'I told you so' when the time comes. I may even gloat."

Corwin continued to stare down at the shattered emperor. "I don't feel anything," he said. "It's so strange. I don't care that all my dreams of empire and influence are spread out on the floor. I don't even feel a sense of loss."

"Good," Megan said. "Maybe you're finally coming to your senses."

He looked at her and was about to say something, and then he locked gazes with Brax. "I know how to save your sister and bring her back," he said to Brax. "That has become clear to me. It would be a way to make some reparations for all the harm I've caused."

"Oh, you have plenty of reparations to make," Brax said. "A few to me, but mostly you owe the people you see around you. I do want you to spill your secret about my sister, though."

"We will have to travel to Drachia," Corwin said.

"Then let us go now," Brax said. "I'm ready."

"No, Brax." I put my hand on his shoulder. "We cannot make that trip just yet. We have to return to Avenus."

"And we have to inform the other realms," Maestru Beatrix said. "They should be first to know that the emperor is dead. Quick, my old students, who is next in line for the Akkadian throne?"

I shook my head. "I honestly don't know who remains alive."

"Sargon didn't name an heir," my brother said. "That was my advice to him. It gave him more power. So there isn't an heir. He killed all his other relations."

"Well, that was excellent advice for Sargon." Archon Thena was holding her spear like she still expected an attack. "But not so good for an empire without an emperor. It makes it much weaker. That said, there is an Akkadian army in Avenus, and we will need a show of force to drive them home licking their wounds. They can sort out what remains of their empire themselves."

"Then let us do that," Brax said. "I'll be happy to light a fire under their tails."

"Can you open a doorway?" the archon said to Corwin.

"And should we trust him to do that?" Megan asked.

"Trust won't matter in this case," Corwin replied. He held up his staff. It looked to be little more than a burnt stick. "I am afraid that it took all the magic invested in my staff to cast that spell on the emperor. I can't open a gateway without it. And carving a new one would take too long."

"Then we will fly," I said.

It took some time to organize ourselves for the journey. We ate several handfuls of cheese and dried meat and went up to the swannery. The swans were not pleased to be saddled, but they didn't maim a single person.

"I will go to Allesaria first," Maestru Beatrix said, holding the reins of one swan. "I still have many contacts there, mostly librarians, but as you know they hold a great deal of power." She didn't seem to jest. "Then next I'll visit Daria and Woden." Just mentioning Thord's home city made a coldness grow in my stomach. "I'll encourage them to organize their militias and the realms will rise again. Maybe even the old realms that existed before the empire destroyed them."

Maestru Beatrix hugged me and Megan, then looked at my brother. She reached out a hand. "I feel like every time I shake your hand you are a different person. So good luck with the new version of yourself, Corwin. If you hurt a hair on their heads, I will kill you."

This wasn't said in a threatening tone, but the steel in her eyes made even me shudder.

"You will have every right to," he answered.

Then Maestru Beatrix turned and climbed onto a swan that didn't even hiss at her—she'd always been good with swans. She was gone a few wingbeats later.

Megan and Archon Thena were able to climb onto two of the swans. The beasts were not happy to have riders, but of all people Corwin calmed them with kind words. He took the final swan and Thena told the remaining senators she would send help. They promised to hammer the remains of Sargon into dust.

"It'll keep us busy," one of the female senators said with a tired grin.

We flew south. My brother called up a wind that was fast yet calm, and it took only a few hours to get to the island. The villages and fields along the way to Avenus were still burning, and it seemed hard to imagine that anyone was alive.

Even from a distance it was clear that the city itself was still in flames, which in some ways surprised me—I had imagined all of it would have been burnt to the ground by now. As we neared the city we saw Immortals and other Akkadian troops marching away from it in scattered groups. "The Akkad army is leaving," Brax said. "The death of Sargon has broken their will."

"I'll organize what forces I can find to harass them," the archon said. "The fewer Immortals and Akkadian foot soldiers who return to their capital, the better it will be for all of us. Come with me to the Carthenon and we can plan from there."

"No," I said. "Not yet. We have to go back to where Sargon's chariot was and look for our fallen comrade."

The archon nodded. "Then good luck with that—Thord was a brave man." She already expected us to only find his body. "I am thankful for your help and will welcome you when you return." Without another word, she turned her swan toward the Carthenon.

Megan, my brother, and Brax and I flew over the broken gates and out toward the flat land where the catapults sat. They were burning and broken, which mean the Avenians had already performed a few counterattacks. Perhaps there were forces hiding in the hills who were now free to attack their enemies. The sight of a dragon and swans in the sky made the few marching Immortals and soldiers move even faster, though many of them didn't break their formations.

We landed near the field of dead white bears. I jumped off of Brax once we were close to the ground, and the others left their mounts and we searched for our friend.

"Thord," I shouted, though my voice was so hoarse it barely carried. "Thord!"

Corwin hunted for him, too, and I saw him bend over to examine something and began moving in his direction, but my brother waved me away. "It wasn't him," he said. He pocketed whatever it was he'd found.

And so I kept walking through the field of dead bears and dead Immortals, moving aside fallen cloaks or broken wagon pieces, looking for Thord. Brax followed a few steps behind me. There wasn't a sign of my friend.

"Here!" Megan cried from several feet away. She had moved the massive arm of a dead bear. "He's over here."

All three of us ran to her. The bear, no longer white, but stained by the red of its own blood, had fallen across Thord. His blade was stuck in its side. Megan was struggling to move the creature, but with a yank from one paw Brax shoved it aside and it rolled out of our way.

Thord was a chalky pale color, his eyes were closed, his face bruised, and his chest didn't move. "Thord," I said. "Wake up. Wake up."

Megan fell to her knees beside him and took his hand. And my brother was at his other side, pressing two fingers against Thord's neck to feel for his heartbeat. We all held our breath for a moment or two so that Corwin could listen. He looked over at Megan and gave a quick shake of his head.

"He's dead," she said.

"He's dead," I echoed. "Thord is dead." I still couldn't bring myself to get any closer. The blood on his clawed face looked fresh. Only a short while ago he had been alive and fighting for his life, blade in hand. And now he was gone.

Brax put a talon on my shoulder and said nothing. For what was there to say?

"He is recently dead," Corwin added. "And that is an important statement to make."

"What do you mean?" I asked.

"Because I can convince him to come back," Corwin said. He pressed his head against Thord's chest and listened for a moment and then began tearing off his chest armor. "He fought these bears until his heart burst. You may not want to watch this part."

He turned to the bear next to him. "I will give him a new heart." And my brother pulled out his dagger and began working at the bear's chest.

"I believe him when he says you don't want to watch

this," Brax said and, reaching out, he pulled both Megan and me away, using his wings to shield us from the sight.

It took some time for Corwin to perform his operation and cast his spells. The sun moved slowly in the sky. Megan and I eventually strode away from Brax. I looked for my dagger, the one Sargon had tossed aside, but even this part of the battlefield was too large to cover. I would have to come back later.

Instead, I followed Megan further away. I found that if we looked toward the hills, with our backs to the city, we could almost pretend a war had never happened. It was a peaceful sight.

"Do you think it will work?" Megan had been biting her lip up until the moment she said those words. The wind adjusted her red hair.

"Inside my brother is the most powerful wizard in Ellos," I said. "A wizard who has ancient knowledge of the dead. So it will work. It must. Though who knows how Thord will be changed by, well, by being dead for a while."

She nodded. "Yes. That's something to think about."

There was even more to think about, I realized.

"Do you care for him?" I asked.

"Of course," she said. "Isn't it obvious?"

"Then I should leave you to him."

"Leave him to me?" She gave me an angry glare, and her nostrils flared, making me think she might strike me. "By the gods, no! I don't want him. He's not a bauble."

"But you have feelings for him. You... you care and he cares about you and..."

She punched my shoulder hard enough to make me stumble. "You are so stupid, Carmen. I don't like him like that."

"You don't like him?" I was embarrassed by how squeaky my voice was.

"I don't like anyone that way. Haven't you figured that out? It's better to be alone." She punched me again in the shoulder. It hurt, but the pain was waking me up. "Don't ever try to fob that stinky Wodenite off on me again."

I didn't know what to say to this. Thankfully, as I rubbed my shoulder, Corwin called out. "Come, come," he said. "Thord wakes."

We walked back, and the three of us looked down at Thord. Brax stuck his head in the circle.

My brother had put his robe over Thord's chest. "You won't want to look into his eyes," he warned. "It will give you nightmares. And... and gas."

"What?" I said. "What in the Hades do you mean?"

"Just remember I warned you."

Thord opened his eyes and I couldn't help but look. They were black. There was no color at all—no whites or pupil. It was as if they had become two pools of ink. I shuddered, for he no longer looked mortal. Even Brax, who had a smart thing to say in every situation, glanced away from that stare.

"You wake me." Thord's voice was gravelly and distant. At least I thought it was him. He sounded the same, but it was hard to know if he was angry or had any emotion at all.

"Yes, you are awakened," my brother said. "You are Thord of the Red Assassins. You are our friend. And we welcome you back to Ellos."

Thord blinked, momentarily covering up those dark, dark eyes.

"You are friends?" he asked. Then he turned his head, and it was hard to tell exactly where he was looking because his eyes were such voids. “What friends would bring me back here?”

He closed his eyes again and continued to breathe, but did not try to wake up.

“He will need to sleep,” my brother said. “Help me get him to the Carthenon.”

35

NOT ENOUGH

In the end, it was Brax who carried him gently in his talons. He set him down in the garden on the top floor of the Carthenon. Words were spoken to the senators there and physicians came to carry Thord away to a healing room.

I watched him go. The words he'd spoken still haunted me. *"What friends would bring me back here?"*

"Do you think he saw the afterlife?" Megan asked. She was obviously equally disturbed by his question.

"He would have stood at the gateway to the next realm," Corwin said. "And heard the singing of his ancestors. That will change a person."

"I hope that what we did was a good thing," I said.

"It was," Megan replied. "He wouldn't want to be away from our companionship. It's better than any heaven." This got a slight chuckle out of me.

"I, for one, am looking forward to seeing him wake," Brax said.

"You are?" I admit his words surprised me.

"Yes." Brax nodded. "He has the heart of a bear now. So maybe he'll be a lot more interesting. It's likely a strange experience. But you know all about having parts from other creatures, Carmen. I'm sure it won't change him."

Before I could answer, Archon Thena came up to us. She had already removed her armor and donned a blue robe, though it had a few bloodstains on it.

"We have sent messages," she said. "Armies are gathering. And the fight for freeing Ellos is here. You are all welcome to stay as long as you need to recover—for the rest of your lives if necessary, for I am officially making you citizens of Avenus."

"A dragon can be a citizen?" Brax raised his eyebrow in that sardonic way.

"Especially dragons," she said. "Your names are written in the rolls as of a few minutes ago. You are one of us now. Always welcome. I have affairs of state to look after, so I must say farewell. But I will join you later this evening or in the morning, depending on timing. I've ordered food to be brought up here." She gestured at the stone benches, stained with smoke and maybe blood. Someone had put cushions on them. "Please seat yourselves. This meal will be just the first of our many thanks to you all. We will be honored to have you anytime."

The food arrived, and to be honest I was shocked at the variety and the freshness. They had just had their city mostly destroyed and still were civilized enough to put together a meal that would make the gods jealous. Even Brax didn't complain about the fact that everything was cooked.

When we were finished, Brax walked up and down beside the table, pacing. "We must go to Drachia," he said. "It is time."

I shook my head. And so did my brother. "No," we said at the same time.

"You two are ganging up on me," Brax said. "This is not a good sign."

"We will have to wait until the morn," Corwin explained. "I need to look in on my patient. And I need sleep. Carmen does, too, and despite your dragony vigor, you also need the rest. Brenna will gladly wait."

Brax only looked from my brother to me and back. He rolled his eye and nodded. "Fine," he said. "Only one more sleep, then."

They gave us mortals rooms on the top floor of the Carthenon—rooms that belonged to the dead archon. Megan shared my room and we collapsed onto a giant bed, the softest I'd ever felt. As night fell, we slept. Brax slept out in the open of the garden.

In the morning, I awoke with a start to see Corwin's face right over mine and couldn't help but reach for the dagger I'd left sheathed on the stool beside the bed. He caught my hand and smiled.

"You'll never have to feel that fear again," he said. "I promise." Then he paused for a second, to create a bit of drama, I assumed. "Thord is awake," was his next sentence. "And he asked for you."

My brother led me to the hospital room. They had opened a curtain enough to let the morning sunshine in. Thord lay back on a pillow. They had changed him into a white robe, his face had been stitched and he had a cast on his arm.

When we entered I saw that his eyes were closed but as I stole near the bed, he opened them. The blackness was gone, except for his pupils, surrounded by that familiar blue.

"You are here," he said. "Good."

"Yes, we are," I said then realized my brother hadn't followed me in. It was only Thord and me.

"I need to talk to you," Thord said.

"Yes. That... that's good."

He struggled to sit up and the motion showed that there were bandages across his chest. He saw my glance. "Yes," he said. "I heard I have a new heart. It is quite the wonder. The Avenian physicians were awestruck by it. I was awestruck by the fact it was a gift from your brother."

"He has changed," I said.

"He has," Thord agreed. "Did you know he spent most of the night by my side?"

I shook my head. The new Corwin was full of wonders.

"Will you be returning to Drachia?" Thord asked.

I nodded. "Brax is eager to see his sister. He will awake soon, and then we will be on the way. Megan taught us how to reach the high air currents that will carry us there at speed."

"And will you come back here when you are done?" he asked.

"Of course," I said.

"And will you be the same?"

"I'm always the same." But even as I said that, I knew I was looking at him through both a mortal and a dragon eye, which showed me the magic that knit the bear's heart into his chest.

"That's not entirely true," he said.

"In my heart," I said, "I don't change."

"Yes, that part is true." He nodded. "It seems so long ago since I loaned you those feathers to make a swan costume to get a swan egg."

"It is a long time ago." I leaned on the bed, moving slightly closer to him. "I am still thankful."

"You have become something amazing," he whispered. "More than an assassin. Something else." And then, before I could reply, he said, "I know there is something between us —feelings." He stopped there, and my mouth was dry. I didn't know what words I would say. "But it's important for you to know that I am not enough for you yet. You are something greater."

"No, that's not true." My voice was quiet.

"Yes, it is true. It is the truth. One day I will find you. Or you will find me. And by then I will be something more. But I need time to figure out exactly what that is." He looked tired saying this.

"How much time?" I asked.

He shrugged and winced a little with the motion.

"Then I will wait to hear from you," I said. "You can send a spellbird to me and, wherever I am, I will come back to you, Thord. I promise."

And then I leaned down and kissed his forehead.

"Good," was all he said.

36

THE BRASS

Traveling to Drachia using the "spellbird" airstreams was one of the most frightening and exhilarating experiences I'd ever had. I rode on Brax and my brother was on the swan he'd chosen from the Red Assassin keep. He hadn't named it yet. But that made sense since he didn't seem to know what to call himself anymore either, though he would answer to Corwin.

At first, after leaving Avenus, we rose higher and higher. I cast the bubble spells so that all of us could breathe—the bubbles formed around our heads and the air smelled fresher. When we had ascended to such a height that the clouds were far below us, we found an airstream that was running north. Brax and I flew into it and, without warning, it accelerated us to a stupendously impressive speed. Corwin followed. Within the stream it was as if the surrounding air was still and the rest of the world turned underneath.

This changes everything, Brax said. *Everything!*

Within minutes we were over the ocean, then halfway up Ellos. A short time later Bitterwaters were below us, but the airstream stayed warm as if it were the breath of a loving goddess. It had taken us days of struggle to wing our way over that dangerous collection of water and ice. And now we were past the Bitterwaters in a few heartbeats.

As Dreki, the great and powerful dragon city with its impressive spires, appeared on the horizon, Brax angled his wings and my brother followed us. We came out of the airstream, slowed to a normal mortal pace and swirled our way down to the palace.

We had sent a spellbird to warn his royal highness Kon of our arrival. We didn't want to be blasted out of the sky by overeager Crimson dragons. So when we touched down on the massive royal balcony, it surprised me to find no one to greet us.

"Where is he?" Brax said. "Keep your guards up. He may have been dethroned and this is a trap."

My brother unclasped a makeshift staff he'd carved from a spear shaft and I set my fingers on my dagger. Brax drew in a lengthy breath.

And then the main door swung open, and trumpets played. Mortals—well, slaves I should say—marched out in their finest white outfits, clutching brass instruments and drums and playing a joyous, pompous tune. Crimson and Obsidian dragons, who marched out in unison and spread in a perfect line, followed them, impressive in both their strength and power and in how incredibly shiny their scales were. The slaves must have been busy waxing them.

I felt dirty and ugly. I hadn't done more than wash my face, let alone comb my hair since the battle. And here before us was all the resplendence of the dragon kingdom. Even the slaves seemed to look down at me.

And finally, out came Kon, a purple robe around his shoulders.

The trumpets stopped playing the moment he was in front of us. "Welcome home, brother," Kon said.

"What is all this?" Brax motioned with a talon. "There's more pomp here than at a Golden dragon's ball."

"I know." Kon huffed out a bored sigh. "Personally, I hate it. But we need practice. This kind of display gets treaties signed. Too many dragons like the show of it all."

I realized again how much Kon looked like Brax. He also looked both healthier and stronger since we'd last seen him —perhaps being a king was good for his scales. And his soul.

"It was an impressive entrance, brother," Brax said. "Will you be dancing next?"

Kon ignored his question. "You look like a broken-winged bat."

"That is exactly how I feel," Brax replied, not seeming to take any offence. "There is much to tell. And you have permissions to give."

Kon's smile showed way more teeth than his brother's. "There is nothing more I love than giving permission to my older brother. Come, come, I am all ears. We shall dine at the royal table, and you can introduce me to this other mortal. You do have a habit of collecting riffraff."

Corwin gave his swan orders to stand in place and then we all followed Kon into the palace and soon were at a table overflowing with food. It was so strange to be eating again so soon, after so many weeks of eating only dried fruit and meat. This table held mostly meat and much of it was cooked, but there were goats chained at one end, which Brax eyed hungrily. I didn't watch what he did next, but my brother glanced that way and paled a little.

I saw Dyn bring in one plate. He gave me a friendly, eager wave and then went back to the kitchen.

Once we were fed, we explained to the king of dragons everything that had happened since we'd left his palace. He listened asking no questions, but several times he looked from me to Brax and then to my brother. When we finished, Kon asked, "And we are to trust this traitor before us?"

Brax sighed. "Carmen is constantly making me do things that are against my nature. But yes, we can trust him. He killed the emperor for us."

"Funny," Kon said. "From your tale it's my sister who killed the emperor."

"That's one way of looking at it," I said. "She was a significant help."

And then my brother cleared his throat. "You can trust me in this," he said. It was almost a whisper.

Kon looked at him for several moments in silence. Oddly enough, the room became silent, too, and I wondered how many of the guards and slaves were listening in on our conversation. Kon picked at his teeth for several seconds, sucking up the chunks of meat that he discovered there.

"So what will it be?" Brax asked. "Will you give us permission?"

"The answer was never in doubt," Kon said. "I gave you permission to start this quest. And now that you're here, my mind hasn't changed. Besides, I've always liked Brenna more than you. So you have my permission to bring her back from the dead."

37

THE HALL OF ANCESTORS

The three of us descended to the Hall of Ancestors, the great domed room below the palace. Again, seeing row after row of dragon statues, a chill ran along my spine. The history of the dragons was such a deep and long one that we mortals looked like mayflies in comparison. My brother glanced from side to side at the statues, each with their own soulstone hanging from their necks. "So many souls waiting to be reborn," he said. "So many. It is astounding."

"That's a good word for it," I said.

Brax was silent and led us toward the pillar at the center of the room. It still glowed with a soft light. Perhaps it had been glowing for thousands of years.

"The magic here," my brother whispered. "Such powerful magic. It, too, is astounding. Even Boqin, inside of me, is astounded."

He was running out of words to describe what he saw.

The corpolium—that is, the three molded beds in the shapes of dragons—waited for us. It wasn't that long ago that I had almost stabbed Brax to death while he lay in one of them. Brax led us to a bed that looked to be the right size for Brenna. He looked pale. Either the light from the column painted him that way, or he was nervous.

"And how exactly, again, will this work?" Brax asked.

"From our discussions, I know that you were very close to understanding the process," my brother said. "Boqin's spirit filled in the blanks for me. It also helped to read the books Goran loaned you."

"But the laws are still immutable," Brax replied. "My understanding of the Elder magic is that we must make a sacrifice."

My brother nodded. "You are correct. But it is all in the way you make that sacrifice," he said. He held out his hand to me. "May I have the soulstone?"

I took it from my neck, holding the soulstone in one hand. The smooth rock was warm to the touch as if Brenna somehow knew where we were and what was happening. My neck and chest felt light. And... and empty, like something was missing. I had grown used to having the soulstone there, a constant reminder of Brenna. "Here it is."

My brother took it gently from me and placed it in a small alcove above the corpolium. It began to pulse with a dim red light.

"But the stories were very clear," Brax said. He looked from the soulstone to Corwin. "None of the readings varied from this point. Someone who loves must sacrifice a life. That is immutable."

"Nothing is immutable," my brother said.

"Ah! More wizard wordplay," Brax said. "I don't trust it."

"Then trust in this," my brother said. "Your love will bring your sister back, and so too will the love of my sister." He drew in a breath. "Will the two of you stand on either side of the corpolium?" We moved into position so we were on either side. "Now please place your hand and a paw on the soulstone."

We did so. It was not that large of a stone, but I could press my hand against Brax's paw and the stone at the same time. The hairs on my arm rose.

"Yes, yes," my brother said. "That is perfect."

"But what are you going to do?" I asked. "What is next?"

"This." Without me noticing, he'd brought his staff out, and it was glowing red. He tapped my shoulder. "You will feel it run through you. Your connection with Brax and with Brenna. You all have the same blood."

I felt it. From my shoulder where he had tapped me, through my arm, into the stone, through Brax, too. We were one.

And then Corwin said: "You will also notice that you, like so many of the statues here, can't move."

I tried to pull my hand away. And Brax hissed in a breath. "Traitor!" he spat the word. "We have been betrayed!" His voice echoed up to the dome ceiling and back.

"Brother," I said. "What is this?"

His face was unreadable, but Corwin reached out and took my hand. I couldn't move my fingers but I felt the warmth of his own. He gave me a squeeze then pulled back. "I lied to you both. A sacrifice must be made. But I cannot ask either of you to give up your lives. It is not necessary, nor is it right."

"What do you mean?" I asked.

"One must die so the other can live," he said. "A willing soul must be sacrificed by someone with love in their heart."

"But there's no one else here," I said.

"And the only one who has love for you," Brax said, "is frozen in place."

"You are both wrong. I am not alone."

I got an inkling of what he meant.

"You can't do this, Corwin," I said. "This wasn't agreed upon."

"No, but it is necessary. And I don't know which voice inside my head I am anymore. But Corwin will make the sacrifice. As you know he—well, I—have always loved myself. So both of us will die in here." He had worked his way past me and Brax to one of the molded beds and then lay down in it. "I am sorry for my trespasses," he said. "It is me, Corwin speaking, just for the record. Goodbye, sister. Goodbye."

Then he lowered out of sight into the corpolium and before I could say another word, I saw my dagger—my second dagger—rise into the air in his hand and then plunge downward.

Nothing happened. There wasn't a sound from him or anywhere else in the hall.

Then the soulstone cracked and fell away and a bright light flew past us. Another cracking followed, but neither of us could turn our head. There was a sound of creaking and a cry out as if a birthing pang. Then silence. Someone was moving behind us.

A shadow fell across Brax and a female voice said, "Never kill my future husband again." A paw smacked Brax full in the face, drawing a little blood. "Got it, brother? Leave it to me next time."

The dragon moved closer. It was Brenna. She looked like him, but was slightly larger. Brax hadn't moved.

Couldn't move.

"Why aren't you fighting back?" she said.

"It's a spell," he answered. Though he was tearing up, and I knew it wasn't from the pain of the cuts on his face.

"A spell?" she asked. "Is Vecterix here?"

"Vecterix is dead," Brax said with little emotion. "The dead man in the corpolium was the wielder."

She looked over toward the corpolium, and from her vantage point could see my brother. "He seems familiar," she said. "Who is he?"

"My brother," I answered. A tingling was beginning along my fingers, signaling that the spell Corwin had cast on us was fading.

"You seem very familiar, too." Brenna scratched her chin with a talon—a family habit, it seemed. "Like you're from a dream. Who are you?"

"I'm Carmen," I said. "A friend of Brax's."

"A mortal friend." Brenna nodded. "Things have changed since I fell asleep." Brenna raised an eyebrow and then looked back toward my brother's body. "And he's dead, you said?"

"Yes." My voice choked a little. I pulled my hand back from Brax and took a wobbling step backwards.

"Well, if he's dead," Brenna continued, "he's not doing an outstanding job of it."

"What do you mean?" I stepped toward her as if I were moving through molasses. My muscles said no, but I told them to take another step.

I reached the corpolium and looked down.

Corwin was there with my dagger in his chest. There wasn't very much blood. And his eyes were open.

"Corwin," I said. "Corwin!"

He slowly looked toward me.

"Corwin is dead." His tone was emotionless. "He is truly gone this time. Even his memories."

"What?" I said.

"Something had to be sacrificed." He sat up slightly and

then groaned. "Will you take this dagger out of me?" he asked.

I pulled it out, and, without thinking, wiped it on my trousers and sheathed it.

"Why aren't you dead?" I asked.

"I am. I was. But what happened here is what I learned from Boqin. My heart stopped. My blood no longer flowed. And Corwin died. Then my heart began again and I… I lived. Please help me out."

I reached out a hand. His fingers were cold, and he seemed weak, but I pulled him out and he stood and surveyed us.

"It worked," he said, sounding a little triumphant. "I'm so very glad it worked."

38

WITH OPEN EYES

The four of us made the long climb through the carved tunnels until we reached the palace. Kon met us in one of the massive halls and there was such emotion on his face that it was truly shocking to me. He embraced his sister. "You are back, you are back, you are back," he repeated over and over again.

"Yes," she said. "And much has changed in the realm since I slept. Father is dead, I hear. And you are king."

Kon let her go. "There is so much for you to learn about. I will tell you all. I truly need you, sister. I have all of Drachia to rule. And your wise help will be immeasurable."

"Yeah," she said, though her tone of voice made it seem she wasn't quite convinced. "I could be an advisor. Or I could rule."

He gave her a shocked look.

"I am kidding, brother." She clapped him on the shoulder hard enough to make him wince. "I shall wield power behind the throne."

He didn't look any happier.

~

There was more food and song that followed, and a Caerulan dragon performed a quickly composed poem about the return of Brenna. Before I knew it I was asleep in a chamber that Brax told me had once been for mortal allies —kings and queens had slept here thousands of years ago. The warm shower and the scented soaps particularly impressed me.

In the morning, I found my brother already saddling his swan.

"Were you leaving without saying goodbye?" I asked.

He shook his head. "I would have found you. I have some fondness for you and recognize our sibling bond. I also have the memories that Nameless had, too."

But not Corwin's, I wanted to add. In some ways that was a good thing. It was also odd to be mourning my brother when he was standing right before me. I supposed in time I could come to terms with that.

"And what will you do?" I asked him.

"I will return to Goran the wizard. To learn. To become who I was meant to be. It will be strange to have the voice of his master, Boqin, inside my head, though I am sure Goran will find that endlessly interesting. But do know that I am no longer Nameless and no longer Corwin."

"Then who are you?" I asked. "What do we call you?"

"I'm going to have to discover that," he said. He gave me a perfunctory hug, as if it was something he thought he should do as opposed to wanting to do it. I hugged back, though, hard. And then he climbed onto the black swan. Without looking back, he was in the air and gone.

~

We stayed at the palace for a full month. I checked the windowsill for spellbirds from Thord every day. Megan sent one to say that all was returning to normal in Avenus and that the kingdoms had thrown off the yoke of the empire. There was word that even the ancient provinces were working toward becoming realms again. The various realms were also hunting for Scyllia, but they had not found her. She didn't mention Thord.

I didn't get a word from him, either. I decided that was all right. Time had to pass. We both had so much to learn about our new lives. And our new selves.

With each day, Brax grew more restless. He had always hated the court and the politics and though he enjoyed his time with his sister, being here was wearing on him.

One afternoon, he found me on the grand balcony. He was holding something in his paw, but he pushed it out of sight behind him.

"What was that?" I asked.

"Oh, nothing," he said.

If he wanted to aggravate me by being secretive I would not fall for it. In fact, I knew the best question to aggravate him. "How is royal court working out?" I asked. My smile was innocent.

"Mind-numbingly boring," he answered. "I still don't have a place in Drachia. Something about me has changed —I am not really at home with the dragons." He gave me a glare. "It is you who has changed me. Thanks so much for that."

"You are so welcome," I responded with fake cheer.

"Have you thought any further about your future?" he asked. He sounded a little hesitant, as if he didn't truly want to know the answer.

"I still don't know where to go or what to do next," I said.

"And I don't know what I'm becoming." I looked down at my arms, remembering that in the blink of an eye they could be covered with scales. "For the first time since I was a child I have no purpose. No goal." I drew in a breath. The air in Dreki, this high up, was fresh. "And to be honest, it feels good."

"Then we should fly," Brax said. "You and I going where the wind takes us. We will find our place somewhere. Maybe moving between the mortal and dragon lands is where we most belong."

I patted his shoulder. "Yes. I like that."

"Good," he said. His tail pushed the item he'd been carrying so it was right in front of my feet. It was a backpack. "I already had this packed. And I said our goodbyes. Kon wasn't sad to see me go."

I laughed as I pulled it on.

"Oh, and one more thing," he said. "There is a secret I've been keeping from you for the last few weeks."

He turned his head so his blind, closed eye was right in front of me. And then he opened it. Inside his socket an eye had grown, but it wasn't gray like his other eye. It looked—it looked like a very large mortal eye. The same color as my mortal eye.

"Surprise, it has grown back," he said. "And I can see through it. I still don't know why it has taken a mortal shape and color. Maybe we are connected in more ways than I'd like to admit." Then he puffed out two little flames from his nostrils. "I just hope it doesn't make me soft-hearted and maudlin."

I laughed. "It won't."

"Good! Then I suggest we should fly. And we will figure this new eye and everything else out as we go along."

I climbed onto his back, and with two powerful movements of his wings we were in the air. I wasn't even certain which direction we were going. But it felt good to be in the sky with the wind in my hair and my hand on Brax's back.

We flew on and on.

ALSO BY ARTHUR SLADE

Crimson. A ruthless queen. An ancient god. One brave girl with an impossible choice...

"A wildly inventive, action-packed fantasy. A darkly fascinating read."

— Kevin Sands, author of *The Blackthorn Key*

Book one in the bestselling young adult series. Over 100,000 copies sold. Modo is the greatest spy of the Victorian era, but it will take all of his skill to survive the Clockwork Guild.

Mission Clockwork

ABOUT THE AUTHOR

Arthur Slade was raised in the Cypress Hills of southwest Saskatchewan and began writing at an early age. He is the author of over twenty books, including *Dust* (which won the Governor General's award), *Mission Clockwork*, and *Amber Fang*. He currently lives in the mythical city of Saskatoon, Canada where he writes on a treadmill desk while listening to heavy metal.

It's true.

Connect with Arthur Slade online:

www.arthurslade.com

art@arthurslade.com

Printed in Great Britain
by Amazon

43559825R00227